W9-AQB-623

DATE D

American Women in the Twentieth Century

Series Editor: Barbara Haber, The Schlesinger Library on the History of Women in America, Radcliffe College

Pulling together a wealth of widely-scattered primary and secondary sources on women's history, *American Women in the Twentieth Century* is the first series to provide a chronological history of the changing status of women in America. Each volume presents the experiences and contributions of American women during one decade of this century. Written by leading scholars in American history and women's studies, *American Women in the Twentieth Century* meets the need for an encyclopedic overview of the roles women have played in shaping modern America.

Also Available:

Setting a Course: American
Women in the 1920s
Dorothy M. Brown

The Home Front and Beyond:
American Women in the 1940s
Susan M. Hartmann

Mothers and More: American
Women in the 1950s
Eugenia Kaledin

Migrant Mother, Nipomo, California,
1936, by Dorothea Lange
*Courtesy of Library of Congress,
FSA Collection*

Holding Their Own
American Women in the 1930s

Susan Ware

Twayne Publishers · Boston

Holding Their Own:
American Women in the 1930s

Copyright © 1982
by G.K. Hall & Co.
All Rights Reserved
Twayne Publishers
A Division of G.K. Hall & Co.
70 Lincoln Street
Boston, Massachusetts 02111

Book production and design
by Barbara Anderson

This book was typeset in
10 point Janson with
display type from the
Morgan Press supplied by
Composing Room of New England.

PRINTED ON PERMANENT/DURABLE
ACID-FREE PAPER AND BOUND IN
THE UNITED STATES OF AMERICA

Library of Congress Cataloging
in Publication Data

Ware, Susan, 1950–
Holding their own.

Bibliography: p. 203
Includes index.
1. Women—United States—History—20th century.
2. Depressions—1929—United States—Psychological
aspects.   I. Title.

HQ1420.W33   305.4'0973   82-6215
ISBN 0-8057-9900-1   AACR2

10   9   8   7   6   5   4

softcover ISBN 0-8057-9902-8

10   9   8   7   6   5   4   3   2   1

TO D.R.W.

Contents

About the Author

Susan Ware graduated from Wellesley College and received the Ph.D. from Harvard University in 1978. She has taught at Harvard University, the University of New Hampshire, and Tufts University, and is currently an Assistant Professor of History at New York University. Her first book was *Beyond Suffrage: Women in the New Deal* (Harvard University Press, 1981). Her most recent work is *Partner and I: Molly Dewson, Feminism, and New Deal Politics* (Yale University Press, 1987).

Preface

This book is intended as a general introduction to women's activities in the United States during the decade of the 1930s. Because it surveys developments in fields as diverse as popular culture, employment, and sexuality, it does not provide comprehensive or definitive answers on all topics. Rather, it introduces the reader to important themes in these areas and provides a synthesis of the existing scholarship. With its bibliography and notes covering both secondary and primary sources, it can serve as a starting point for further investigation.

After years of neglect, the topic of women in the 1930s is suddenly receiving substantially more attention from historians. New research by Alice Kessler-Harris, Lois Scharf, Winifred Wandersee, and others, as well as many of the biographies in the recently published *Notable American Women: The Modern Period*, has greatly widened our knowledge of women's activities in this decade. Whenever possible, I have incorporated this new scholarship into the text. The general survey of developments for women in the 1930s presented in *Holding Their Own: American Women in the 1930s* is a first step toward the more detailed analaysis of the decade that will be possible when the findings of all such new studies become available.

Writing a survey of developments for women over the course of a decade is an inherently difficult undertaking. Many trends and forces that affect women's lives do not fit neatly into segments decade by decade: continuity rather than change is the rule. On the other hand, there are good reasons for taking a decade-by-decade approach to women's history. Conclusions from the 1930s can be fit into the broader patterns of twentieth-century women's history. Moreover, freezing women's roles and activities over a ten-year period allows a broad analysis of the multiple influences on women's lives. The interconnections between popular culture and attitudes toward women, between governmental initiatives and women's participation in the arts, between feminism and college life can be concretely analyzed. In the specific case of the 1930s, such an approach allows historians to survey in some depth the impact of the Great Depression on various facets of women's lives. More than any other general theme, the role of the Depression in shaping American culture and society in the 1930s molds this book.

Susan Ware

Prologue:
The 1930s

Decades have become a convenient way of compartmental-
izing the American past. Labels like the Twenties, the Fifties, or
the Sixties immediately suggest a certain interpretive framework—flappers and gin fizzes, complacency and gray flannel
suits, protest and social change. As America moves from one
decade to the next, the country seems to confront new problems
and challenges in ten-year cycles. While distinguishing characteristics certainly shape individual decades, historians must be wary
of placing too much emphasis on what is new and distinctive about
each succeeding decade. Such an excessive categorization hides the
strong continuities that have shaped American history from decade to decade, especially in the twentieth century.

Some decades have more unity and cohesion than others: this is
certainly true of the 1930s. Bounded on one side by the stock
market crash of October 29, 1929, and on the other by the bombing
of Pearl Harbor on December 7, 1941, the decade of the 1930s was
dominated by the gravest economic crisis the United States had
ever faced. Caroline Bird said of the period between 1929 and
1941, "During those long intervening years of standstill everybody
and everything marked time. . . ."[1] One early casualty was the
carefree self-confidence that had characterized the prosperous
1920s. Never has a decade been snuffed out so quickly as the 1920s:

it was almost as if people felt that the Depression was punishment for the excesses of the previous decade. Only with the mobilization of resources for World War II did the United States finally pull out of the Depression.

Few people had predicted the stock market crash of 1929, and certainly no one suspected that the country would be locked in a depression throughout the 1930s. Once the crash came, the economy went into a tailspin. Prices on the New York Stock Exchange show the declines dramatically: American Telephone, from a September 3, 1929, high of 304 to a low of $70\frac{1}{4}$ in 1932; General Electric, from $396\frac{1}{4}$ to 34; General Motors, from $72\frac{3}{4}$ to $7\frac{5}{8}$; United States Steel, from $261\frac{3}{4}$ to $21\frac{1}{4}$. A more telling symptom of the decline than the stock market collapse was the halving of national income between 1929 and 1932; by the winter of 1932–33, industrial output had practically ground to a halt. United States Steel cut its full-time payroll from 225,000 in 1929 to zero on April 1, 1933; the ranks of part-time employees fell to barely half of their 1929 totals. In 1934, national income was $10 billion less than in 1931, just above half the 1929 level. Instead of snapping out of the downturn, the economy slipped deeper and deeper into a prolonged depression. Frederick Lewis Allen observed that "perhaps the worst thing about the Depression was its inexorable continuance year after year."[2]

Agriculture was one of the areas hardest hit by the Depression. Farm prices plummeted in reaction to the stock market crash: farm income dropped 20 percent in 1930, and 30 percent again in 1931. Farmers had huge surpluses, but consumers could not afford to buy their crops. The drop in farm income meant that many farmers could no longer meet mortgage payments, and they watched helplessly as their homes and farms were foreclosed and auctioned off. By 1932, farmers were organizing "farm holidays" (strikes) to protest declining farm income. Compounding these problems, the 1930s brought serious drought, making farming even more difficult in the dust storms that choked the Midwest. This, in turn, fueled a steady stream of migrants to the promised land of California. John Steinbeck's *The Grapes of Wrath* (1939) provided a fictional portrait of one Dust Bowl family's struggle after they lost their land.[3]

Families were struggling in the urban areas as well. At its peak in 1933, unemployment affected between 12 and 15 million American workers; during the rest of the decade, the number of unemployed hovered around 8 million. At times, 25 percent of the workforce was out of a job. Caroline Bird recalled, "Everyone knew of someone engaged in a desperate struggle. . . ." Men and women felt superfluous when they wanted to work but for month after month could not find jobs. "There is something about the anniversary of your layoff which makes you feel more helpless," one man remembered. People learned to get by with less, and they even got used to hunger. Public officials liked to say that no one had starved, but cases of starvation were documented. The psychic damage such conditions inflicted on the spirit is impossible to measure.[4]

One persistent irony of the Depression was the vast economic dislocation: want in the midst of plenty. While crops rotted in the fields because farmers did not have enough money to harvest them, people starved in the cities. People wore threadbare clothing, while bales of cotton stood unsold in southern commercial centers. Thousands of shoe workers were laid off, while people walked the streets in cardboard shoes.

While the economic system at times seemed to have broken down completely, these contradictions never led to a sustained questioning of the American capitalist system. Instead, people blamed themselves. Even at the lowest ebb of the Depression, the mood of the country was never revolutionary. Ed Paulson remembered, "Ours was a bewilderment, not an anger. Not a sense of being particularly put upon. We weren't talking revolution; we were talking jobs." In a cartoon from the 1930s, a squirrel asks an old man on a park bench why he had not saved for a rainy day. "I did," replies the old man apathetically.[5]

The Depression's impact spread inexorably. While hard times had predated the 1929 crash for groups like coal miners and blacks, in 1930 and 1931 the Depression reached wider groups of Americans. One writer remembered, "You could feel the depression deepen. . . ." The winter of 1932–33 saw the worst despair. Herbert Hoover's Republican principles limited his response to the Depression: he supported federal grants to corporations to get industrial production moving again, but balked at direct federal relief to the unemployed. The dole would destroy their character, Hoover avowed. By 1932–33, however, private charity and state and local welfare councils had exhausted their resources. The unemployed had no place to turn.[6]

Against this backdrop, Franklin D. Roosevelt became president. Since the Republicans had smugly claimed credit for the prosperity of the 1920s, Herbert Hoover found it difficult to escape the blame for the Depression. During the 1932 campaign, Roosevelt promised bold new action, but little of the New Deal was actually spelled out. In fact, one of Roosevelt's campaign pledges was to cut government spending by 25 percent. Roosevelt easily won the general election winning 427 electoral votes to Hoover's 39.[7]

At his inauguration on March 4, 1933, Roosevelt made what one historian has called "his greatest single contribution to the politics of the 1930s: the instillation of hope and courage in the people." Mentioning few specific programs in his speech, Roosevelt nonetheless convinced the country that he would provide the necessary leadership to end the Depression. In fact, throughout the 1930s the New Deal was almost totally dependent on Roosevelt's ability to inspire confidence in the American public. While the New Deal did much to save faith in the American system, only World War II finally pulled the United States out of its ten-year slump.[8]

The New Deal went through several stages. The early days of the Roosevelt administration produced an outpouring of legislation which suggested bold new solutions to the problems of the Depression. The Triple-A farm program planned crop reduction through price supports; the federal government cooperated with business in the National Recovery Administration (NRA) codes; new laws regulated the banking industry and Wall Street. Public works programs and federal aid to the unemployed were initiated. In addition, creative experiments like the Tennessee Valley Authority (regional planning and cheap hydroelectric power run by a government-owned company) and the Civilian Conservation Corps (unemployed young men living in camps in the woods while doing reforestation work) caught the public's imagination. The first one hundred days of the Roosevelt administration also saw the end of Prohibition, a welcome relief to many Americans.

The New Deal moved into a second phase in 1934 and 1935. Conditions had improved slightly after 1933, and rising expectations fueled impatience with the slow progress of recovery. Leaders like Huey Long, Father Coughlin (who received more mail than any other person in America in 1934), and Dr. Francis Townsend gained large followings. Governor Floyd Olsen of Minnesota and California gubernatorial candidate. Upton Sinclair pressed for more radical solutions. A general strike in San Francisco in 1934 was but one of a series of radical-led strikes in that year. The 1934 election results reflected these rising concerns, and Roosevelt was pushed to the left. In the next session of Congress, the New Deal went significantly beyond the programs of its first one hundred days, undertaking social security legislation, expanded relief under the Works Progress Administration (WPA), and banking and tax reform. Moreover, Congress passed the 1935 National Labor Relations Act (also known as the Wagner Act), which put the weight of the federal government behind the recognition of unions. Support for the emerging labor movement was one of the decade's most lasting achievements.[9]

In 1936, the New Deal was truly at "high tide." Franklin Roosevelt was immensely popular, and in 1936 he rode to a stunning electoral victory, taking every state but Maine and Vermont. For the rest of the 1930s, however, the New Deal stagnated. Now that the sense of emergency from the early 1930s had passed, a loose conservative coalition in Congress began to balk at Roosevelt's liberal programs. In 1937, Roosevelt made an ill-conceived attempt to pack the Supreme Court with justices more sympathetic to the New Deal's social legislation, an action which further alienated Congress. Perhaps the gravest mistake of the Roosevelt administration was its decision to cut back government spending in the summer of 1937, precipitating a recession almost as severe as that of 1932–33. Unemployment soared to 11 million; the stock market fell 43 percent; industrial production fell to the lowest levels of 1933. Only when Roosevelt increased government spending in early 1938 did the economy pick up again. That the economy had fallen half as much in nine months in 1937–38 as it had from 1929 to 1933 shows how far from understanding the causes of the Depression the New Dealers still were. However much the New Deal had restored hope to the American people, it utterly failed to curtail the Depression.[10]

The economy, unemployment, and the New Deal response to the Depression are only one part of the story of the 1930s. For many Americans, life continued fairly normally. Some escaped contact with the Depression entirely or were only marginally affected, and a lucky few even managed to strike it rich in the midst of the economic dislocation. For many Americans in the 1930s the diversions of popular culture and amusement were just as absorbing as the latest unemployment figures or the profusion of alphabet agencies in Washington. Popular culture and entertainment distracted Americans from the hard times all around them.

During the 1930s and into the 1940s, movies reached their peak of influence, with an average weekly audience of 85 million. Mae West, W. C. Fields, Greta Garbo, Marlene Dietrich, Joan Crawford, Claudette Colbert, Clark Gable, the Marx Brothers, Shirley Temple, Cary Grant, Jimmy Stewart, Bette Davis, and Katharine Hepburn were the decade's most popular stars. They appeared in such successful Hollywood genres of the 1930s as the gangster movie, the screwball comedy, the Busby Berkeley extravaganza, and Walt Disney cartoons. While the films produced in the 1930s often give little indication that there was a depression on, movies played a key role in preserving national cohesion, as Robert Sklar observed: "Hollywood directed its enormous powers of persuasion to preserving the basic moral, social, and economic tenets of traditional American culture." By providing cheap family entertainment and reinforcing traditional ideals, movies made an important contribution to the 1930s. To film buffs, the legacy has been of lasting value.[11]

Radio went big time in the 1930s as well. "Amos 'n' Andy" was the most popular show of the decade, with millions tuning in each week to the exploits of the Kingfish and the Fresh Air Taxicab Company. Charlie McCarthy and Edgar Bergen, daytime radio dramas like "Ma Perkins," and serial dramas like "The Lone Ranger" (which had 20 million listeners by 1939) provided cheap home entertainment for many American families. Even FDR got into the act with his fireside chats. Radio also produced one of the biggest hoaxes of all times—Orson Welles's October 31, 1938, broadcast of H. G. Wells's "The War of the Worlds." Panic-stricken listeners actually believed that Martians had landed in New Jersey. No one doubted any longer the power of radio.[12]

Other diversions abounded. Even though automobile sales dropped during the Depression, more cars were on the road in 1937 than in 1929. There were also more roads for people to drive on, including the Merritt Parkway in Connecticut, which was specifically limited to pleasure vehicles. If a family could afford a vacation in 1932, they could go to Lake Placid for the Winter Olympics or to Los Angeles for the Summer Games. The 1933 World's Fair in Chicago, ill-named the Century of Progress (planning had begun before 1929), drew millions of visitors; so did the 1939 New York World's Fair, organized around the theme of the World of Tomorrow. A big hit was the General Motors Futurama pavilion, which depicted life in 1960. Another forerunner of things to come was the first public exhibition of television.

Like other decades, the 1930s had its fads and amusements. Miniature golf, contract bridge, and Monopoly were sensations during the Depression. Six-day bicycle races, dance marathons, and rollerskating caught the public's attention. Professional sports became more popular than ever. Babe Ruth's domination of the game of baseball was being challenged by Lou Gehrig; Bobby Jones reigned in golf, and Bill Tilden in tennis. Benny Goodman was the King of Swing, and "Brother, Can You Spare a Dime?" was one of the decade's most popular hit songs. Another timely tune was "Who's Afraid of the Big Bad Wolf?" from the Walt Disney cartoon *Three Little Pigs*. Released in May 1933, the song's upbeat tone mirrored the excitement of the early days of the Roosevelt administration.

Women's fashions underwent noticeable changes in the 1930s. One observer quipped that "indeed so striking was the change between the ideal figure of 1929 and that of 1933 that one might almost have thought a new anatomical species had come into being." Instead of the boyish, low-waisted, no-hipped styles of the 1920s, 1930s fashions emphasized curves and fuller bosoms. New foundation garments and uplift bras supplied what nature had forgotten: the 1930 Sears catalog reminded women, "The new mode calls for a definitely indented waistline, long tapering hips and the molded bust. To wear the new frocks, you must wear the smart, new corsets." Paralleling the decline in economic fortunes, skirt lengths fell to within a foot of the ground for everyday wear by 1933. Suits were more tailored and severe, and padded shoulders first appeared on Schiaparelli models. By the late 1930s, skirt lengths began to rise again, approaching the short lengths of the previous decade. To conserve fabric during wartime, skirts stayed short, and styles kept the functional and tailored look developed over the previous ten years.[13]

During the Depression, many people had a superabundance of leisure time, and reading became a popular pastime. The phenomenal success of Harvey Allen's gothic tale *Anthony Adverse* (1934) was topped a scant three years later by Margaret Mitchell's monumental saga of the Old and New South, *Gone With the Wind*. Pearl Buck's *The Good Earth* (1931) took readers to far-away China, and Sinclair Lewis's *It Can't Happen Here* (1935) showed that fascism might not be as alien to the United States as the country believed. Dale Carnegie's 1936 runaway bestseller, *How to Win Friends and Influence People*, struck a responsive chord among the insecure American middle class. John Steinbeck's poignant portrayal of the Joad family in *The Grapes of Wrath* (1939) introduced millions of readers to the plight of migrant workers in California.

Tabloid newspapers still dominated the printed media. Sensation-seeking journalists found plenty of stories to divert their readers from hard times and depression: the 1932 kidnapping of the Lindbergh baby, Amelia Earhart's disappearance on a round-the-world flight in 1937, the Hindenburg disaster on May 6, 1937, the gunning down of John Dillinger ("Public Enemy Number One") by the FBI and the birth of the Dionne quintuplets in 1934, the abdication in 1936 of Edward VIII from the English throne to marry the twice-divorced American Wallis Simpson. Tabloids were not the only print media to cover these stories. During the 1930s, *Life*, *Look*, *Fortune*, and *Esquire* commenced publication.

Increasingly as the 1930s wore on, domestic stories shared the stage with grim news from abroad, specifically the rise of fascism in Europe and the Far East.[14] In one of those coincidences whose significance becomes apparent only in hindsight, the German Reichstag granted total power to Adolf Hitler just one day after Franklin Roosevelt was inaugurated as president of the United States. After 1933, Hitler's anti-Jewish policies and repression increased. While Japanese expansion continued unchecked in the Far East, Mussolini annexed Ethiopia in 1935 and Hitler moved into the Rhineland in 1936. That same year the Spanish Civil War erupted, pitting the forces of fascism (General Franco, backed by Hitler, Mussolini, and the Catholic Church) against the Spanish Republican government, supported by the Soviet Union and several thousand idealistic American volunteers fighting with the Abraham Lincoln Brigade. By 1939, Franco's victory was assured.

In the late 1930s, the world moved closer to war. In 1938, Western allies hoped to appease Hitler at Munich by allowing him to annex the Sudetenland section of Czechoslovakia, but their plan backfired. Once Hitler realized that no country would likely take action against his aggression, he became bolder. In 1939, he took over the rest of Czechoslovakia. In August 1939, the world reeled from the announcement of the Nazi-Soviet pact, which left Hitler free to attack Poland. In retaliation, Britain and France declared war on Germany. In April 1940, Hitler moved swiftly, crushing Denmark, Norway, the Low Countries, and France, all within seven weeks. Now only Britain stood between the United States and Hitler's plans to conquer the world.

Throughout these ominous developments in Europe and the Far East, American public opinion remained steadfastly isolationist. Disillusionment with American participation in World War I, a conviction that wars were conducted for the profit of munitions makers, and a preoccupation with domestic events fueled this staunch isolationism. Strict neutrality legislation after 1935 hampered U.S. efforts to influence international developments.

By 1939, however, Franklin Roosevelt and others realized that American entry into the war was inevitable. Concern over European developments was a major factor in Roosevelt's decision to seek a third term in 1940. He moved cautiously in his public pronouncements, but behind the scenes he began to aid Churchill and the Allies. A lend-lease agreement with Britain in 1940 bypassed the neutrality guidelines and brought the United States closer to the contest as the main ally of Britain. In the end, the act which propelled the United States into war came not from Europe but from Asia, with the surprise Japanese attack on Pearl Harbor on December 7, 1941. Because Japan was allied with Germany and Italy, America now found itself involved in a truly global war.

American participation in World War II has had a profound impact on American society since 1940, especially in the field of foreign relations. The isolationism of the 1930s did not return when World War II ended: America now considered itself the police officer of the free world. Another unexpected by-product of the war was that the mobilization of resources snapped the economy out of the Depression. In 1941, the economy finally approached its 1929 levels.

The Depression was over, but not forgotten. Every great social and economic disaster has long-term effects. Activist Larry Van Dusen observed, "Any great economic upheaval, I think, alters patterns."[15] Perhaps the greatest alteration from the 1930s concerned the role of the federal government: the modern welfare state was born of the Depression. During the 1930s, the federal government became an institution which touched the lives of most American citizens for the first time, taking on new responsibilities for guaranteeing the security and livelihoods of citizens, supporting the right of labor to organize, and managing the economy. The modern Presidency took root as well, spurred by the charismatic personality of Franklin D. Roosevelt. These institutional changes are a firm legacy of the 1930s.

The decade left another legacy, a psychological one which Caroline Bird has called "the invisible scar." Bird believes that the total human bill for the Depression has never been totaled up. The hurt and humiliation of hard times did not suddenly disappear with the return of a steady income, and many "survivors" of the Depression retained the deep-seated fear of losing things of value. Larry Van Dusen put it well: "The Depression left a legacy of fear, but also a desire for acquisition—property, security. I now have twenty times more shirts than I need, because all during that time, shirts were something I never had." Virginia Durr noticed a similar reaction: "The great majority reacted by thinking money is the most important thing in the world. Get yours. And get it for your children. Nothing else matters. Not having that stark terror come at you again."[16] For many Americans, that was what the 1930s were all about.

Notes and References

1. Caroline Bird, *The Invisible Scar* (New York, 1966), pp. xi–xii.
2. William E. Leuchtenberg, *Franklin D. Roosevelt and the New Deal, 1932–1940* (New York, 1963), pp. 18–19, 94; Frederick Lewis Allen, *Since Yesterday: The 1930's in America* (New York, 1939), pp. 49, 59. These two books are excellent introductions to the 1930s, and much of the general information in this chapter is drawn from them, especially Leuchtenberg.
3. Paul Conkin, *The New Deal*, 2d ed. (Arlington Heights, Ill., 1975), pp. 38–39.
4. Ibid., p. 67; Bird, *Invisible Scar*, pp. 18, 23–24, 29; Leuchtenberg, *FDR and the New Deal*, p. 118.
5. Leuchtenberg, *FDR and the New Deal*, p. 26; Studs Terkel, *Hard Times: An Oral History of the Great Depression* (New York, 1970), p. 31; Bird, *Invisible Scar*, p. 33.
6. Bird, *Invisible Scar*, p. 18; Leuchtenberg, *FDR and the New Deal*, p. 18.
7. Leuchtenberg, *FDR and the New Deal*, p. 11.
8. Ibid., p. 42; Conkin, *The New Deal*, p. 1.
9. For general background on the early New Deal in addition to Leuchtenberg and Conkin, see Frank B. Freidel, *Franklin D. Roosevelt: Launching the New Deal* (Boston: Little, Brown, 1973), and Ellis W. Hawley, *The New Deal and the Problem of Monopoly* (Princeton: Princeton University Press, 1966).
10. Leuchtenberg, *FDR and the New Deal*, p. 167; Conkin, *The New Deal*, pp. 92–93. See also James T. Patterson, *Congressional Conservatism and the New Deal* (Lexington, Kentucky: University of Kentucky Press, 1967).
11. Robert Sklar, *Movie-Made America: A Cultural History of American Movies* (New York, 1975), p. 175; Allen, *Since Yesterday*, p. 224. The Sklar book is an excellent introduction to movie culture in the 1930s.

12. Unless otherwise noted, all the material on popular culture is drawn from Allen, *Since Yesterday*.

13. Allen, *Since Yesterday*, pp. 111–12; Sears, Roebuck catalog quoted in Lois Banner, *Women in Modern America: A Brief History* (New York, 1974), p. 197; Alice Lessing, *Sixty Years of Fashion, 1900–1960: The Evolution of Women's Styles in America* (New York, 1963).

14. Leuchtenberg, *FDR and the New Deal*, in chapters 9, 12, and 13, provides a convenient summary of international developments.

15. Terkel, *Hard Times*, p. 108.

16. Bird, *Invisible Scar*, pp. xi–xii; Terkel, *Hard Times*, pp. 108, 462.

Mother of eleven at rural rehabilitation center, Tulare, California
1938, by Dorothea Lange
Courtesy of Library of Congress
FSA Collection

Chapter One

Women Face
The Depression

In 1933, Eleanor Roosevelt's *It's Up to the Women* attempted to show women how they could pull the country through its economic crisis. According to Eleanor Roosevelt, women were often called on to carry heavier burdens for weathering such crises than men: "The women know that life must go on and that the needs of life must be met and it is their courage and determination which, time and again, have pulled us through worse crises than the present one." It was to these women that Eleanor Roosevelt addressed her pleas. While women cannot claim credit for ending the Depression, the country could never have survived the 1930s without women's collective contributions.[1]

Eleanor Roosevelt wrote in *It's Up to the Women*, "Practically every woman, whether she is rich or poor, is facing today a reduction in income." She felt sympathy for women from wealthy backgrounds whose families had sometimes lost their entire fortunes in the stock market crash. Even if they were more fortunate, they still suffered. As Eleanor Roosevelt pointed out, if one has always gone skiing in the winter, or headed south for a warm-climate vacation, if a maid has always appeared when one rings, it seems a real hardship to give up such things. Louis Adamic, whose *My America: 1928—1938* contains many poignant glimpses of American life during the Depression, felt similar compassion for the wealthy classes: "There is no doubt that some of these women—to say nothing of the men—suffered as much on account of economic reverses as most of the unemployed men's wives whose plight actually was much worse than theirs."[2]

The very rich have always been a small minority of the American population, and the experiences of certain wealthy women should not be counted as typical. In fact, many well-to-do people escaped entirely the devastating changes the Depression forced on other segments of society. But the vast majority of American women were neither very rich nor very poor. Somewhere in the middle, they were struggling to get by with less. For most American women, the experience of the Depression did not mean having a million-dollar trust fund lost in the stock market or being taken out of a fancy boarding school because the family could no longer pay the bills. On the other hand, neither did it ordinarily mean living in cardboard "Hoovervilles" or going on relief. The typical woman in the 1930s had a husband who was still employed, although he probably had taken a pay cut to keep his job; if the man lost his job, the family often had enough resources to survive without going on relief or losing its possessions. Life was not easy for women in these situations, but the picture was not uniformly bleak.

The old saying "Use it up, wear it out, make it do, or do without" provided the title for Jeane Westin's oral history of how women survived in the 1930s. *Making Do* characterizes the lives of many middle-class women in that decade. These women practiced small economies like buying day-old bread, warming several dishes in the oven at once to save gas, and relining coats with old blankets. Sheets were split down the middle and resewn to equalize wear; adult clothing was cut down to child size; broken crockery, string, and old rags were saved in case they might come in handy some day (they usually ended up in the attic). Such families still had food on their tables, but the meat was of a cheaper cut; the family went to fewer movies; if they had a car, they went on fewer Sunday drives; if they could not afford a large apartment, they moved to a smaller one. Eleanor Roosevelt summarized the day-to-day lives of these women: "It means endless little economies and constant anxiety for fear of some catastrophe such as accident or illness which may completely swamp the family budget." The line between making do and doing without was often a fine one in the 1930s.[3]

During the 1930s, over half of the families in the country had incomes between $500 and $1,500 yearly. In 1935–36, the median family income was $1,160; $2,500 a year placed a household in the top tenth percentile and guaranteed a very comfortable life-style. Only these higher incomes were subject to taxation in the 1930s. One woman recalled, "You know what our big wish was? That someday we would be making so much money we'd have to pay income tax. In those days that meant you'd really arrived."[4]

Given a yearly income of approximately $1,100 to $1,200, the average family had between $20 and $25 a week to feed, clothe, and provide shelter for itself, making budgets an obvious necessity. This was usually women's responsibility, since women were estimated to control the spending of at least 80 percent of the family's income. Government guidelines recommended setting aside 35 percent of family income for food, 33 percent for shelter, and a scant 0.4 percent for taxes. Clothing allowances were more individual. Eleanor Roosevelt noted that a coat would usually last two seasons, and suggested that a new hat often made people think one's entire outfit was new. Not everyone was so enamored of budgets. Humorist Will Cuppy quipped, "In order to run a budget, you have to have money. . . . I don't feel that I can afford one right now—there are so many other things I need worse."[5]

Making do on $20 a week was aided by deflation, which caused food prices to drop in the early 1930s. With some creative shopping and cooking, a woman could feed a family of six on $5 a week, with milk at 10¢ a quart, a loaf of bread 7¢, butter 23¢ a pound, and two pounds of hamburger for 25¢. But women had to watch every penny. One woman recalled that she and a friend would go shopping together each week and split the two pounds of hamburger a quarter would buy, taking turns each week paying the extra penny.[6]

Recipes for nutritious yet inexpensive meals provided another way to cut down on food costs. Major food companies like General Mills sponsored radio programs like the "Betty Crocker Hour," which gave out recipes and money-saving hints while promoting the sponsor's products. Blanche Eddy recalled, "I used to listen to Aunt Susan on WKY in Oklahoma City. She came on Monday through Friday at 10:30 a.m., and I'd always stop my housework and write down her recipes." Women shared recipes among themselves, such as this imitation mincemeat called Green Tomato Mincemeat:

> 1 pk green tomatoes
> ½ pk apples
> ½ c butter
> 5 c white sugar
> 2 t cinnamon
> ½ t cloves
> 1 box raisins
> 1 c cider vinegar

> Grind tomatoes and apples, mix other ingredients, and cook for two hours. Place in nine-inch pie shells and bake at 375° until done. Makes six or seven pies.[7]

Another favorite was called Poor Man's Cake:

> 1 c sugar
> 2 c raisins
> 1 t cloves
> ½ c lard
> 2 c water
> 1 t nutmeg
> pinch of salt

> Boil all ingredients 3 minutes. Cool. Add 2 teaspoons baking powder, 1 teaspoon soda, 3 cups flour. Mix and bake in medium oven about 45 minutes.[8]

Jeane Westin found that many women discarded their old recipes as soon as the Depression ended. Some, however, still maintain today that the substitutes were better than the real things.[9]

When a salesperson (or a transient) asked at the door in the 1930s, "Is the lady of the house at home?", she usually was. Middle-class women's lives revolved around their homes. For one thing, more and more women were "doing their own work." Domestic service continued to decline in the 1930s, and only a small minority of households had full-time help. Partly this was a matter of economy—families could no longer afford to pay their servants. But just as important was the introduction of labor-saving devices into the home which made it possible for women to do their own housework. Ruth Cowan has observed, "The ideal housewife of the 1920's and 30's did not have servants, or to put it another way, the servants she had were electrical, not human."[10]

During the 1920s and extending into the 1930s, much of women's household labor was changed dramatically, especially by the introduction of electricity. By 1925, more than half the homes in America had been wired; the figure was even higher for urban areas. Electrification allowed such changes as a motor for the ubiquitous sewing machine, small appliances like irons, toasters, and wafflers, as well as major appliances like washing machines, refrigerators, and vacuum cleaners. Even with these appliances, the typical woman was spending sixty-one to sixty-three hours a week on housework.[11]

The 1930s housewife could also take advantage of changes in meal preparation, traditionally one of the most time-consuming of women's household chores. More food was available precooked or in cans. In the 1930s, the housewife could choose from among twenty-one varieties of Campbell's soups, six kinds of Jell-O, Chase and Sanborn coffee in cans, and such new packaged dry products as Cream of Wheat, Kellogg's Corn Flakes, or Post Grape-Nuts Flakes. Products such as Heinz spaghetti, Libby's corned beef and chili con carne, Van Camp pork and beans, and Del Monte peaches, pineapples, and other fruits were all readily available. Recipes now included directions for "canned or fresh," or just assumed the woman would be using ingredients out of a can. This changeover was not complete (one woman recalled, "I don't remember ever seeing my mother use a can opener"), but it did signal a decline in home canning and preserving.[12]

During the early- to mid-twentieth century, cooking and cleaning became easier when gas stoves replaced coal or wood-burning stoves in many kitchens. (Electric stoves were still too unwieldy in the 1930s.) Telephone shopping increased, and more supermarkets opened. More women bought ready-made clothing, finding it cheaper and easier than making their families' clothes, especially with items like children's clothing. Likewise, home baking declined, with the storebought loaf of bread comparable, occasionally even superior, to what a housewife could produce after spending an entire day baking.[13] These general trends in household technology continued to influence women's roles in the 1930s in spite of the Depression. Functions previously performed by the isolated woman were removed from the home: the housewife now bought such goods, rather than producing them herself.

The 1930s, however, did see a temporary slackening of this great American love affair with technology and gadgetry. Women in the Depression made do by substituting their own time and labor for goods and services that previously had been bought with cash. Ruth Milkman's research on women's work, both paid wage labor and unpaid domestic work, has emphasized how women "took up the slack" in the economy of the 1930s by expanding their unpaid labor in the home. Out of necessity, many women returned to home canning, sewed all their family's clothes instead of buying them ready-made, and baked bread at home instead of buying it at the store. Milkman concluded that many families maintained their former standards of living despite decreased incomes only because women substituted their own labor for goods and services previously purchased.[14]

The Depression also had a strong impact on demographic factors affecting the family. The marriage, divorce, and birth rates all fell dramatically in the early 1930s and did not begin to rise again until 1934. The marriage rate had been 10.14 per 1,000 persons in 1929, but was down to 7.87 per 1,000 by 1932. By 1938, according to one estimate, 1.5 million people had been forced to postpone marriage due to hard times. Moralists feared a rise in premarital and extramarital sexual activity, but no such dramatic increase was noted at the time. "Girls adapted by turning down the heat," one commentator explained.[15]

Caroline Bird remembered that the burning question facing young people was whether they could afford to get married on $15 a week. But many couples did not have even that much. Schoolteacher Elsa Ponselle noted that temporary postponements of marriage often became permanent, especially among those in her field: "Do you realize how many people in my generation are not married? . . . It wasn't that we didn't have a chance. I was going with someone when the Depression hit. We probably would have gotten married. He was a commercial artist and had been doing very well. . . . Suddenly he was laid off. It hit him like a ton of bricks. And he just disappeared." Cohort figures confirm Elsa Ponselle's experience. Among women who never married, the proportion of single women who were between twenty-five and thirty in 1935 is about 30 percent higher than the proportion of single women in the similar cohort five years earlier.[16]

Not only was it too expensive to get married: it was too expensive to get a divorce. In "Middletown" (Muncie, Indiana), the divorce rate fell 43 percent from 1928 to 1933, one of the few good things Middletown folks had to say about the Depression. Nationally the divorce rate dropped from 1.66 per 1,000 population in 1929 to 1.28 by 1932, before beginning to rise again. Besides sticking together when times got rough, couples often stayed married because it was easier to get on relief if one had a family to support.[17]

Another demographic factor very sensitive to hard times was the birth rate. During the early 1930s, the birth rate fell below the replacement level for the first time in U.S. history. From 21.3 live births per 1,000 population in 1930, the rate fell to 18.4 by 1933. Just as couples consciously postponed marriage, so too did they put off having children. At the least, families lowered their sights to two children. A common cliché was, "I don't want to bring children into a world that has no use for them." Pregnancy was often treated as a misfortune, rather than a joyous event, and in many circles abortion emerged as an acceptable (if illegal) alternative. Yet it cost only $65 to have a baby in a good New York hospital in 1935, and by then the birth rate was on the upswing.[18]

Besides changing expectations about childbearing, the increased availability of birth control played a large role in the elimination of unwanted fertility. By 1940, dissemination of birth-control information to married couples was legal in all states but Massachusetts and Connecticut; a 1936 Gallup poll showed that 63 percent favored the teaching and practice of birth control. Contraceptives were available through the mail, even from the Sears, Roebuck catalog, and in gas-station restrooms. Contraceptive manufacture was one industry that never felt the effects of the Depression: business was booming. Even in Middletown, contraceptives were widely available.[19]

A final factor may have contributed to the downturn in births—
a decline in sexual relations. Sketchy evidence suggests that due to
the tensions of hard times, sex within marriage decreased. One
woman observed, "They're not men anymore, if you know what I
mean." Fear of pregnancy was a major factor, but feelings of
inadequacy on the part of the male and lack of respect for the
unemployed man from his wife also played roles. And perhaps the
women were so tired by all their making do that they were too tired
for making love.[20]

In general, the Depression affected the family, and by extension
women's roles, in one of two ways. Louis Adamic observed, "On
the one hand, thousands of families were broken up, some permanently, some temporarily, or were seriously disorganized. On
the other hand, thousands of other families became more closely
integrated than they had been before the Depression." Many of
Adamic's examples support the latter interpretation: when unemployment and hard times struck, family members pooled their
resources and worked together to make whatever sacrifices were
necessary. Eleanor Roosevelt saw many families brought even
closer together by the experience. With money short, families
turned to cheap entertainment like staying home to listen to the
radio, a popular family pastime. Church attendance rose, and
women found comfort and consolation in their religion and wom-
en's church groups. Americans turned inward during the Depression, and women's roles at the center of the family took on even
greater significance.[21]

While most women's lives in the 1930s centered around their
homes and families where they struggled to make do during the
Depression, for many Americans the crash in 1929 did not signal a
significant change in their lives. Times had always been hard. One
person recalled, "I've been in a depression ever since I've been in
the world." A black man in Chicago told Studs Terkel, "The
Negro was born in the depression. It didn't mean too much to him,
the Great American Depression, as you call it. There was no such
thing. It only became official when it hit the white man." Caroline
Bird summed this up well when she said, "The Depression did
not depress the conditions of the poor. It merely publicized
them."[22]

The lives of rural women, for example, had continuities which transcended the economic dislocations of the 1930s. While the urban population had steadily increased throughout the twentieth century, a rural life-style still characterized a significant minority of American women in the 1930s. Conditions had always been difficult on farms, especially for women. Rural women's lives were ruled by low income and poverty, overdependence on cash crops like cotton and tobacco, high fertility, isolation, and the lack of conveniences—all conditions which predated (and postdated) the 1930s.

James Agee and Walker Evans have provided perhaps the most widely known portrait of farm tenancy in the 1930s in *Let Us Now Praise Famous Men*, which, despite its title, contains much information about women's family roles in the rural South. An even more complete picture of the white tenant farm woman is Margaret Jarman Hagood's classic 1939 study, *Mothers of the South*. Hagood provided a general definition of men's and women's roles in the typical southern tenant farm family: "The modal pattern is for the woman to do everything inside the house, for the man to occupy himself on the farm, and for both to share the intermediate duties centering around the backyard and relating chiefly to the care of the livestock. So far this sounds fairly evenly balanced, but the wife does field work also for about half the year in addition to her traditionally allocated sphere of labors. The return of services she gets from her husband for her farm work is never equal to it in amount."[23] Women had triple responsibilities: the household, childbearing and raising, and actual farm work.

Southern farm women had primary responsibility for all household chores, which were performed in homes typically lacking electricity and running water. (Before the rural electrification program in 1935, only one out of ten American farms had electricity; by 1941, four out of ten had electric power.) Women cooked on wood stoves and made most of their family's clothes on foot-powered treadle sewing machines. Washing was by far the heaviest chore, the one most disliked by farm women. Husbands' overalls and babies' soiled diapers were the hardest to get clean.

The complaints about soiled diapers point to the second main component of the farm woman's life—the bearing and raising of children. Hagood noted the very high fertility of these southern farm women: an average of 6.4 live births per married woman, not counting stillbirths or abortions. This was significantly higher than the national average of 2.19 children. Large families provided extra hands for household and farm chores, but southern women rarely expressed desires to have more children. Since their knowledge of contraception was quite sketchy, however, these southern women were able to exercise little control over their own fertility.

Women's primary responsibility for household and child-care duties was widespread in the 1930s, shared by southern and northern, rural and urban, black, white, and chicana women alike. One thing which set rural women apart was their participation in actual farm work. While not usually counted for census purposes as employment outside the home, women's economic contributions were vital to the farm family income. Southern women did not really see helping in the fields as work in itself: "I was brought up to it" or "I've always done it" were typical comments.[24]

Hagood found that seven-eighths of the farm women she studied preferred fieldwork to housework. They enjoyed the companionship in the fields; they liked the smell of tobacco. But women also appreciated the clearly defined nature of fieldwork: "In the field there's just one thing and you can finish it up; but here in the house there's cooking, cleaning, washing, milking, churning, mending, sewing, canning, and always the children—and you don't know what to turn to next." Unfortunately, many southern women still retained full responsibility for the household and for childrearing. Even when wives worked in the fields, husbands rarely reciprocated by helping out around the house.[25]

Nora Miller's 1935 study, *The Girl in the Rural South*, offers a complementary picture of rural white women, with special emphasis on young girls between school and marriage. Miller found prospects bleak for rural girls. The average girl left school at age fourteen or fifteen when her home responsibilities had grown so large that she could no longer keep up with her course work, or when she simply lost interest in school. Between quitting school and leaving her family to set up her own household after marriage, the young girl functioned as an unpaid domestic servant and farm laborer within the family, with little time or money for social life and recreation. No wonder marriage, even at the young age of seventeen or eighteen, was seen as a release.[26]

The Depression affected the aspirations and expectations of rural girls in several ways. After World War I, more rural girls left their farms to continue their schooling in towns, or more typically, to find wage-paying jobs in nonrural areas. This trend continued into the 1930s, especially as farm families tried to earn extra income by sending the eldest daughter into the city to work, often as a domestic servant. One study found that more women than men migrated from drought-stricken midwestern farms, and at an earlier age. With the economic declines of the Depression, however, many rural girls found that 'they were unable to get jobs. Moreover, rural girls who had left the farm in the 1920s and early 1930s were often forced to return to rural life because they could no longer be self-sufficient in the cities.[27]

Lowered expectations and thwarted dreams made for poor adjustment to the rural life-style. Nora Miller described one such couple. The girl had wanted a business career but had accepted marriage instead. Her husband was dissatisfied as well: "The boy farms because he can do nothing else. The couple will talk about the careers they might have had and think of the farm as a place where they landed because careers were closed to them, and it will be hard for either of them to put his best into making a success of farming or of farm homemaking."[28]

Margaret Hagood and Nora Miller studied white southern farm women, yet many of their generalizations apply to rural black women as well. Hard times were their usual lot, so the impact of the Depression was less acute at first. Maya Angelou described her early childhood in Stamps, Arkansas, in the 1930s in her autobiography *I Know Why the Caged Bird Sings*: "The country had been in the throes of the Depression for two years before the Negroes in Stamps knew it. I think that everyone thought that the Depression, like everything else, was for the white folks, so it had nothing to do with them. . . . It was when the owners of cotton fields dropped the payment of ten cents for a pound of cotton to eight, seven and finally five that the Negro community realized that the Depression, at least, did not discriminate."[29]

In other ways, rural black and white women's lives in the South in the 1930s were similar. Both differed from the conventional white pattern in that wives (and children) worked alongside men in the fields in addition to carrying out their household responsibilities. In the black family, the role of the woman was especially strong: "The women are the stable element," a 1934 study concluded. Two-thirds of the families in that study had both parents living together with their children. There was pride in large families, and children were seen as an economic asset. A good thing, as one woman remarked: "Jest been having chillun all my life."[30]

The strong cultural definitions of men's and women's roles were tempered by the realities of agricultural life. Women's own earning power (women's earnings were often more sustained and dependable than men's) gave women an important advantage if, by choice or necessity, they needed to farm without their men. Mosel Brinton's 1935 letter to the U.S. Department of Agriculture describes one Georgia woman who planned to make it on her own:

> *Dear Friends:*
> *I am a widow woman with seven head of children, and I live on my place with a plenty of help. All are good workers and I wants to farm. I has no mule, no wagon, no feed, no grocery, and these women and men that is controlling the Civil Work for the Government won't help me.*
> *Because I am a woman. I wants to ask you all to please help me to make a crop this year and let me hear from you on return mail. Yours for business.*
>
> Mosel Brinton
> *Please answer me on return mail.*[31]

For hundreds of years, black Americans had been almost totally confined to the South, where slavery, and then sharecropping and Jim Crow laws, circumscribed their lives. Starting around World War I, blacks began to leave the South for better jobs in northern cities. As in most migrations, more men than women migrated initially. During the 1930s, some 400,000 blacks migrated north, bringing the total of blacks living outside the South to 3 million by 1940. Yet that was still a small minority: in 1940, 77 percent of the country's black population lived in the South.[32]

The pull of the North was work, but as usual, blacks were relegated to the lowest-status, lowest-paying jobs. This was especially true of black women, who were overwhelmingly concentrated in domestic service in the 1930s. Sales and clerical jobs were reserved for white women, and higher-paying factory jobs were closed to blacks of both sexes. The only time black women got into factories was as unskilled scrubwomen or floor sweepers. With husbands' wages so low, and a family to support, black women were forced to work outside the home and did so at twice the rate of white women. In 1938, 38 percent of all black women were employed outside the home.[33]

Because of the economic and social conditions under which they were forced to live, black women generally were exempted from the protected and passive role expected (but not necessarily adhered to) by the white American female. Struggling to better herself and her family gave the black woman a strength and perseverance that have not gone unnoticed. Maya Angelou paid tribute: "The fact that the adult American Negro female emerges a formidable character is often met with amazement, distaste and even belligerence. It is seldom accepted as an inevitable outcome of the struggle won by survivors and deserves respect if not enthusiastic acceptance."[34]

Maya Angelou's praise of the strength of black women has not always been shared. During the 1930s, the ongoing debate over the matriarchal family structure of black households began with the publication of sociologist E. Franklin Frazier's *The Negro Family in the United States* (1939). Yet perhaps some of the debate over whether black families are matriarchal is simply the result of white male sociologists' inability to envision a family structure where women make such vital economic contributions. Certainly the large number of black women who worked and raised families, a trend underway by the 1930s, presaged the postwar increase in white married women who worked outside the home. The economic contributions of both members of black families may signify a more egalitarian partnership in marriage as well. But one should never lose sight of the burdens that the black woman, urban or rural, northern or southern, has labored under—in Maya Angelou's phrase, "caught in the tripartite crossfire of masculine prejudice, white illogical hate and Black lack of power."[35]

American women in the 1930s thus experienced both continuities and changes in the decade. The Depression, a major new factor, had its largest impact on urban women. Other segments of society saw their lives less changed by the conditions of the Depression. One thing that remained constant throughout the 1930s was the clear division of roles within most American households. The man was the breadwinner and the woman ran the household. Of course, such roles were not unique to the 1930s, but few challenges to these age-old definitions emerged during the decade. In many ways, the Depression actually reinforced and strengthened these traditional ideals.

Robert and Helen Lynd observed these roles very clearly in *Middletown in Transition*, the 1937 sequel to their pioneering study of Muncie, Indiana. According to the Lynds, "The worlds of the two sexes constitute something akin to separate subcultures. Each involves an elaborate assignment of roles to its members and the development of preferred personality types emphasizing various ones of the more significant role attributes." Men's primary role was that of breadwinner and provider for the family. Men were to earn money to pay for food, clothing, shelter, and their children's education; they were to make enough money so that their wives did not have to work outside the home. Men represented the family in civic affairs and public life. Men had no responsibility for household chores, except for certain things like mowing the lawn or getting the car repaired.[36]

The women's role neatly complemented this. Eleanor Roosevelt wrote in *It's Up to the Women* that " . . . the women, the wives and mothers, are the inspiration of the homes, the persons for whom the men really work." The husband earned the income, the wife spent it and ran the household. Cleaning, marketing, and child care were women's responsibilities. Women were strongly encouraged to limit their aspirations to husband, family, and domesticity; work outside the home, especially for married women, was discouraged.[37]

While the 1930s present strong evidence of continuities in women's roles, the decade also suggests that women's experiences differed significantly from men's. Women's lives were probably less disrupted by the Depression than men's. Recollections like this were common: "When hard times hit, it didn't seem to bother mother as much as it did my father." If a family moved from the farm to the city, the men's work roles changed dramatically, while the women's stayed relatively the same. When unemployment took away men's jobs, it took away their roles as breadwinners for their families. Women's lives had stronger continuities: even if their husbands were unemployed, the women still had primary responsibility for the household. Caroline Bird wrote, "Even when there was not a cent in the house they had an occupation. They were still in command of 'their' homes."[38]

Observers from the 1930s often noticed these differences. In *Middletown in Transition*, Robert and Helen Lynd noted: "The men, cut adrift from their usual routine, lost much of their sense of time and dawdled helplessly and dully about the streets; while in the homes the women's world remained largely intact and the round of cooking, housecleaning, and mending became if anything more absorbing." According to the Lynds, the Depression put far more pressure on male roles than female. They even suggested that some of the tensions of women's roles in modern society were eased by women's increased contributions to family survival in the 1930s.[39]

Some of the greatest strain occurred when the man suddenly found himself around the house all the time. The unemployed man's constant presence underfoot often led to irritability; sometimes the man began to feel that his wife and children were looking at him "funny." There usually came a point when he was asked to help out with the household chores, the ultimate "woman's job." Some men pitched in cheerfully; others helped only begrudgingly. In one study, Mr. Raparka agreed to scrub the floors and help with the washing, but balked at hanging the clothes outdoors to dry because the neighbors might see him. Louis Adamic found another case where such chores caused deep resentment and bitterness: "Time hung on his hands. In the morning before she left for work his wife told him to make the beds. The children, seeing him in this new role, sometimes laughed at him. I came upon a man who, making the beds one day, was so enraged by his son's laughter that he had nearly killed the child."[40]

Most studies emphasize that this role reversal was desired neither by men nor women, partly because many wives found that their husbands were not very good housekeepers. E. Wright Bakke concluded, "His ineptness and the mistakes he makes as frequently lead to conflict as to satisfaction. After a while, the wife is glad to have him out from under foot and do the work herself." This inability of husbands and wives to exchange roles easily suggests why more women did not seek work if their husbands lost their jobs. As one case study concluded, "When he works and comes home tired, she is waiting for him and they have a nice talk together. But the other way around it was quite different."[41]

In her 1940 study, *The Unemployed Man and His Family*, Mirra

Komarovsky found that in the great majority of cases the husband maintained his dominance and authority over the family even without contributing income to the household. Only in 25 percent of the sample did unemployment significantly lower the status of the husband within the family or undermine the male's predominant role as decision-maker. Old patriarchal patterns proved stronger than temporary reverses.[42]

Even when husbands saw their dominant position in the family undermined by hard times, their lost authority did not necessarily accrue to women, either temporarily or on a permanent basis. The Lynds found that Middletown's conception of male-female roles and attributes remained basically unchanged in spite of women's larger roles in the Depression. Ruth Milkman noted that instead of leading to their increased stature within the family, women's extra contributions to family life actually served to reinforce their traditional identification with the domestic sphere. In most crises and emergencies, women are called upon to assume extra responsibilities, but rarely do these temporary advances become permanent.[43]

These cultural definitions from the 1930s bear remarkable similarities to those Betty Friedan described in her 1963 book, *The Feminine Mystique*. Friedan contrasted the claustrophobic world of the suburban housewife of the 1950s with the supposedly freer, more independent world of women of the 1930s (at least the one Friedan gleaned from the women's magazines of the period she read). Ruth Schwartz Cowan, who has studied the impact of technology on women's roles in the household, disagrees sharply with Friedan's assessment, concluding that the 1920s and 1930s "laid the trap" for the feminine mystique of the 1950s. According to Cowan, "The mystique makers of the 20's and 30's believed that women were purely domestic creatures, that the goal of each normal woman's life was the acquisition of a husband, a family, and a home." The housewife in the 1930s gladly did her own housework: "Housework was no longer regarded as a chore, but as an expression of the housewife's personality and her affection for her family. . . . Clearly, tasks of this emotional magnitude could not be relegated to servants." The 1930s were well on the way toward the feminine mystique of the 1950s.[44]

Perhaps in the long run the Great Depression did not change ordinary women's lives to any significant degree. Women simply did what they had always done: work hard and put the concerns of their families first. They did not even question their extra responsibilities in the 1930s. One woman noted that her father was changed by the Depression, but "My Mother? I think she accepted things as they came. She was busy, and I suppose that is an answer—she always had work to do."[45] Another woman recalled her own experience at length:

> I did what I had to do. I seemed to always find a way to make things work. I think hard times is harder on a man, 'cause a woman will do something. Women just seem to know where they can save or where they can help, more than a man. It's just a worry for him, and he feels so terrible when he can't take care of his family.
>
> My husband got very despondent, you know. Oh, he'd say you can't have this and you're not getting that, and I don't want to hear about this; just fighting against it all the time. A woman, like I said, can take more. I always said that she can stand more pain.[46]

Blanche Eddy summed up women's roles succinctly: "We had no choice. We just did what had to be done one day at a time."[47]

During the 1930s, therefore, strong concensus shaped women's proper roles in society. This concensus, propagated by the media, religion, and other institutions of culture, guided men and women alike. Women had complete responsibility for the domestic sphere and played a critical role in holding families together against the disintegrating forces of the Depression. But while women had primary responsibility for the household in theory and practice, many American women did not limit themselves to their homes. As always, American women's lives have encompassed far more than cooking, cleaning, and child care. The Depression propelled many women into new patterns of behavior that might not have occurred otherwise. Women's activities outside the home—especially their participation in the workforce, in the professions, in politics and social reform, and in fine arts and popular culture—add further dimensions to the experience of women in the depression decade of the 1930s.

Notes and References

1. Mrs. Franklin D. Roosevelt *[sic]*, *It's Up to the Women* (New York, 1933), p. ix.

2. Ibid., pp. 1–2; Louis Adamic, *My America: 1928–1938* (New York, 1938), pp. 288–89.

3. Jeane Westin, *Making Do: How Women Survived the '30s* (Chicago, 1976); Caroline Bird, *The Invisible Scar*, p. 226; Roosevelt, *It's Up to the Women*, p. 8.

4. Winifred D. Wandersee Bolin, "The Economics of Middle-Income Family Life: Working Women During the Great Depression," *Journal of American History* 65 (June 1978):62; Westin, *Making Do*, p. 71.

5. Roosevelt, *It's Up to the Women*, pp. 40–45; Cuppy quoted in Bolin, "The Economics of Middle-Income Family Life," p. 67.

6. Westin, *Making Do*, p. 27.

7. Ibid., p. 35.

8. Ibid., p. 37.

9. Ibid., p. 35.

10. Allen, *Since Yesterday*, p. 347; Ruth Schwartz Cowan, "Two Washes in the Morning and a Bridge Party at Night: The American Housewife Between the Wars," *Women's Studies* 3 (1976):148.

11. Cowan, "Two Washes," pp. 159–64; Ruth Schwartz Cowan, "A Case Study of Technological and Social Change: The Washing Machine and the Working Wife," in Mary Hartman and Lois W. Banner, eds., *Clio's Consciousness Raised: New Perspectives on the History of Women* (New York: Harper and Row, 1974), p. 148.

12. Cowan, "Two Washes," p. 160; Westin, *Making Do*, p. 37.

13. Robert S. Lynd and Helen Merrell Lynd, *Middletown: A Study in Contemporary American Culture* (New York, 1929), p. 155.

14. Ruth Milkman, "Women's Work and Economic Crisis: Some Lessons of the Great Depression," *Review of Radical Political Economics* 8 (Spring 1976):81–85.

15. Allen, *Since Yesterday*, p. 107; Milkman, "Women's Work and Economic Crisis," p. 83; Bird, *Invisible Scar*, pp. 234–35.

16. Bird, *Invisible Scar*, p. 233; Terkel, *Hard Times*, p. 389; Milkman, "Women's Work and Economic Crisis," p. 83.

17. Robert S. Lynd and Helen Merrell Lynd, *Middletown in Transition: A Study in Cultural Conflicts* (New York, 1937), p. 166; Allen, *Since Yesterday*, p. 109.

18. Milkman, "Women's Work and Economic Crisis," p. 84; Bird, *Invisible Scar*, pp. 44, 238–39.

19. Bird, *Invisible Scar*, pp. 42–43; Lynd and Lynd, *Middletown in Transition*, p. 167.

20. Mirra Komarovsky, *The Unemployed Man and His Family* (New York, 1940), pp. 28, 130; Adamic, *My America*, p. 293; Milkman, "Women's Work and Economic Crisis," p. 84; Westin, *Making Do*, p. 5.

21. Adamic, *My America*, pp. 283, 287; Roosevelt, *It's Up to the Women*, p. 8; Westin, *Making Do*, pp. 240–41, 250–69, for women and religion.

22. Terkel, *Hard Times*, pp. 198, 82; Bird, *Invisible Scar*, p. 30.

23. James Agee and Walker Evans, *Let Us Now Praise Famous Men* (New York: Random House, 1941); Margaret Jarman Hagood, *Mothers of the South: Portraiture of the White Tenant Farm Woman* (Chapel Hill, N.C., 1939), pp. 158–59. Unless otherwise cited, the material on southern rural women is drawn from Hagood.

24. Hagood, *Mothers of the South*, p. 89.

25. Ibid., p. 90.

26. Nora Miller, *The Girl in the Rural Family* (Chapel Hill, N.C., 1935), p. 93.

27. Mary W. M. Hargreaves, "Darkness Before the Dawn: The Status of Women in the Depression Years," in Mabel Deutrich and Virginia Purdy, *Clio Was a Woman: Studies in the History of American Women* (Washington, D.C., 1980), p. 183.

28. Miller, *The Girl in the Rural Family*, p. 64.

29. Maya Angelou, *I Know Why the Caged Bird Sings* (New York, 1969), p. 41.

30. Charles S. Johnson, *Shadow of the Plantation* (Chicago, 1934), pp. 48, 29, 54, 60.

31. Quoted in Gerda Lerner, *Black Women in White America: A Documentary History* (New York, 1972), p. 399.

32. Godfrey Hodgson, *America in Our Time* (New York: Doubleday, 1976), pp. 54–62, provides a general overview of the migration north in the 1940s and 1950s.

33. Mary Ryan, *Womanhood in America: From Colonial Times to the Present*, 2d ed. (New York, 1979), p. 213.

34. Angelou, *I Know Why the Caged Bird Sings*, p. 231.

35. E. Franklin Frazier, *The Negro Family in the United States* (Chicago: University of Chicago Press, 1939); Angelou, *I Know Why the Caged Bird Sings*, p. 231.

36. Lynd and Lynd, *Middletown in Transition*, p. 176.

37. Roosevelt, *It's Up to the Women*, p. 20.

38. Westin, *Making Do*, p. 120; Bird, *Invisible Scar*, p. 48.

39. Lynd and Lynd, *Middletown in Transition*, pp. 178–79.

40. Adamic, *My America*, pp. 283, 286; E. Wright Bakke, *Citizens Without Work: A Study of the Effects of Unemployment upon the Worker's Social Relations and Practices* (New Haven, 1940), p. 136; Ruth Shonle Cavan and Katherine Howland Ranck, *The Family and the Depression* (Freeport, N.Y., 1938), p. 83.

41. Bakke, *Citizens Without Work*, p. 198; Komarovsky, *The Unemployed Man and His Family*, p. 76.

42. Komarovsky, *The Unemployed Man and His Family*, p. 23.

43. Lynd and Lynd, *Middletown in Transition*, pp. 202–203; Milkman, "Women's Work and Economic Crisis," p. 85.

44. Cowan, "Two Washes," pp. 148–51. For Friedan's views on the 1930s, see *The Feminine Mystique* (New York: W.W. Norton, 1963), chapter 2.

45. Westin, *Making Do*, p. 128.

46. Ibid., p. 34.

47. Ibid., p. 9.

Women Needle Workers, Cincinnati, Ohio, 1935
Courtesy of Harvard Business School

Chapter Two

Women at Work

American women have always worked, and the 1930s proved no exception to this general rule. While the great majority of American women worked as unpaid domestic laborers within their homes, almost 25 percent, a sizable minority, worked outside their homes for wages during the decade. Contrary to widely held views, women workers were not devastated by the Depression. Although American society was often blatantly hostile to the idea of women working in the 1930s, women fared better than men during the Depression in many cases. Moreover, women workers benefited from new federal relief programs and the dramatic growth of unions in the 1930s. In general, women continued to increase their participation in paid wage labor outside the home, a trend which has characterized women's work throughout the twentieth century. In the 1930s this progress on the job occurred despite much public hostility, and in the face of severe economic dislocations.

Women's experiences in the 1930s are best understood within the broader framework of patterns in women's employment over the last one hundred years. Table 2-1 shows the percentage of women age fourteen and older in the labor force, and the percent change by decade. Equally relevant is women's percentage of the total work force (see Table 2-2). While some of the biggest jumps

TABLE 2-1.

Percentage of Women in the Labor Force, and Percentage Change by Decade

YEAR	PERCENT OF WOMEN AGE 14 OR OLDER IN THE LABOR FORCE	PERCENT CHANGE BY DECADE
1900	20.4	
1910	25.2	23.5
1920	23.3	7.5
1930	24.3	4.3
1940	25.4	4.5
1950	29.0	14.2
1960	34.5	19.0

Source: Valerie K. Oppenheimer, *The Female Labor Force in the United States: Demographic and Economic Factors Governing its Growth and Changing Composition* (Berkeley: Institute of International Studies, University of California, 1970), p. 3.

TABLE 2-2.

Women in the Labor Force

YEAR	PERCENTAGE OF ALL WORKERS	PERCENTAGE OF ALL WOMEN
1890	17	18
1900	18	20
1920	20	23
1930	22	24
1940	25	28
1945	36	37
1950	29	32
1955	31	34
1960	33	36
1970	40	44

Source: Lois W. Banner, *Women in Modern America: A Brief History* (New York: Harcourt Brace Jovanovich, 1974), p. 256.

occurred in years beyond the scope of this study (1900 1910, the postwar period), women increased their participation even in the depression decade of the 1930s. The percentage of women who were working increased from 24.3 percent to 25.4 percent. By 1940, women made up 25 percent of the labor force, as compared to 22 percent in 1930. Married women's participation increased at an even more dramatic rate.

While the number of women working has grown steadily throughout the twentieth century, such figures mask important changes both in the kinds of work women were doing, and in the characteristics of the women workers themselves. In 1900, almost all women who worked had jobs as domestic servants, farm laborers, unskilled factory operatives, or teachers. By 1940, clerical work was emerging as an important occupation for women. This shift was part of the general increase—from 28.2 percent in 1910 to 45 percent in 1940—of women in nonmanual occupations. Increasingly women's work included white-collar jobs like secretary, typist, and salesperson.[1]

The age and marital status of women workers also underwent significant changes. In 1900 the average woman worker was young (under twenty-five), single, and poor, often an immigrant or the child of immigrant parents. By 1950, the average woman worker was in her forties, married, and just as likely to be from the middle class as the working class. During the 1930s more older women, and especially married women, sought or held jobs, showing that this trend was well underway before the dramatic changes that World War II brought for the female work force.[2]

According to the 1930 census, nearly 11 million women were gainfully employed, 24.3 percent of the women in the country. For every seven men employed, there were two women. While a greater variety of jobs had opened up for women since the 1890s, three of every ten women workers in 1930 were still in domestic and personal service (see Table 2-3). Over the previous thirty years, women had increased their participation in clerical and white-collar work, while their numbers in factory employment had not risen as dramatically. In professional service, women remained heavily concentrated in certain fields: three-quarters of women professionals in 1930 were schoolteachers or nurses. With the growth of urban centers, the proportion of women who worked

TABLE 2-3.

Gainfully Employed Women, 1930

	PERCENTAGE OF GAINFULLY EMPLOYED WOMEN
All occupations	100.0
Agriculture	7.3
Professional service	14.5
Clerical occupations	18.9
Manufacturing	17.5
Domestic and personal service	29.7
Trade	9.1

Source: Mary Elizabeth Pidgeon, "The Employed Woman Homemaker in the United States: Her Responsibility for Family Support," *Women's Bureau Bulletin #148* (Washington, D.C.: Government Printing Office, 1936), p. 4.

as agricultural laborers steadily declined, down to 7.3 percent of all women workers employed by 1930.

Ten years after the 1930 census, the picture of women's work had not changed dramatically, as it rarely does in the course of a single decade. The 1940 census counted 13 million women workers, 25.4 percent of all women aged fourteen and older. Domestic service led the field with 1.4 million women (90 percent of all domestic servants); stenographers, typists, and secretaries numbered just under a million. While the 1930 and 1940 census categories are not exactly comparable, the intervening decade saw a slight decline in women in professional service and an increase in clerical work, while manufacturing stayed about the same. Domestic service also experienced a large drop (see Table 2-4). In general, out of every ten women workers in 1940, three were in clerical or sales work, two were factory operatives (concentrated in the apparel and textile industries), two were in domestic service, one was a professional (usually a teacher or nurse), and one was a service worker.

TABLE 2-4.

Women's Occupational Groups, 1940

OCCUPATIONAL GROUP	PERCENTAGE OF GAINFULLY EMPLOYED WOMEN
Professional	11.7
Semiprofessional	.9
Farmers and managers	1.3
Proprietors, managers	3.6
Clerical, sales, and kindred	28.0
Craftsmen, foremen	.9
Operatives	18.5
Domestic service	17.9
Service, other personal (cleaning, waitresses, cooks, beauticians, practical nurses)	11.3
Farm laborers—wage	.9
Farm laborers—unpaid family workers	1.9
Laborers, except farm	1.0
Occupations not reported	2.1

Source: Janet Hooks, "Women's Occupations through Seven Decades," *Women's Bureau Bulletin #218* (Washington, D.C.: Government Printing Office, 1951), p. 18.

In general, women's working conditions in the 1930s were characterized by long houfs and low wages. According to the U.S. Department of Labor's Women's Bureau, over half of all employed women were working more than fifty hours a week, with more than one-fifth laboring in excess of fifty-four hours. The strain of tending a loom or working a steam-powered laundry machine for such long periods of time made women prone to such diseases as tuberculosis and pellagra. Employers preferred to hire energetic young women as workers, and many a worker found herself considered "old at thirty."[3]

Figures from the Social Security Administration in 1937 showed that women's average yearly pay was $525, compared to $1,027 for men. The average annual income of household workers in 1940 was $312.60. The Depression put even more pressure on women's already low pay, and women's wages dropped to the point that, even though employed, many women could not even meet basic living costs. The Consumers' League of New York reported the situation of Mary Smith in the early 1930s: "She averaged $4 a week. She spent 20 cents a day for carfare, 25 cents for lunch and 25 cents for the care of her children in the nursery— 65 cents a day, $3.90 a week, for the privilege of working." This left only one dime for all her other living expenses.[4]

Working women, especially if they were married, faced strong public hostility to their very participation in the work force. Several polls conducted during the 1930s show the depth of public feeling on the subject. A 1936 *Fortune* poll asked: "Do you believe that married women should have a full time job outside the home?" Fifteen percent approved, 48 percent disapproved, and 37 percent gave it conditional approval. The three most frequently cited reasons for opposing married women's work were that it took jobs otherwise filled by men, that the woman's place was in the home, and that children were healthier and home life happier if women did not work.[5]

That poll showed at least conditional support for women working. A 1936 Gallup poll asked if wives should work if their husbands had jobs, and 82 percent of all Americans said no. (George Gallup observed that he had "discovered an issue on which voters are about as solidly united as on any subject imaginable—including sin and hay fever.") Other polls showed that the lower the husband's salary, the more tolerant Americans were toward married women working. If husbands earned more than $1,600 a year, 67 percent supported laws to prohibit wives from working. When the figure for the husband's wages was lowered to $1,000, support for such restrictions dropped to 56 percent.[6]

The attempt to make women the scapegoats for the Depression rested on shaky ground. Women worked because they had to; dismissing women from jobs probably created more distress than it relieved. When King County, Washington, passed a law banning married women from local government employment, it gained a total of fifty jobs. This did little to help the 83,000 unemployed in that county alone. In addition, men rarely replaced women in the vacated jobs because of the strong segregation by sex built into the occupational job structure. Ruth Shallcross observed in 1940, "Few of the people who oppose married women's employment seem to realize that a coal miner or steel worker cannot very well fill the jobs of nursemaids, cleaning women, or the factory and clerical occupations now filled by women."[7]

Such rational inquiry into the causes and effects of women's work was rarely heard in the 1930s. Public opinion led legislatures and organizations to restrict the rights of married women to work, with teachers the hardest hit. A 1930–31 National Education Association survey found that of 1,500 school systems contacted, 77 percent would not hire married women and 63 percent dismissed women teachers if they married. A 1939 survey by the National Industrial Conference Board showed that 84 percent of insurance companies, 65 percent of banks, and 63 percent of public utilities had restrictions on married women working. The New England Telephone and Telegraph Company let go its married women workers in January 1931. Both the Northern Pacific Railway and the Norfolk and Western Railway Company dismissed sizable proportions of their married women workers in 1931.[8]

Even the federal government restricted the employment of married women. Section 213 of the 1932 National Economy Act prohibited more than one member of the same family from working for the civil service. Since women usually made less than their husbands, they were usually the ones who lost their government jobs. (In addition, the Comptroller General ruled in 1933 that female government employees had to take their husbands' names and report that change to their department or face disciplinary action.) That even the federal government allowed such a misguided law as Section 213 to run for five years (a provision which did nothing to reduce unemployment among men or women and which singled out for special, and unequal, treatment a small and vulnerable group of workers) shows the depth of these sentiments in the depression decade.[9]

Such public hostility makes the increase in the number of married women workers which occurred in the 1930s even more significant. In one sense, the increase was part of a long-term trend. In 1900, 5.6 percent of the nation's married women worked; the figure climbed to 10.7 percent in 1910, 11.7 in 1930, and 15.2 in 1940. The rise from 1930 to 1940 was an increase of nearly 50 percent, at a time when the number of married women increased by only 15 percent. By 1940, married women made up 35 percent of the female labor force, a gain from 29 percent in 1930 and 15 percent in 1900. While married women posted significant increases, the number working still comprised a small minority (only 15 percent) of married women. Even at the lowest income levels, only 25 percent of married women worked, and it was still unusual for women with very small children to work outside the home. Clearly, pervasive cultural values kept the vast majority of married women in the home.[10]

On the other hand, the Depression probably propelled more married women into the work force. If a husband lost his job, his wife often looked for a position to take up the slack. If the husband's earnings were too low to support the family, the additional family worker was much more likely to be the wife than one of the family's children. In addition, not only women from families of direst poverty sought work in the 1930s. Winifred Wandersee Bolin discovered that by 1940 over 40 percent of gainfully employed married women were married to men who earned $1,000 or more in 1939. With a median family income in 1935–36 of $1,160, such women were assured at least a fairly comfortable living standard. In part, they were working to maintain the high standard of consumption to which they had become accustomed during the 1920s. Raised expectations about what were "necessities" for family life sent a certain group of married women into the work force: "values, rather than absolute need" were the primary factor.[11]

In the majority of cases, however, women worked in the 1930s out of economic necessity. This was especially true of black women, who made up one out of every six women workers in the United States in 1930—a total of 2 million black women. Because their economic needs were more acute, almost 40 percent of all black women worked, compared to less than 20 percent of all white women. A study of New Orleans, Atlanta, and San Antonio confirmed that black women had a consistently higher tendency to remain in the work force after marriage. Cultural considerations, however, restricted the wage force participation of chicana women.[12]

The position of black women, always difficult, became even more tenuous during the Depression. The Women's Bureau concluded, "To their lot, therefore, have fallen the more menial jobs, the lower paid, the more hazardous—in general, the least agreeable and desirable." In 1935, 25 percent of all black women workers were on relief, two-fifths of them economic heads of households. While white women benefited from New Deal labor legislation such as minimum wage laws and social security, black women lagged behind, since agricultural work and domestic service were exempted from such laws. Black women also faced racial discrimination on New Deal programs for which they were eligible.[13]

According to the 1930 census, nine-tenths of black women worked in agriculture or domestic service. Domestic service has been the primary wage role for most black women in the twentieth century: in 1930, 60 percent of black women workers were engaged in domestic or personal service. Yet the position of the Negro domestic declined during the Depression, as employers were no longer able to afford servants and began to "do their own work." For those household workers who could get jobs, the typical wage was $5 to $6 for a week that averaged seventy-two hours. Women who took in laundry in their homes undercut wages of women in power laundries. One of the few occupations on the increase for black women in the 1920s and 1930s was beauty service.[14]

The twenty years between 1910 and 1930 also saw a 100 percent increase in the number of black women in professional service, yet in 1930 only 5 percent of gainfully employed black women were in white-collar occupations. Three-fourths of black professional women were teachers, one-tenth trained nurses. Black teachers

were paid considerably less than whites of both sexes. Black
women were beginning to enter the clerical field, but mainly in
offices already predominantly Negro. A few black women were in
retail trade as well.[15]

In general, black women's wages were much lower in the South
than the North, mainly because of southern women's heavy concentration in agricultural work. In 1930, almost 500,000 black
women worked in agriculture, making it the second-largest occupation for black women. As the 1930s progressed, many agricultural workers saw their standard of living decline as sharecropping
came to predominate in the South. The position of black males and
females declined proportionately more than that of southern
whites, according to a U.S. Department of Agriculture report. For
women who worked as cotton pickers in one Louisiana parish,
their average yearly earnings were $41.67 (men's earnings were
$120.19), with most women averaging less than ninety days of
work a year.[16]

Compared to work in domestic service and agriculture, manufacturing jobs would have been a great step forward, yet in the 1920s
and 1930s the number of black women employed in industry was
very small. The only jobs that black women could get in industry
were menial or unskilled; the semiskilled and skilled jobs were
reserved first for white men and then for white women. Black
women (100,000 in 1930) were employed in the largest numbers in
the tobacco, clothing, food, textile, lumber, iron and steel, and
printing industries. Linked to their low numbers in industry was
the fact that few black women belonged to unions.[17]

Women have always faced problems on the job, problems which
transcend race: low wages, sexual harassment and discrimination,
and poor working conditions. The Depression exacerbated these
problems. One hazard was irregular or part-time employment. A
worker recalled, "In those days nobody worked a whole year at a
time. You worked a few weeks and then you had layoffs for a
month or two and then you got another job and you worked a few
weeks." Women's Trade Union League data from autumn 1936
showed that workers ordinarily worked only between twenty-six
and thirty-five weeks a year in the garment, glove, textile, and
millinery industries. Many seasonal industries were also large
employers of women. Canning of fruits and vegetables occurs

mainly in August and September; candy-making peaks before Christmas and Easter; meatpacking peaks from January to March; department stores have a pre-Christmas rush. Women played large roles in all these industries.[18]

While irregular or part-time employment was a problem for many women workers, at least those women had jobs. During the Depression many women who wanted and needed to work could not find employment. The Women's Bureau estimated that at least 2 million women were out of work in January 1931. Grace Hutchins, whose anticapitalist perspective made her less tolerant of the system's failings, claimed that more than 2.5 million women were unemployed in 1931 and that the number had grown to at least 4 million by autumn 1933. To make matters worse, about one-tenth of all jobless women in 1930 were also heads of household; between 20 and 50 percent of the unemployed women had responsibilities for dependents. As a general rule, about one out of five women normally employed was out of work at any given point in the 1930s.[19]

While most public attention focused on the needs of the unemployed man, the plight of jobless women was especially acute during the Depression. Women's Trade Union League president Rose Schneiderman emphasized, "After all, they are not like men. They just cannot go around with a suit of clothes and one shirt." Schneiderman and other public figures feared jobless women would turn to women's perennial last resort, prostitution, in order to earn a little money. But even prostitution was affected by the Depression. Meridel LeSueur observed, "Like every commodity now the body is difficult to sell and the girls say you're lucky if you get fifty cents."[20]

Meridel LeSueur's "Women on the Breadlines," which appeared in *New Masses* in January 1932, gives a grim account of women trying to scrape by in the cities during the Depression. LeSueur set her story in the waiting room of a city employment office: "I am sitting in the city free employment bureau. It's the Woman's Section. We have been sitting here now for four hours. We sit here every day, waiting for a job. There are no jobs." (Such sentiments earned LeSueur a short lecture from the editors of *New Masses* for her "defeatist" attitudes, although they published the piece anyway.) LeSueur realized how invisible the jobless women were:

It's one of the great mysteries of the city where women go when they are out of work and hungry. There are not many women in the bread line. There are no flop houses for women as there are for men, where a bed can be had for a quarter or less. You don't see women lying on the floor at the mission in the free flops. They obviously don't sleep in the jungle or under newspapers in the park. There is no law I suppose against their being in these places but the fact is they rarely are.

Yet there must be as many women out of jobs in cities and suffering extreme poverty as there are men. What happens to them? Where do they go? Try to get into the Y.W. without any money or looking down at the heel. Charities take care of very few and only those that are called "deserving." The lone girl is under suspicion by the virgin women who dispense charity.[21]

LeSueur continued from her own experience: "I've lived in cities for many months broke, without help, too timid to get in bread lines. I've known many women to live like this until they simply faint on the street from privations, without saying a word to anyone. A woman will shut herself up in a room until it is taken away from her, and eat a cracker a day and be as quiet as a mouse so there are no social statistics concerning her."[22]

Often the problem of joblessness was compounded by having no place to live. Elizabeth Conkey, commissioner of public welfare for Chicago, estimated that hundreds of homeless women spent night after night in Chicago's parks. Grace Hutchins estimated that between 100,000 and 150,000 homeless women were wandering through the country. A count of women hoboes in 800 cities found almost 10,000 women on a given night asking for help and shelter at Salvation Army stations, certainly a mere fraction of the total number of women on the road. The YWCA estimated that in March 1933, 145,000 women were homeless and footloose.[23]

Thousands of these women had no other choice than to hit the road as hoboes—"sisters of the road," as the men called them. Thomas Minehan, a social scientist who hoboed around the country for several months collecting information, estimated that girls made up one out of every twenty tramps on the road. Most of them were under eighteen. Like boys, these young girls left home because their families did not have enough money to feed an extra mouth and because they could not find jobs. The girls donned overalls and took off, rarely staying more than a week in one place.

Usually they traveled in pairs, either with another woman or a man, and lesbian couples were not uncommon. Whatever these women's sexual orientation, prostitution was an easy option; in return the men provided shelter and food. In any case, there were few scruples about sex on the road. The lives of these girls were probably no worse than what they had experienced at home or in the desperation and loneliness of a large city. Moreover, hoboing gave young girls an opportunity for adventure and wanderlust usually reserved for males.[24]

Bertha Thompson's *Autobiography of Box Car Bertha* (1937) gives a vivid personal account of one sister of the road. Thompson was thirty years old and had been on the road for fifteen years when she collaborated on the book with Dr. Ben Reitman (also known as the lover of Emma Goldman). Bertha got her nickname from her shape and her early propensity for spending a lot of time in box cars. Seeking freedom, adventure, and the camaraderie of a life on the road, Thompson alternated hitching rides in box cars with working for an abortionist, being a prostitute, and having a baby (which she promptly took home to her family in—where else?—a box car). In the early 1930s, she began working in Female Transient Bureaus, where she helped the "great army of women" who had taken to the road because of the Depression. According to Thompson, "Their stories were very much the same—no work, a whole family on relief, no prospects of marriage, the need for a lark, the need for freedom of sex and of living, and the great urge to know what other women were doing." These young women, "sure that their sex would win them a way about," were too restless to settle down in one place.[25]

These descriptions of jobless, homeless women and the estimates of at least 2 million women unemployed show the grim side of life in the Great Depression. Indeed, several government studies done in the 1930s suggested that women had suffered more acutely than men in the Depression. A 1931 Women's Bureau study concluded that "relative to the extent of employment of either sex, fluctuations and declines frequently have affected women to a greater extent than they have men; that women to a greater extent than men are employed at the peak periods in certain high seasonal industries and later laid off; and that the industries and occupations in which the variations are most extreme often are exactly those within which women workers must make their livelihoods." In addition, a 1934 report in the U.S. Department of Labor's *Monthly Labor Review* concluded that women's unemployment "developed early and that it was more pronounced in some industries and groups than in the population generally."[26]

Current historians and sociologists have also theorized that women fared worse than men in the Depression. Marxist-feminist writers including Juliet Mitchell and Margaret Benston have argued that women function as a "reserve army" for the work force: during times of labor scarcity, women are drawn into the labor market, only to be expelled in times of labor surplus.[27] According to this scenario, women should have been expelled from the work force during the Depression. Yet while historians agree that in periods of expansion such as World Wars I and II, women are drawn into the work force, there is less agreement that women are pushed out in times of contraction. During the decade of the Great Depression, the percentage of women employed actually increased. Women escaped expulsion from jobs during the 1930s in part because the economy had become so strictly segregated into "women's jobs" and "men's jobs" that men rarely took over jobs previously held by women. Jobs stereotyped as women's work, therefore, gave women a certain amount of protection even in the midst of a severe economic contraction like the Depression.[28]

Historian Alice Kessler-Harris has elaborated on these themes in her broader studies of women's work over the last century. Kessler-Harris suggests that the Depression affected men and women differently, accelerating female incorporation into the wage force yet confirming segmentation by sex. In this case, segmentation of the work force by sex was part of a long-term process, not a response to the Depression. Women's Bureau studies confirm that men do not take over women's jobs except in mixed sectors. When there is a choice, employers prefer to hire men; once a job is "all female," men no longer apply. This protects women, but at the expense of reinforcing prevailing stereotypes about what is "women's work."[29]

Ruth Milkman has provided an even more extensive analysis of women's work in the Great Depression. Milkman stresses the sexual division of the work force: "the sex-typing of occupations created an inflexibility in the structure of the labor market which prevented the expulsion of women from it in the manner Benston suggests. It was not because of the fact that women's labor power is cheaper than men's, but rather because women's work is so rigidly sex-typed, that women enjoyed a measure of protection from unemployment in the Great Depression." Milkman cites the 1930 census as evidence that "insofar as their paid labor force participation was concerned, women were less affected than men by the contraction." The unemployment rate for women was 4.7 percent versus 7.1 percent for men. Women fared better because the occupations in which they were concentrated (clerical, trade, and service occupations) contracted less than those in which men were concentrated (manufacturing, for example).[30]

Milkman does admit that the gap between male and female unemployment may be closer than her data suggest. For example, women are frequently undercounted in employment statistics; census counters often assumed that the woman who answered the door during the day was a homemaker, not an unemployed worker. Also, women work part-time more often than men, gaining employment but not necessarily enough to live on. In addition, Milkman tentatively posits "a gradual deterioration of women's situation relative to men's as the Depression deepened," perhaps because more women had entered the labor force for the first time due to the economic pressures of the Depression. By the 1940 census, women's unemployment (7.5 percent) was still lower than men's (8.6), but the gap had narrowed.[31]

Julia Kirk Blackwelder's study of women in the work force in Atlanta, New Orleans, and San Antonio from 1930 to 1940 confirms Milkman's thesis on several key points. Blackwelder found that "the burdens of poverty and unemployment fell unevenly among ethnic groups," primarily because of occupational segregation, with its almost "caste-like regard" for gender and ethnicity. This affected women's labor force participation: "As particular occupations which were strictly labeled by gender or ethnicity rose or fell in strength, the *number* of jobs available to one ethnic group or female workers advanced or declined, and labor force participation among that group manifested a consequent gain or loss." Blackwelder also confirmed that unemployment in all three cities in 1930 and 1940 was higher among men than women.[32]

While the evidence is sometimes contradictory, its general direction is clear. Women were not expelled from the labor force during the Depression. In fact, they made both numerical and proportional increases during the decade, confirming that women's work is crucial (not marginal) to the functioning of the American economic system. Much of this progress was linked to the rigid and stable occupational structure of the economy: certain essential jobs (such as clerical work, and domestic and personal service) were so clearly marked as women's work that the economy could not survive without women's contributions in these areas. As the Depression increased the strain on family resources, more women entered the labor force in the 1930s seeking income. Due to widespread stereotyping of jobs, and women's own expectations of what jobs they were qualified for, women were often able to find work even in the midst of the Depression. Life was not easy for working women in the 1930s, but like their sisters who remained housewives in the decade, they were "making do."

While conditions remained poor for many women workers in the Depression, women were no longer totally dependent on their own resources. Starting in 1933, the federal government greatly expanded its responsibility for providing relief and assistance to male and female workers alike. The New Deal's steps unfolded gradually. Some measures, like the Civilian Works Administration or the Works Progress Administration, were temporary public works programs designed to get the country through the worst of the Depression. Other pieces of New Deal legislation, such as the 1935 Social Security Act, the 1935 National Labor Relations Act, and the 1938 Fair Labor Standards Act, were permanent measures. By the end of the 1930s, the modern welfare state had been born.

While the New Deal pushed the federal government in new directions, the coverage of these new programs was never complete. Many workers were left outside the scope of the relief programs and social security. In the case of blacks, the exclusion was often the result of deliberate discrimination. But for women, who likewise did not always receive their full share of the benefits, the discrimination was less calculated. Unless reminded, policymakers simply forgot that women, too, were hurt by the Depression. The New Deal did take the needs of women into consideration, but its record was far from perfect.

The National Industrial Recovery Act was probably the most important piece of legislation to come out of the first one hundred days of the Roosevelt administration. Passed in May 1933, the act set up the National Recovery Administration (NRA), whose main function was to negotiate codes designed to rekindle production. These codes established production goals, fixed prices, and allocated resources within specific industries. Comprising almost one-quarter of the work force, women workers were vitally affected by the NRA codes. As with all the New Deal programs, the record on women was mixed.

Even though the NRA codes operated for only two years, the Women's Bureau concluded that "enormous advances were made for employed women in a raising of their wages, a shortening of their hours, and an increase in their employment." For the first time, maximum hour and minimum wage provisions were mandated for all workers, male and female alike. These provisions usually benefited women more than men, especially in the area of wages. Since women have traditionally been concentrated in the lowest-paying jobs, they stood to gain more from minimum wage standards.[33]

The NRA codes were designed to cover most major industries, and their potential reach was enormous. Reformers were delighted that with one piece of mandatory national legislation, they accomplished more for wages and hours than they had been able to secure piecemeal over the previous thirty years. Rose Schneiderman, a tireless advocate of better working conditions for women throughout her long career, served on the Labor Advisory Board that framed the NRA codes and called the NRA the "high spot" in her career: "Here was an opportunity to help working women such as had never existed before." Even militant feminists of the National Woman's Party like Maud Younger applauded the NRA code provisions. By setting standards for all workers and by abolishing sweatshop conditions, the NRA made the need for protective laws for women less compelling.[34]

The NRA codes did contain significant drawbacks. For example, they affected only half of the women in the work force. While most women in manufacturing and trade were covered, other areas where women predominated, notably domestic service, professional service, agriculture, and clerical work, received little or no protection.

An even greater problem was the pay differential (from 5¢ to 25¢ an hour) mandated in one-quarter of the codes. The official NRA explanation cited "long established customs" which allowed women to be paid less than men for doing substantially the same work. Organizations like the Women's Trade Union League, the National Consumers' League, the Business and Professional Women, the National League of Women Voters, and the Young Women's Christian Association registered loud complaints about the lower pay scale, but the women's protests had no effect on the discriminatory codes. Still, while one-quarter of the codes contained such provisions, three-quarters did not, suggesting that in the long run the gains for the majority of women workers probably outweighed the discrimination that a minority faced. Even with lower minimum wages, most women found they were earning more money than ever before.[35]

The NRA codes regulated working conditions of women who were employed, but had little to offer to the 2 million women who lost their jobs and were forced to seek relief. The New Deal undertook responsibility for unemployed women during the 1930s, but unlike the NRA codes, which treated men and women alike, the relief agencies assumed that women had special needs and abilities. Separate programs were devised to deal with these unemployed women, staffed and run mainly by women administrators, but the New Deal relief agencies only went so far.

One of the earliest relief agencies, the Civilian Works Administration (CWA), was planned as a temporary expedient to get the country through the winter of 1933–34. The CWA had 4 million people at work in January 1934, but only 300,000 of them were women. The CWA concentrated on large-scale construction and public works projects, work which throughout the 1930s was considered unsuitable for women. Women fared slightly better in the Federal Emergency Relief Administration (FERA), which from 1933 to 1935 dispensed federal money to run state relief projects. In 1935, women made up 12 percent of the workers on FERA jobs. Later that year FERA was replaced by the Works Progress Administration (WPA), which oversaw federal relief programs, rather than granting money to the states. Throughout the 1930s, the women's relief programs were in the capable hands of Ellen Sullivan Woodward and her predominantly female staff at the Women's and Professional Projects division in Washington.[36]

Women who qualified for relief often faced difficulty finding project assignments, since women were not considered suitable for the construction projects which dominated relief projects for men. One regional director of women's work wrote to Eleanor Roosevelt: "One can put practically all of the men eligible for work in a community to work on a couple of major work projects. Not so with women. To care for one hundred women in a county we will have perhaps a dozen projects differing in nature." Successful women's programs included research and clerical work; library projects; recreational activities; health projects; nutrition projects; canning projects; community service centers. By far the largest component of the WPA women's program was the sewing room, where old garments were repaired or new ones were sewn from surplus materials. These products were then distributed to relief families. In 1936, 56 percent of all women on the WPA worked in sewing rooms. One female WPA official summarized their importance succinctly: "For unskilled men we have the shovel. For unskilled women we have only the needle."[37]

Women also faced problems getting on relief in the first place. Since only one member of a household was eligible for a WPA job, women had to qualify as the economic head of a household before they would be certified. Women with husbands who were physically able to work but had been unable (or unwilling) to find jobs were not eligible, since the WPA automatically considered those men the heads of household. Women on the WPA also lacked appropriate work experience. Because the Depression forced many women into the work force for the first time or encouraged them to reenter after a long absence, women's projects often had to include sustained on-the-job training. Women comprised between 13 and 19 percent of the total WPA rolls, with a peak of 405,700 women employed in December 1938. Women were not grossly underrepresented on the WPA, but they did have to struggle for recognition and benefits.[38]

One final aspect of New Deal relief policy shows the limits of steps taken to meet the needs of unemployed women. One of the most popular of the early New Deal programs, the Civilian Conservation Corps (CCC), sent unemployed youth to live in camps in the woods and work on outdoor projects like reforestation and soil conservation. The CCC was specifically limited by law to men only, and critics asked, where was the "she-she-she"? The federal government did set up resident camps for women, but on a drastically reduced scale. Hilda Worthington Smith, who was in charge of the camps for unemployed women at FERA and WPA, complained to Eleanor Roosevelt: "The CCC camps with their millions of dollars for wages, educational work, travel, and supervision constantly remind me of what we might to do for women from these same families. As so often the case, the boys get the breaks, the girls are neglected." In the ehd, 8,000 young women (compared to 2.5 million young men in the CCC) attended these camps before the program was suddenly dissolved in 1937 for budgetary reasons.[39]

Several other pieces of New Deal legislation affected the woman worker or the woman on relief. The Social Security Act provided maternal and pediatric programs and grants for mothers with dependent children. But many provisions of the act discriminated against female wage earners, especially if they were married. Large groups of employed women, notably domestic servants and agricultural workers, were left outside the coverage of the Social Security law completely. In addition, the act offered no protection to women who chose homemaking as their career. The 1938 Fair Labor Standards Act also contained provisions of benefit to women workers, making permanent the hours and wages regulation begun with the NRA codes. Like the NRA, both men and women benefited from these regulations, but again, coverage was limited to a minority of the work force.[40]

Perhaps the law with the greatest significance for women workers was the 1935 National Labor Relations Act, often referred to as the Wagner Act. Drawing on the experiences of Section 7(a) of the National Industrial Recovery Act which placed the federal government behind workers' efforts to bargain collectively, the Wagner Act gave a crucial boost to the emerging labor movement in the 1930s. In fact, the growth of organized labor was one of the most far-reaching changes of the entire decade.

For women workers, the 1930s witnessed a major breakthrough in the labor movement, although much still remained to be done at the end of the decade. Gains for women were part of a general revitalization of the labor movement after 1934, rather than a specific drive to recruit more women workers into the labor movement. Whatever the reasons, the progress was significant. In 1929,

the Women's Trade Union League, an organization loosely affiliated with the American Federation of Labor and the only national
group dedicated to organizing women workers, estimated that
only 250,000 women workers of 4 million women who were eligible belonged to unions. By 1939, according to Women's Bureau
estimates, 800,000 women belonged to unions, a sizable increase.
Women's experiences in unions show both the importance and the
limits of these new breakthroughs for women. Their stories also
restore to labor history the lives of individual women who made
important contributions to this cause in the decade of the 1930s.[41]

The International Ladies Garment Workers Union (ILGWU)
has traditionally been a union with strong female representation,
since women have predominated in the textile and garment manufacturing work force. Growing out of a series of successful strikes
in the early twentieth century, notably the uprising of 20,000 shirt-
waist workers in New York in 1909, the ILGWU became a major
union, peaking at 105,000 members in 1920. But symptomatic of
the general reverses experienced by labor during the 1920s, the
ILGWU went into a steep decline, wracked by mounting debts,
falling membership, and internal dissension over the issue of Communist influence. By 1933, the ILGWU claimed only 40,000
members, was deeply in debt, and could only watch helplessly as
the Depression brought deteriorating conditions to the garment
trades, including the reappearance of sweatshops and piecework
rates of pay. With the guarantees of Section 7(a) of the National
Industrial Recovery Act, the ILGWU once again took the offensive and set out on a massive organizing drive in sixty cities. Its
most dramatic victory occurred in New York, where 60,000 new
workers joined the union. By 1934, ILGWU membership stood at
200,000, an increase of 500 percent over one year. This made the
ILGWU the third-largest union in the American Federation of
Labor.[42]

Although women made up almost half of the membership in the
ILGWU, the union leadership remained male-dominated during
the 1930s. (This pattern of male leadership was repeated in other
unions where women predominated at the rank-and-file level.)
David Dubinsky's name is most often linked with the ILGWU,
but Pauline Newman, Fannia Cohn, Angela Bambace, and Rose
Pesotta were quite active in the union in the 1930s. Pesotta's

experiences reflect the successes and problems women faced as union organizers.[43]

Rose Pesotta, a Russian Jewish immigrant who had come to the United States around 1912, became interested in union activities while working in the garment trade. During the 1920s, she attended the Bryn Mawr Summer School for Industrial Workers, which had a strong impact on many labor women. Pesotta was fired in 1933 from her job in a Los Angeles garment factory and blacklisted for her union activities, but she kept up her attempts to organize women garment workers in San Francisco, Seattle, Portland, Puerto Rico, Boston, Buffalo, and Montreal during the rest of the 1930s. Her philosophy was, "To us no strike is ever lost. Whatever the immediate outcome, we eventually win."[44]

During the 1930s, Pesotta moved into union leadership positions. She became the only woman vice president of the General Executive Board of the ILGWU and served for three full terms. Pesotta also continued as a full-time organizer. As part of the war effort, she returned to work as a garment worker in the 1940s and declined a fourth term on the General Executive Board in 1944. Pesotta, who was not noted for championing women's causes within the union, commented on her retirement, "Ten years in office had made it clear to me that a lone woman vice president could not adequately represent the women who now made up 85 percent of the International's membership of 305,000."[45]

One innovative undertaking of the ILGWU was *Pins and Needles*, a show it staged in 1937 as part of its Labor Stage division. The cast of this musical revue was made up of garment workers, who received the same pay for their theatrical work as they would have in their regular factory jobs. There was no "star" in the production, just an energetic group of singers and dancers. The show was a great hit, and had a three-and-one-half-year run, grossing $1.5 million. In February 1938, the cast staged a command performance for Franklin and Eleanor Roosevelt at the White House.[46]

The ILGWU tried to remain neutral in the schism that emerged in the revitalized labor movement in the 1930s, but all unions were forced to take sides eventually. The American Federation of Labor (AFL), a more traditional and conservative force in the labor movement, tended to concentrate on the elite of the work force—skilled workers and craftspeople in specific industries. By 1935, certain elements in the AFL, notably John L. Lewis of the United Mine Workers, wanted the AFL to commit itself to organizing on an industry-wide basis, rather than by specific crafts or trades. This involved organizing unskilled as well as skilled workers, and offered larger roles for women and blacks, two groups not usually welcomed by the conservative AFL leadership. After a scuffle at the 1935 AFL convention, the Committee on Industrial Organization (CIO) was formed to pursue full-scale mass industrial organization. David Dubinsky and the ILGWU at first sided with the CIO, but declined to become a permanent part of the new labor group in 1938. After pursuing an independent course for two years, the ILGWU rejoined the AFL in 1940. In aligning itself with the AFL, the mass-based ILGWU was an exception. Most of the successes for women workers came from the emerging CIO.[47]

The CIO was committed to organizing workers without regard to sex, race, or skill. Its first targets were the rank and file workers in the automobile, textile, and electrical unions, where large numbers of women worked. The textile industry had traditionally proved very hard to organize because of the different areas involved (cotton, woolen/worsted, rayon, silk, and hosiery) and because four-fifths of the cotton mills were in the South, an area long hostile to unionization. A strong textile union, the United Textile Workers, claimed 110,000 members in 1920 but declined drastically during the ensuing decade, crippled by lack of support and a series of unsuccessful strikes which dropped membership below 13,000 in 1930. The conservative AFL-tone of the United Textile Workers leadership strongly contributed to the decline. Although the NRA helped the United Textile Workers build its membership to 200,000, it fell quickly back to 20,000 after losing a major textile strike in 1934. The lesson seemed clear: the AFL's approach to textile organizing was not working.

The CIO responded by forming the Textile Workers' Organizing Committee (drawing on a similar device used to mobilize steelworkers), with support of seasoned labor leaders like Sidney Hillman of the Amalgamated Clothing Workers. TWOC's fortunes went up and down: it quickly reached 130,000 workers by June 1937 and climbed to 200,000 by September 30, only to see big setbacks in late 1937. By 1939, only 7 percent of the South's 350,000 mill hands had been unionized. The Textile Workers

Union of America counted 120,000 members in 1943, a sixfold increase since pre-CIO levels of 20,000, but there still was (and is) a long way to go.[48]

An active CIO supporter in the southern textile drive in the 1930s was public relations officer Lucy Randolph Mason. Mason had become general secretary of the National Consumers' League in 1932 after the death of its guiding spirit, Florence Kelley, but left the Consumers' League in 1937 to work with the new CIO. Mason functioned more as a roving ambassador than as an organizer, touring the South in her blue Plymouth coupe. Because of her impeccable Virginia lineage (a descendant of George Mason, John Marshall, and Robert E. Lee), Mason could intercede with dubious southern officials on behalf of the emerging textile movement. In addition to her public relations work for the CIO, Mason was also instrumental in the passage of a resolution supporting collective bargaining by the Southern Baptist convention in 1938.[49]

Another woman active in textile organizing was Dorothy Bellanca of the Amalgamated Clothing Workers of America (ACWA), the union most closely associated with Sidney Hillman. Bellanca's family had come to America from Latvia in 1900, and as a young girl she had worked in clothing shops and factories. By 1914 she was an active trade unionist, with her main focus on women workers in the men's clothing industry. Active throughout the 1920s and 1930s, Bellanca concentrated her attention on shirt workers in the Northeast from 1932 to 1934; by 1934, nearly 30,000 shirt workers belonged to the ACWA. Besides organizing for the ACWA, Bellanca also did work for the Consumers' League, Women's Trade Union League, and the CIO Textile Workers Organizing Committee. Bellanca was widely respected as one of the most effective women organizers of the period, and played roles in most of the major battles for women textile workers in the 1930s. Like Rose Pesotta, she was the only woman vice president on the executive board of the Amalgamated Clothing Workers of America, where she served from 1934 until her premature death in 1946 at the age of fifty-two.[50]

After textiles, the CIO waged a major and decisive campaign in the automobile industry in 1937. While women did not make up more than a fraction of the industrial auto work force (and a discriminated minority at that: women received 12½¢ an hour in the General Motors A/C Sparkplug plant, while men received 42¢),[51] they played crucial roles in the Flint, Michigan, sit-down strikes that resulted in the formation of the United Auto Workers (UAW).

One form of women's participation was the Women's Auxiliary, founded by fifty wives, daughters, girl friends, and female employees of General Motors in Flint. These women maintained a first-aid station during the strike and provided food, meals, and coffee for the pickets. They ran day-care centers and a speakers' bureau, helped out with the picketing, and distributed literature. Their theme song was:

> The women got together and they formed a mighty throng;
> Every worker's wife and mom and sister will belong;
> They will fight beside the men to help the cause along,
> Shouting the Union forever!

The CIO was not the first organization to grasp the importance of women's support during strikes. The radical Trade Union Unity League (TUUL) had successfully organized wives and daughters into auxiliaries in exclusively male industries like coal in the early 1930s; TUUL organizer Anna Burlak was often in charge of these projects. Meridel LeSueur's "I Was Marching," a description of women's roles in a 1934 Teamsters' strike in Minneapolis, gives a stirring portrait of another Women's Auxiliary.[52]

In the Flint strike, the Women's Emergency Brigade complemented the Women's Auxiliary and was even more militant in pursuing its objectives. Founded by twenty-three-year-old Genora Johnson, wife of one of the General Motors strikers, this group eventually mobilized five hundred women from the community. The Flint Women's Emergency Brigade wore distinctive red berets and armbands; their sisters from the Detroit auxiliary wore green berets. The Women's Emergency Brigade took responsibility for the picket line several days a week, often singing old labor (and suffrage) standards like "Hold the Fort" and "We Shall Not Be Moved." On Women's Day in Flint, more than 7,000 women marched in the streets surrounding Fisher Body Plant #1.

Often more militant action was undertaken. Women broke windows to keep sit-down strikers from being gassed inside the plants, or took injured pickets back to the first-aid station after violence occurred. In one case, a diversion created by the women allowed the successful takeover of a new plant by sit-down strikers. In several instances, the organized presence of these women, the wives and sisters of the strikers, played a major part in preventing further bloodshed.[53]

While the women of the Auxiliary and the Emergency Brigade allied themselves with the CIO, the union deserves little credit for these spontaneously formed groups. As Genora Johnson recalled, "This was an independent move. It was not under the direction of the union or its administrators—I just talked it over with a few women—the active ones—and told them this is what we had to do." The women could no longer simply sit on the sidelines. Journalist Mary Heaton Vorse described their courage: "They were fearless and seemingly tireless. One and all were normal, sensible women who were doing this because they had come to the natural conclusion that it must be done if they and their children were to have a decent life." Mrs. Violet Baggett of the Detroit Women's Emergency Brigade wrote to her local CIO paper about her involvement: "Just being a woman isn't enough any more. I want to be a human being. I'm ready and glad to wear my green beret and Women's Emergency armband anytime, anywhere I'm needed."[54]

But the Women's Auxiliary found it difficult to maintain its effectiveness and cohesion after the emergency of the strike situation had passed. This was partly a natural letdown after the intensity of the strike, but more fundamentally the women realized that male union leaders had no use for the women once the strike was over. Genora Johnson recalled, "The brigade disbanded with the victory. . . . [T]he husbands began saying, 'Well, you women did a wonderful job, but now your duty is back there getting those kids in school, getting the wash done, and regular meals again. . . .'" In effect, Johnson remarked, the union said to the women, "Thank you, ladies, so much," but now things can go back to normal. Lack of gratitude from the union, however, never took away the women's pride in their accomplishments. Genora Johnson spoke for all of them: "It's a measure of the strength of those women of the Red Berets that they could perform so courageously in an atmosphere that was often hostile to them. We organized on our own without the benefit of professional leadership, and yet, we played a role, second to none, in the birth of a union and in changing working families' lives forever."[55]

The growth and legitimization of the labor movement as a permanent part of the American political and economic system was one of the most significant changes of the 1930s, and women shared in this progress. Yet by the end of the decade much still remained to be done, with inadequate resources for the job. The National Women's Trade Union League (WTUL) in the 1930s illustrates both the strengths and weaknesses of attempts to unionize women workers in the decade.

The WTUL, originally founded in 1903, was a unique attempt at cross-class cooperation, its membership and leadership composed jointly of women workers and wealthy reformers. The WTUL shared twin goals of encouraging the unionization of women workers and promoting legislation of benefit to working women, such as the minimum wage, regulation of hours, and the banning of night work. As such, the WTUL was the only national organization dedicated to unionizing women workers. Unfortunately, the WTUL received little help, and a good deal of hindrance, from the AFL, with which it was affiliated. Even at its height, this small private organization could not realistically bear the brunt of promoting the unionization of 12 million women in the work force. This was especially true in the 1930s, when the WTUL's finances were in bad shape (its total budget was $10,000) and it could barely afford to keep one full-time organizer in the field. During the 1930s the WTUL worked closely with the ILGWU, and also approached laundry workers and hotel workers. Under WTUL organizer Eleanor Mishnun, there were small breakthroughs, but they were limited to the New York area. Another goal, passage of a New York law mandating a forty-eight-hour work week for women workers, was finally achieved after twenty-five years. Unfortunately, what the WTUL could accomplish was merely a drop in the bucket.[56]

When women were lucky enough to get into regular unions in the 1930s, they faced many problems. Most unions were dubious about female members; the traditional attitude that "woman's place is in the home" (rather than as a permanent member of the work force) was firmly entrenched in male union leadership. Many industrial unions had separate locals for men and women; union-approved contracts allowed unequal pay scales and the maintenance of separate seniority lists for women workers.[57]

Women were also noticeably underrepresented in union leadership. The ILGWU, a predominantly female union, had only one female member (Rose Pésotta) on its general board throughout the 1930s; Sidney Hillman's Amalgamated Clothing Workers Union (where, like the ILGWU, the majority of members were women) had only a few token women like Dorothy Bellanca as officers. Only fourteen out of 477 delegates to the 1938 AFL convention were women. The CIO fared little better, even though one-fifth of its membership came from predominantly female industries. Mary Anderson of the Women's Bureau complained to Eleanor Roosevelt about how difficult it was to work with the male unionists: "I suppose it is too much to expect these men will ever put us on a par with them. It will be the next generation, maybe even the next, before that will happen."[58] Anderson's prophecy is still unfulfilled.

An even greater problem than discrimination against women in the unions was the large number of women workers left outside the labor movement entirely. The Women's Bureau estimated that no more than one out of fifteen women workers belonged to the AFL or the CIO; Grace Hutchins estimated that at least 5 million women were eligible for union membership but were ignored by the predominantly male leadership. The approximately 800,000 women who enjoyed union protection at the end of the decade (an increase of 300 percent over ten years earlier) must be balanced against the millions of women who still had no union to protect their rights.[59]

Overall, women at work survived the Depression in much better shape than has previously been suggested. To be sure, it was at a cost of 2 million women unemployed, several hundred thousand on the road, and with an increase in women's concentration in the lowest-paying, lowest-status jobs. But in the midst of the greatest economic crisis this country has ever seen, in the face of strongly hostile public opinion, women actually increased their participation in the work force from 24.3 to 25.4 percent, a numerical gain of more than 2 million women workers. The decade saw a dramatic (50 percent) increase in the number of married women who were working, and women made important strides in the emerging labor movement. In general, women as a group seem to have been less affected by unemployment than men. Like the housewives whose lives stayed the same while men's roles were threatened, women's lives on the job were less disrupted by the Depression. The 1930s did not see drastic losses for women at work, and women certainly held their own. They might even have taken a small step forward.

Notes and References

1. William H. Chafe, *The American Woman: Her Changing Social, Economic, and Political Role, 1920–1970* (New York, 1972), p. 55.

2. Robert W. Smuts, *Women and Work in America* (New York, 1959), pp. 38, 58–66.

3. Grace Hutchins, *Women Who Work* (New York, 1934), pp. 31, 159.

4. Chafe, *The American Woman*, p. 61; Hutchins, *Women Who Work*, pp. 134–35, 153. The mistake in arithmetic occurs in the original source.

5. Valerie Kincade Oppenheimer, *The Female Labor Force in the United States: Demographic and Economic Factors Governing its Growth and Changing Composition* (Westport, Conn., 1976), pp. 44–45, 53.

6. Chafe; *The American Woman*, p. 108; Oppenheimer, *Female Labor Force*, p. 53.

7. Ruth Shallcross, *Should Married Women Work?* (Washington, D.C., 1940), p. 17.

8. Shallcross, *Should Married Women Work?*, pp. 5, 9; Chafe, *The American Woman*, p. 108; Hutchins, "Women Who Work", *International Pamphlets*, no. 27 (New York, 1934), p. 12.

9. Sarah Slavin Schramm, "Section 213: Woman Overboard," unpublished paper presented at the Berkshire Conference on the History of Women, October 1974, p. 2. See also chapter 3 of Lois Scharf, *To Work and To Wed: Female Employment, Feminism, and the Great Depression* (Westport, Conn., 1980).

10. Chafe, *The American Woman*, pp. 56–57; Winifred D. Wandersee

Bolin, "The Economics of Middle-Income Family Life," pp. 60–61.

11. *Women's Bureau Bulletin #148*; Bolin, "The Economics of Middle-Income Family Life," pp. 62, 69, 70.

12. Julia Kirk Blackwelder, "Women in the Work Force: Atlanta, New Orleans, and San Antonio, 1930 to 1940," *Journal of Urban History* 4 (May 1978):339.

13. Jean Collier Brown, "The Negro Woman Worker," *Women's Bureau Bulletin #165* (Washington, D.C., 1938), p. 1.

14. Ibid. For one black woman's description of life as a laundry worker, see the oral history interview with Sylvia Woods in Alice and Staughton Lynd, eds., *Rank and File: Personal Histories by Working Class Organizers* (Boston, 1973).

15. *Women's Bureau Bulletin #165*, pp. 8–13.

16. Ibid., pp. 6–8.

17. Ibid., pp. 8–13.

18. Lynd and Lynd, *Rank and File*, p. 23; Mary Elizabeth Pidgeon, "Women in the Economy of the USA: A Summary Report," *Women's Bureau Bulletin #155* (Washington, D.C., 1937), p. 39.

19. Mary Elizabeth Pidgeon, "Employment Fluctuations and Unemployment of Women: Certain Indications from Various Sources, 1928–1931," *Women's Bureau Bulletin #113* (Washington, D.C., 1933); Hutchins, *Women Who Work*, p. 181.

20. Federal Emergency Relief Administration, *Proceedings of the Conference on Emergency Needs of Women* (Washington, D.C., 1933), p. 16; Meridel LeSueur, "Women on the Breadlines," *New Masses*, January 1932, in Harvey Swados, ed., *The American Writer and the Great Depression* (Indianapolis: Bobbs-Merrill, 1966), p. 186.

21. LeSueur, "Women on the Breadlines," pp. 187–88.

22. Ibid., p. 188.

23. Hutchins, *Women Who Work*, p. 187.

24. Thomas Minehan, *Boy and Girl Tramps of America* (New York, 1934). See also Callman Rawley, "A Glimpse of the Unattached Woman Transient in New Orleans," *Family* 15 (May 1934):84–86.

25. Bertha Thompson, as told to Ben Reitman, *Sister of the Road: The Autobiography of Box Car Bertha* (New York, 1937), pp. 251–52.

26. *Women's Bureau Bulletin #113*, p. 4; "Unemployment Among Women in the Early Years of the Depression," *Monthly Labor Review* 38 (1934): 790–95.

27. See, for example, Juliet Mitchell, *Woman's Estate* (New York:Penguin, 1971), and Margaret Benston, "The Political Economy of Women's Liberation," *Monthly Review* 21 (1969), reprinted in Edith Altbach, ed., *From Feminism to Liberation* (Cambridge: Schenkman, 1971).

28. Even during the 1930s, the view that women were doing better than men found support. See Harriet Byrne, "The Effects of the Depression on Wage Earners' Families: A Second Survey of South Bend," *Women's Bureau Bulletin #168* (Washington, D.C., 1936), p. 17; *Women's Bureau Bulletin #155*, pp. 35–45; Mary Elizabeth Pidgeon, "Trends in the Em-

ployment of Women, 1928−1936," *Women's Bureau Bulletin #159* (Washington, D.C., 1938); Sophonisba P. Breckinridge, *Women in the Twentieth Century: A Study of Their Political, Social, and Economic Activities* (New York, 1933), pp. 233−34, 242.

29. Alice Kessler-Harris, "A History of Women Workers: The Great Depression as a Test Case," Radcliffe Institute, March 9, 1977; *Women's Bureau Bulletin #155*, p. 44.

30. Milkman, "Women's Work and Economic Crisis," pp. 75−76.

31. Ibid., pp. 79−80.

32. Blackwelder, "Women in the Work Force," pp. 331−32, 342, 353−54.

33. Mary Elizabeth Pidgeon, "Employed Women Under N.R.A. Codes," *Women's Bureau Bulletin #130* (Washington, D.C., 1935), p. 2.

34. Rose Schneiderman (and Lucy Goldwaithe), *All for One* (New York, 1967), p. 9; Maud Younger, "The NRA and Protective Laws for Women," *Literary Digest* 117 (June 2, 1934):27.

35. *Women's Bureau Bulletin #130*, pp. 5−7, 111; Younger, "The NRA and Protective Laws for Women," p. 27; Genevieve Parkhurst, "Is Feminism Dead?" *Harper's Magazine* 170 (May 1935):743.

36. Ellen Woodward, "This New Federal Relief," *Independent Woman* 13 (April 1934):104; *Women's Bureau Newsletter* 15 (December 1, 1935); Donald S. Howard, *The WPA and Federal Relief Policy* (New York: Russell Sage Foundation, 1943), p. 280.

37. Report on Women's Work in the WPA, from Dorothy Nyswander to Eleanor Roosevelt, September 29, 1935, quoted in Susan Ware, *Beyond Suffrage: Women in the New Deal* (Cambridge, Mass., 1981), p. 109.

38. Howard, *The WPA and Federal Relief Policy*, pp. 278−80, 345.

39. Ibid., p. 282; Hilda Worthington Smith to Eleanor Roosevelt, May 15, 1940, quoted in Ware, *Beyond Suffrage*, p. 114. See also Hilda W. Smith, "Educational Camps for Unemployed Girls," *New York Times Magazine*, January 15, 1936.

40. Scharf, *To Work and To Wed*, pp. 127−30, 133−34.

41. Chafe, *The American Woman*, pp. 68, 86; "The Woman Wage Earner: Her Situation Today," *Women's Bureau Bulletin #172* (Washington, D.C., 1939). See also Philip Foner, *Women and the American Labor Movement, From World War I to the Present* (New York, 1980).

42. Chafe, *The American Woman*, pp. 66−67, 83; Irving Bernstein, *The Turbulent Years: A History of the American Worker, 1933−1941* (Boston, 1970), pp. 84−89.

43. For a discussion of these three women, see Alice Kessler-Harris, "Organizing the Unorganizable: Three Jewish Women and Their Union," *Labor History* 17 (Winter 1976):5−23. See also Barbara Sicherman and Carol Hurd Green, *Notable American Women: The Modern Period* (Cambridge, Mass., 1981).

44. Rose Pesotta, *Bread Upon the Waters* (New York, 1944), 158; *NAW: The Modern Period*, pp. 541−42.

45. Kessler-Harris, "Organizing the Unorganizable"; Pesotta, *Bread Upon the Waters*, p. 395.

46. Bernstein, *Turbulent Years*, pp. 682–83. *Pins and Needles* was recently revived on Broadway.

47. Bernstein, *Turbulent Years*, is an excellent introduction to the rise of the CIO in the 1930s and its split from the AFL.

48. Bernstein, *Turbulent Years*, pp. 616–19; Chafe, *The American Woman*, pp. 83–84.

49. Lucy Randolph Mason, *To Win These Rights: A Personal History of the CIO in the South* (New York, 1952); *NAW: The Modern Period*, pp. 461–62.

50. Herbert Gutman, "Dorothy Jacobs Bellanca," in Edward T. James, ed., *Notable American Women, 1607–1950: A Biographical Dictionary* (Cambridge, Mass., 1971), 1:124–26.

51. Westin, *Making Do*, p. 311.

52. James J. Kenneally, *Women and American Trade Unions* (St. Albans, Vt., 1978), pp. 166–67; Meridel LeSueur, "I Was Marching," in *Salute to Spring* (New York, 1940).

53. Kenneally, *Women and American Trade Unions*, pp. 166–67; Westin, *Making Do*, pp. 308–18.

54. Westin, *Making Do*, p. 314; Mary Heaton Vorse, *Labor's New Millions* (New York, 1938), pp. 76, 80–81. See also the documentary film *With Banners and Babies* (1977), where forty years later these women, many wearing their old red berets and armbands, recreated their roles in the strike while looking over old clippings of their activities.

55. Westin, *Making Do*, pp. 317–18.

56. For background on the Women's Trade Union League, see Schneiderman, *All for One*; Chafe, *The American Woman*, pp. 69–76.

57. Chafe, *The American Woman*, pp. 77–78.

58. Ibid., p. 86; *Women's Bureau Bulletin #172*; Kenneally, *Women and American Trade Unions*, p. 160.

59. *Women's Bureau Bulletin #172*; Hutchins, *Women Who Work*, p. 260; Chafe, *The American Woman*, p. 86.

Newly elected officers of the freshman class, Radcliffe College, 1934–1935   *Courtesy of Radcliffe College Archives*

Chapter Three
Youth, Education, and Careers

The Depression hit the nation's 21 million youth aged sixteen to twenty-four especially hard. In 1936 Maxine Davis traveled 10,000 miles talking to the nation's young people; *The Lost Generation* chronicled the despair she had seen. Davis described youth as "runners, delayed at the gun": "The depression years have left us with a generation robbed of time and opportunity just as the Great War left the world its heritage of a lost generation." Some 250,000 young boys and girls, average age eighteen, took to the road, hoping to find things better somewhere else. For those who stayed behind, coming of age during the Depression meant lowered expectations, doing without, just getting by. It was hard to be optimistic about chances for the future when one out of four workers was out of a job. No wonder a special 1938 issue of *Life* magazine devoted to "The Youth Problem" concluded that " . . . by and large, U.S. youths today are a sober lot."[1]

With outside prospects so bleak because of the Depression, many young people responded by staying in school for a longer period of time. Middletown posted a sharp increase in high-school enrollment, although boys' enrollment in high school increased more than girls'. (Boys traditionally have dropped out of high school to work earlier than girls; their sisters were more likely to graduate from high school, marking time until marriage.) High schools were bulging in the 1930s because they were warm, free, and a place to go instead of work. These extra students put an additional strain on inadequate budgets and overworked (and underpaid) teachers.[2]

In 1940, 587,718 men and 642,757 women graduated from high school; women comprised 52.3 percent of the total. High school was becoming the major influence on growing up for the nation's youth. In 1930, barely half of the youngsters between fourteen and eighteen attended high school; by 1940, three-quarters shared this experience. Peer culture, rather than parents, community, or church, influenced youth attitudes and set standards of behavior. Conformity became the norm: reading the same funnies, wearing the same clothes, hanging out at the corner drugstore. Popularity was crucial to social acceptance, and no one felt the pressure more acutely than adolescent girls (the word teenager was not yet widely used). A young girl wrote to a newspaper advice column in the late 1920s: "Please help me out. I am not very popular, and yet, according to people I have met, I am pretty. I am five feet eight, with short brown hair, greenish eyes, good color, and inclined to be fat. I do not use cosmetics and don't talk much. It is hard for me to make friends, but I have some. How can I become popular?" With movie stars setting new (and often unattainable) standards for personal attractiveness, these young girls were caught in a trap.[3]

While more students were graduating from high school, that usually marked the end of their formal education. During the 1920s, college had become an accepted stage between adolescence and adult responsibilities for white middle-class men and women, but college students remained a small minority among the eighteen-to-twenty-one-year age group. In the 1930s, scraping together the money to go on to college became even more difficult. For many young men and women alike, any college other than the "college of hard knocks" (to use Jeane Westin's phrase) was out of the question during the Depression. Caroline Bird noted that this country "lost a generation of college graduates in the classes of the early thirties. Almost everyone knew someone who couldn't go to college because of the Depression."[4]

The experiences of female college students in the 1930s, however, were probably influenced more by broader trends affecting women's participation in higher education than by the specific dislocations of the Depression. Only a small minority of American women in the 1930s, between 10.5 and 12.2 percent, attended college (see Table 3-1). The other significant characteristic of higher education for women in the 1930s was that while the absolute number of women enrolled in colleges increased, women's percentage of total college enrollment dropped from 43.7 percent in 1930 to 40.2 percent by 1940.

Throughout the twentieth century, the vast majority of women college students have attended coeducational institutions (see Table 3-2). During the 1930s, only one out of six attended a women's college, although prestigious eastern colleges like the Seven Sisters garnered a far greater share of public attention. The 1938 *Life* issue on youth concentrated on eastern women's colleges like "smart Vassar, scholarly Bryn Mawr, or womanly Wellesley." Sarah Lawrence "girls" were also featured, often identified as daughters of prominent business or professional men. According to *Life*, Sarah Lawrence was distinguished by "its attractive campus, pretty girls and unusual pedagogic methods." Sarah Lawrence and Bennington, founded in 1928 and 1932, respectively, were among the few new colleges, single-sex or coeducational, established in the late 1920s and 1930s. Both stressed field work, creative arts, few required courses, and close contact with faculty, instead of the more traditional education found at other women's colleges.[5]

Almost anyone who went to college in the 1930s had to make some sacrifices, even at the elite eastern women's colleges. Tuition and expenses at a school like Wellesley ran $1,000 a year, well beyond most family budgets in the 1930s. Vassar College had to spend more money on food because students could not afford to eat out; self-help dorms were instituted to cut down on expenses for Vassar students. In contrast to the expensive women's colleges, tuition at a land grant college might be only $25 a semester, allowing many women to work their way through college. Grants from the National Youth Administration often made the difference between graduating and dropping out; in 1936–37, the NYA helped 450,000 young people, approximately half of them women. Averaging $15 to $16 a month, this financial aid took the form either of direct grants to students or work-study programs through colleges and universities. Sacrificing to stay in college often made

TABLE 3-1

Women Enrolled in Institutions of Higher Learning, Regular Session, 1870–1958

YEAR	NUMBER OF WOMEN ENROLLED (1,000s)	PERCENT OF ALL WOMEN AGED 18–21	PERCENT OF ALL STUDENTS ENROLLED
1870	11	0.7	21.0
1880	40	1.9	33.4
1890	56	2.2	35.9
1900	85	2.8	36.8
1910	140	3.8	39.6
1920	283	7.6	47.3
1930	481	10.5	43.7
1940	601	12.2	40.2
1950	806	17.9	30.2
1958	1,148	23.0	35.2

Source: Mabel Newcomer, *A Century of Higher Education for American Women* (New York: Harper and Brothers, 1959), p. 46.

TABLE 3-2.

Women Enrolled in Institutions of Higher Learning, according to Type of Institution, 1869–1957

	PERCENTAGE DISTRIBUTION	
YEAR	COEDUCATIONAL INSTITUTIONS	WOMEN'S COLLEGES
1869–70	41.1	58.9
1879–80	60.4	39.6
1889–90	70.1	29.9
1899–1900	71.4	28.6
1909–10	75.8	24.2
1919–20	81.3	18.7
1929–30	82.9	17.1
1939–40	82.3	17.7
1949–50	88.0	12.0
1956–57	90.4	9.6

Source: Mabel Newcomer, *A Century of Higher Education for American Women* (New York: Harper and Brothers, 1959), p. 49.

students eager to learn and dedicated to their studies—which was much appreciated by the faculty at women's colleges and state universities alike.[6]

One characteristic of women who went to college in the 1930s was their seriousness of purpose. One woman said, "I think we were a more sedate group—the class of '37. Our parents had really sacrificed to send us to college." Caroline Bird remembered "social significance" as the key words at Vassar: "We felt that something basic was wrong with the set-up and it was up to us to find out what was wrong and do something about it." Another woman recalled, "During the thirties when I went to college, the women I knew were ambitious—and serious about it." Economics was one of the most popular subjects, and the New Deal stimulated interest in current affairs, politics, and the social sciences.[7]

The strong emphasis on social significance did not, however, make the campuses of the 1930s hotbeds of radicalism. While William Randolph Hearst portrayed campuses as teeming with Communists, *Fortune* concluded that the colleges were only a little, "a very little," to the left of the country as a whole. College students were a "cautious, subdued, unadventurous generation," which *Fortune* editors likened to a turtle. Committed radicals on campus were a small minority. Maxine Davis in her travels around the country found little evidence of widespread radicalism on campus: "the average undergrad seems to be more agitated about his girl and the team than he is by the United Front."[8]

Caroline Bird remembered a mood of social protest at Vassar, although she admitted radical activists were still a minority: "There were as many politically apathetic girls at Vassar in 1935 as there are now, but the active ones were more active then." Vassar women engaged in social protest by tying heavy brown twine in their hair for the traditional Daisy Chain ceremony, picketing Poughkeepsie factories, and spending summers tutoring in Kentucky. One woman returned with the comment, "Love does not exist among the lower classes." One campus heroine married a political refugee (in name only) to secure him American citizenship. Vassar women, coming from well-heeled families, often felt guilty about their privileges, and they tried to take their social consciences back home on vacation to their Republican parents. A 1936 Vassar cartoon captured the gulf in social consciousness:

"How can I explain the position of organized labor to Father when you keep passing me the chocolate sauce?"[9]

Pauline Kael's memories of Berkeley in the mid-1930s contain a similar mix of radicalism and conservatism. Kael described Berkeley as a "cauldron" in the 1930s: "You no sooner enrolled than you got an invitation from the Trotskyites and the Stalinists." Balancing that was the conservatism of the rich kids from the fraternities and sororities who dominated campus activities; Kael resented such symbols of affluence as cashmere sweaters and pearls almost as much as she did the sorority women's lack of social consciousness. Kael recalled that fraternity boys served as strikebreakers in San Francisco, and were always available to the college administration to put down radical student movements. It was a "miracle" when a liberal was elected student body president.[10]

Pauline Kael's perception of the power of fraternities and sororities was well founded. While their influence had declined slightly from the 1920s, they were still major forces on coeducational campuses. Fraternities and sororities represented another side of college life in the 1930s—the nonacademic side—which existed, even flourished, in spite of the Depression. This was the world of "Betty Coed, popularized female counterpart to Joe College in scores of thirties movies, ads, and stories."[11]

As always, college women's lives revolved around much more than just classes. The college proved an ideal arena to encourage women's athletic prowess and grace as part of the larger curriculum. Physical educators disapproved of the male model of competitive athletics for women, however, promoting instead the more genteel approach described in the *Sportswoman*, published from 1924 to 1936 by the U.S. Field Hockey Association and the Lacrosse Association. Competition was downplayed in favor of enjoyment of the sport and development of sportsmanlike conduct. Colleges instituted play days where women from several colleges were mixed together on color teams to play various sports or recreational activities. In 1936, 70 percent of colleges surveyed utilized college play days instead of meeting head to head in interscholastic contests. From play days emerged sports days, when teams were allowed to represent specific schools. To lessen the competitive aspects, however, winners were often not even announced that day. Another tactic was the "telegraphic" meet:

teams competed at their own schools and then compared scores by telephone or telegraph. During the 1920s and 1930s, according to historian Stephanie Twin, female athletics "blossomed"; the most popular college sports were basketball, tennis, archery, swimming, softball, and field hockey.[12]

While sports were important to female college students in the 1930s, many women remembered other aspects of college life more vividly. A 1937 study showed that college women talked about personalities, sex, careers, and religion, in that order. Social activities, especially dances, were very popular, and most college women had at least one formal gown. One woman remembered, "I didn't have an extensive wardrobe of school clothes, but I always had a bunch of beautiful formals. Now they *were* important." While Radcliffe still required hats and gloves for a trip down to Harvard Square, the preferred everyday dress style on most campuses was saddle shoes, anklets, and cardigan sweaters buttoned up the back. *Fortune* observed that women at eastern schools cultivated a "casual, even untidy, appearance" of tweed skirts, handknit sweaters, low-heeled shoes, and little makeup, while girls in western schools were more likely to wear slacks.[13]

As might be expected, southern schools emphasized the social graces for women even more than their northern counterparts. One woman, who described herself as "brought up like Scarlett O'Hara before Margaret Mitchell even thought of her," remembered her days at Southern Louisiana University as an endless social whirl. The point of college? Not to get an education, but "hunting husbands": "Every girl was crazy to get pinned." Being named Sweetheart of Sigma Chi was the high point of her collegiate experience. This woman later became active in the civil rights movement, but admitted she had no social consciousness in the 1930s: "I wasn't even allowed to breathe on my own."[14]

By the 1930s, sex was taken more for granted on college campuses than ever before. What had seemed shocking in 1923 was not even cause for comment ten years later. As *Fortune* put it succinctly, "Sex is no longer news," which was news in itself. Historians used to credit the 1920s with a dramatic change in sexual mores, but now believe that among certain groups (especially the white urban middle classes) this change was well underway before 1920. By the 1930s, many of these changes in sexual behavior had reached broad sections of the nation's youth, especially in colleges and probably including high schools as well. The changes were especially striking for young women. The new patterns of female behavior encompassed wearing makeup and drinking in mixed company. Smoking, which was once seen as disgraceful, was now acceptable, even sexy, for the liberated woman. But the most striking new mores involved sexual relations.[15]

"Joe and Jane petting on the back seat of an automobile are unimportant. Five million boys and girls petting on public highways have national significance. They indicate a social revolution in manners and morals. Courtship has left the family roof and taken to the road." So opens Dorothy Dunbar Bromley and Florence Britten's *Youth and Sex*, a 1938 study of 1,364 college students. The Bromley-Britten study uncovered strong evidence of new patterns of morals, but also definite standards of permissible behavior. While parents worried about what was going on in the back seats of all those cars, their children had the situation under control.[16]

Bromley and Britten found greater changes in the attitudes and behavior of young women than men, although girls still had considerably less sexual freedom than boys. One-half of the male students and one-quarter of the female had had premarital sex. For college women, their sexual partners were usually their fiancés: love, and a clear commitment to matrimony, justified the intimacy. *Fortune* summarized this new standard: "reasonable restraint, particularly on the part of the girls, before marriage, and fidelity on both sides after marriage."[17]

Among college students, knowledge of birth control was sketchy. Students received little sex instruction from their parents, and picked up most of their (mis)information from friends. Many couples relied on condoms, now conveniently available in gas stations. If sexual activity resulted in pregnancy, desperate college students could usually find an illegal abortionist for between $100 and $150, but such operations often left a girl with a ruined reputation. She was lucky if only her reputation had been damaged. Between 8,000 and 10,000 women died from botched abortions each year. Like today, many college students depended on luck as well as artificial means to avoid pregnancy.[18]

The studies of sex on college campuses in the 1930s concentrate on heterosexual practices, but do pay attention to homosexuality as well. One early study of women's sexuality was Katherine Davis's

Factors in the Sex Life of Twenty-Two Hundred Women (1929). Davis found that 50 percent of the women surveyed had at one time experienced "intense emotional relations with other women." Of these, one-quarter admitted that the relationship had progressed to overt homosexual behavior. Bromley and Britten did not find such a high incidence, but they accepted crushes on other women as a normal and common part of female development. Four percent of the women in their sample admitted homosexual experience, although all but one had "outgrown" it. Bromley and Britten noted that lesbianism was still frowned upon on campuses, and suggested it was less prevalent than a decade earlier, "when a few campus leaders in several of the larger women's colleges made it something of a fad."[19]

New Girls for Old (1930), by Phyllis Blanchard and Carolyn Manasses, was less judgmental about the lesbian life-style. One-third of their sample had had crushes on girls, and 20 percent still preferred girls to boys. Blanchard and Manasses predicted an increase in women seeking intimate companionship with other women as the number of professional women who chose not to marry grew: "The new freedom of woman and her ability to achieve economic independence should favor the homosexual types in making life adjustments."[20]

The 1920s and 1930s came at an interesting crossroads in the history of female sexuality. The late nineteenth and early twentieth centuries had been what Barbara Miller Solomon has called a "golden age for spinsters." Women expected to find spiritual and emotional (and possibly sexual) fulfillment from other women; even married women looked to women for their deepest and most intimate friendships. Many women, especially the college educated, decided to stay single. Along with this decision often went a commitment to social reform or a career in the professions or academic life. These women combined active professional careers with warm and satisfying personal lives, either with a single female companion or with a group of like-minded women friends. This was a respectable and fulfilling life-style for women.

By the 1920s, women who had chosen to live such lives found themselves increasingly out of step with society. The proportion of never-married women fell from around 20 percent in the late nineteenth century to 5 percent by the mid-twentieth. Instead of being looked on as role models, these older women increasingly found themselves objects of scorn and pity: spinsters were seen as neurotic and unfulfilled because they had not participated in the heterosexual experience now so highly valued by society. With the increasing preoccupation on intimate heterosexual relationships, Mary Ryan notes, "the American woman's attention was focused more and more intently upon her private interaction with men." The main casualty was the strong "homo-social" bonds (to use Carroll Smith-Rosenberg's phrase) which drew middle-class women together in deep and intimate friendships in the nineteenth century.[21]

Women of an older generation were confused and saddened by the 1920s' preoccupation with sex. In "A New Generation of Women" (1923), Charlotte Perkins Gilman bemoaned the "physical indecencies of our misguided young people." She singled out the birth control movement for special scorn: "It has come to be, as it were, a free ticket for selfish and fruitless indulgence, and an aid in the lamentable misbehavior of our times, affecting both men and women." Jane Addams shared Gilman's concern, writing, "Perhaps this astounding emphasis upon sex was less comprehensible because of the unique element in the social situation during the last half century regarding the role played by the educated unmarried woman," herself being one of the best examples. Emily Balch disapproved of the emphasis on sex as "practically the whole center of life." These women felt like relics from an earlier age.[22]

The question whether it is appropriate to refer to these late-nineteenth-century single women as lesbians is as yet unresolved. Certainly very few of them consciously identified themselves as lesbians, no matter how woman-centered their personal and professional lives might have been. Yet the growing societal emphasis on heterosexual behavior must have caused women, young and old, to examine yearnings for other women in a different light. Linda Gordon specifically linked this heterosexual preoccupation with perceptions about lesbianism. Gordon noted that the twentieth-century changes in sexual behavior were almost exclusively limited to nonmarital heterosexual activity, which in turn indirectly affected lesbian activity:

> Indeed, so specifically heterosexual was this change that it tended to intensify taboos on homosexual activity and did much to break patterns of emotional dependence and intensity among women. Greater freedom of emotional and sexual expression with men made women

view their time spent with women friends as somehow childish in comparison, or at least less sophisticated and less adventurous. In other words, the sexual revolution produced a social as well as sexual emphasis on heterosexuality.

Drawing on Katherine Davis's 1929 study, Gordon concluded that "lesbian activity did not seem to increase for women born after 1890." Women could and did continue to live together as friends or lovers, often arousing less suspicion and legal persecution than male homosexuals, but by the 1930s their choices put them increasingly out of step with society.[23]

This shift in attitudes had long-range implications both for female sexuality and for women's roles in American society. With the heightened emphasis on heterosexual love, women were increasingly defined by their special "feminine" psychology. Freudian theory could easily be applied in a conservative, antifeminist manner: women were to seek out heterosexual intimacy, which in American society meant marriage, which in turn included the responsibilities of wifehood and motherhood. By the 1940s, psychologists defined motherhood as the "ultimate fulfillment of female sexuality." Women who chose not to marry were seen as neurotic, selfish, and sex starved because they were not fulfilling their biological destinies as women. The single woman lost out in this reorientation.[24]

While this emphasis on fulfilling women's biological destiny through marriage and family was most prevalent in the 1950s, it was already quite strong in the 1930s. Unlike turn-of-the-century feminists who used their college educations as stepping stones to professional careers, an overwhelming majority of college women in the 1930s saw marriage as the main goal of their lives. *Life* captioned it succinctly in side-by-side pictures of students: "Boy's goal: a profession." "Girl's goal: still a home." Most women expected to work for several years after college, but only until they married and began to raise families. The median age for marriage for Vassar women dropped steadily, from twenty-eight in the 1920s to twenty-four by the 1930s and twenty-two by the 1950s. Sixty percent of women surveyed in *Fortune* wanted to marry within one to two years of graduation: the figure for men was 50 percent. The increasing numbers of college women who married in turn provided fuel for the assertion that college women were less interested in careers than previous generations. While such trends had begun by the 1920s, perhaps earlier, they continued during the Depression.[25]

The media offered many examples of women's supposed disillusionment with careers. *Fortune* breezily stated in 1938, "Fifteen years ago, when college girls sat up to the late hours of the night, they talked about careers and living their own lives. The trek to Greenwich Village was on. Today the prospect of marriage and children is popular again." When a number of women published articles describing changed expectations for their sex, their sentiments gained widespread credence. In a 1934 article entitled "In Praise of Domesticity," Harriet Bradley Fitt stated, "Twenty years ago, we all believed in the economic independence of women. Domesticity was regarded with impatience. . . . We all expected to have careers, and we all hoped to be distinguished as the leading woman in this or as the first woman in that. It was part of the doctrine that we should marry and have children, but that these incidents should not stand in the way of our work." By 1934, Fitt had chosen a different route, as the title of her article suggested. Phyllis Blanchard and Carolyn Manasses in *New Girls for Old* came to a similar conclusion: "For the modern girl, working has lost the glamor which surrounded it in the days when women had to struggle against odds for this means of self-expression. It is no longer the ultimate aim of life, but has taken a subsidiary place." What young girls wanted after college was love, marriage, and creative work, in that order.[26]

A glimpse of what actually happened to the Class of '34 appeared in a 1949 *New York Times Magazine* article by John Willig. Willig utilized fifteenth reunion questionnaires from 784 Seven Sisters graduates to trace their experiences after college through 1949. After graduation, it was almost a year before the average woman found a job. Twenty-five percent of graduates found jobs in offices, 24 percent in teaching, 10 percent in sales work, 9 percent in social work, and 29 percent reported miscellaneous occupations. They earned a top annual wage of $1,927, or $37 a week, a very good salary in those days.

Willig continued, "For most of the class of '34, however, a job was only a stop-gap before marriage." By autumn 1938, the majority of the class had married. In 1949, 82 percent were still married (only 7 percent had been divorced), mainly to successful business and professional men. The predominant experience of the Class of '34 was as housewife: only 12 percent of these women were working outside the home in 1949. Almost 90 percent of these women had children, and in 1949 many still had preschool children at home. For the most part, these women felt that marriage was more important than a career, although they did think the two could be combined once children were older. It also helped if the woman had lots of energy, a cooperative husband, good household help, and a part-time career that remained subordinate to her marriage. Interestingly, Willig found more than just scattered evidence of recurring frustration, boredom, and dissatisfaction, precursors of the "problem that has no name" that Betty Friedan described in *The Feminine Mystique* in 1963.[27]

While many college women opted for marriage over career in the 1930s, the trend was never universal. Women continued to enter the professions, joining those who had pioneered in these fields between 1900 and 1930. Moreover, an increasing number of professional women combined marriage and career—almost one-quarter by 1930.[28] Public confessions to the contrary, there is strong evidence of women's persistence, even progress, in the professions in the 1930s. Once again, women were hurt by the Depression, but not destroyed by it.

Analyzing women and the professions in the 1930s is a complicated task, involving conflicting evidence and interpretations. Many historians have sketched a bleak picture, concentrating on two main themes. First, they claim that women's roles in the professions had been declining since the 1920s, supposedly because the younger generation was less interested in feminism and careers than older pioneers in the fields of suffrage and education had been. Second, women's chances were drastically (and adversely) affected by the Depression, which made an already tenuous situation even worse. Barbara Harris summed up both views: "If the 1920's saw a slowing down of the entrance of women into the professions, the 1930's spelled disaster. Under the impact of the depression, hostility to female employment reached new levels of intensity." William Chafe cites figures which show that the percentage of women workers engaged in the professions fell from 14.2 percent in 1930 to 12.3 percent by 1940. The 1940 figure was only 0.4 percent higher than the 1920 figure of 11.9 percent.[29]

Other historians have begun to question such negative interpretations of women's opportunities in the 1920s and 1930s. Frank Stricker argues in "Cookbooks and Law Books: The Hidden History of Career Women in Twentieth Century America" that the same data can be interpreted in a nonregressive manner. He is especially critical of the view that women became disillusioned with careers in the 1920s because the feminist movement went out of vogue. Noting that the evidence on career women returning to domesticity (cookbooks instead of law books) is often highly impressionistic, he cites a 1939 issue of *Harper's Magazine* which prominently featured an anonymous article called the "Lady in the Shoe," in which a woman explained why she had given up her job. In the same issue, however, the editors summarized an informal survey of ten career women which showed that eight of the ten were certain they would not quit their jobs. Evidence for persistence in the face of adverse conditions as well as disillusionment with careers clearly exists.[30]

Stricker does not dispute that setbacks occurred in the period after 1920. During the 1930s, the absolute number of female professionals increased by only 8.5 percent, the smallest decennial increase to that point. Yet declines occurred in different fields at different times. According to the Women's Bureau, the situations of teachers, professors, music teachers, actresses, entertainers, artists, and physicians worsened during the 1930s, with teaching probably the hardest hit. On the other hand, nurses, social workers, and librarians experienced progress.[31]

Table 3-3 summarizes the general trends for women in selected professional occupations throughout the twentieth century, as well as women's experiences in the professions between 1930 and 1940. The figures show slight increases in some fields, slight decreases in others, and stabilization in the rest. They also offer strong testimony to the overwhelming concentration of professional women in certain "female" fields such as librarianship, nursing, and social work.

Women faced strong prejudice as they strove to establish their professional identities. Surveys by the National Federation of Business and Professional Women and the American Association of University Women showed clear discrimination based on sex, marital status, and age which resulted in restricted advancement and lower salaries. Women might sell bonds on Wall Street, but

TABLE 3-3.

Women in Selected Professional Occupations

	PERCENTAGE OF ALL WORKERS						
OCCUPATION	1900	1910	1920	1930	1940	1950	1960
Lawyers		1.0	1.4	2.1	2.4	3.5	3.5
College presidents, professors		19.0	30.0	32.0	27.0	23.0	19.0
Clergy	4.4	1.0	2.6	4.3	2.2	8.5	5.8
Doctors		6.0	5.0	4.0	4.6	6.1	6.8
Engineers					0.3	1.2	0.8
Dentists		3.1	3.2	1.8	1.5	2.7	2.1
Biologists						27.0	28.0
Mathematicians						38.0	26.4
Physicists						6.5	4.2
Librarians		79.0	88.0	91.0	89.0	89.0	85.0
Nurses	94.0	93.0	96.0	98.0	98.0	98.0	97.0
Social workers		52.0	62.0	68.0	67.0	66.0	57.0

Source: Cynthia Fuchs Epstein, *Woman's Place: Options and Limits in Professional Careers* (Berkeley: University of California Press, 1971), p. 7.

they were not listed as account executives on company forms, nor did they receive the same pay as male bond sellers. Banks hired women to deal with female clients, but never promoted them past assistant cashier (which became a "woman's position" in banking). Even in teaching, where women made up more than 80 percent of the teachers, only one out of sixty-three superintendents of schools was female. Moreover, the salaries of women in the professions were consistently below those of men. In 1939, male teachers averaged $1,953, women, $1,394; male social workers received $1,718 to women's $1,442. Eighty percent of those responding to an American Association of University Women survey reported they received less pay than men for equal work.[32]

The Depression threatened, but did not completely undermine, women's tenuous position in the professional world. In 1931, the American Woman's Association surveyed 1,939 members of the Federation of Business and Professional Women about their experiences in the early part of the Depression. Between November 1929 and February 1931, 6.2 percent of those surveyed reported "no job," a warning that "no woman, however trained and affluent, is secure against the avalanche of unemployment." The study found that women who earned between $1,000 and $2,000 in 1929 had a one in ten chance of unemployment in the spring of 1931; those who earned $5,000 to $6,000, one in fifteen; those earning $10,000 and up, one in five chance. (The percentage of unemployment was highest in the top income level, but the actual number of unemployed was much greater in the lower brackets.) One-quarter of the women saw their earnings fall from 1929 to 1931, another common occurrence during the Depression.[33]

By 1934, when the American Woman's Association published a follow-up study, the unemployment rate had doubled. In addition to the 13 percent unemployed, 30 percent of those surveyed had experienced some unemployment over the last several years. Older women were especially vulnerable. Women's unemployment continued to be lower than men's, but the situation was still critical since half the women surveyed were supporting dependents. Sixty percent of those surveyed faced salary cuts or a decline in earnings during the Depression, although as professional women their average salaries (around $2,500) were still significantly higher than those of average female workers.

A strong note of betrayal runs through this 1934 study. These women had entered public life in the flush of postsuffrage optimism: "They belonged to a generation of women which stressed and exalted in the importance of jobs for women, and they had known the crest of the wave that began for women workers during the world war." In the 1930s, professional women in this country increasingly made comparisons to developments in Europe, where women were being told to return to the home and leave the jobs to men. The American Woman's Association called for all women to work together to fight fascism and ensure woman's basic right to work and hold a job outside the home.[34]

The teaching profession was one area where women lost ground during the 1930s. From 1920 to 1940, the number of teachers who were women fell from 85 percent to 78 percent, halting the century-old trend toward feminization of the teaching force. The absolute number of women teachers also showed a decline: 635,207 in 1920; 853,976 in 1930; 802,264 in 1940. Decreasing budgets from lower tax revenues coupled with increased attendance put an almost unbearable strain on school systems, and women teachers bore the brunt of cutbacks. A National Educational Association survey showed that in 1930–31, 77 percent of school districts would not hire married teachers for new positions; 50 percent of the school systems dismissed women teachers when they married. In spite of these prohibitions, the proportion of schoolteachers who were married went from 17.9 percent in 1930 to 24.6 percent in 1940.[35]

The Depression also speeded up a trend in the field of education already underway—the increase in educational standards for teachers. The difficulty of finding jobs encouraged prospective teachers to stay in school longer; school districts could now insist on a college degree without even raising salaries or improving working conditions. By the time the Depression ended, the new standards were widely accepted.[36]

A similar improvement in educational standards occurred in the field of nursing. Before the 1930s, student nurses provided almost all the nursing services in hospitals, while certified nurses worked in private homes taking care of those who could afford their services. The Depression dried up the supply of wealthy private patients, and graduate nurses asked to stay on at hospitals at the jobs they had done as student nurses. From 1929 to 1937, the number of graduate nurses on hospital staffs grew from 4,000 to 28,000. The wages were often no better than what they had earned as student nurses, but few could be choosy in the midst of the Depression. At least hospital employment was regular: private duty nurses rarely worked twelve months a year, even in good times. The services of these trained nurses improved the quality of care offered in the country's hospitals. When the Depression ended, hospitals were so dependent on this new class of nurses that a return to the old system was never considered. The number of nurses grew from 228,737 in 1930 to 362,897 in 1940.[37]

Women fared less well in gaining footholds in traditionally male professions. In law, women faced substantial discrimination which effectively limited their participation in that profession. Women were excluded from many of the major law schools altogether (Harvard did not admit women law students until the 1950s) or were forced to compete against each other with restricted quotas (5 percent or lower) for female admissions. Once they passed the hurdle of law school, women faced further prejudice. Women lawyers were often assigned to traditionally "female" areas of the law such as domestic relations, family law, probate, and wills and trusts. Major corporate law firms rarely hired women, and as late as 1937, prominent women lawyers like Dorothy Kenyon were excluded from membership in the New York City Bar Association. Nevertheless, the number of women lawyers and judges rose from 3,385 in 1930 to 4,447 in 1940, and women's proportion of the legal profession grew from 2.1 to 2.4 percent. A symbolic gain for women in the law was Florence Allen's nomination to the United States Court of Appeals for the Sixth Circuit in 1933, a first for women, and the highest any had risen in the federal judiciary. Allen was mentioned as a possible nominee for the United States Supreme Court in the late 1930s, but nothing came of the effort.[38]

The position of women doctors was perhaps even more tenuous. Women's participation in medicine had been declining since the late nineteenth century, and the absolute number of women physicians was smaller in 1930 than it had been in 1900. In 1930, there were 6,825 women doctors in this country, 4.4 percent of the nation's total; in 1940, there were 7,708 women doctors, 4.6 percent of the total. Like lawyers, women doctors faced strict admissions quotas in medical schools (usually 5 percent); certain prestigious medical schools like Harvard did not admit women students until World War II dried up the supply of bright, zealous young men. Besides barriers to medical school, prospective women physicians faced a new obstacle in the 1920s and 1930s. With a rise in standards for the entire medical profession, internships were becoming mandatory for professional advancement, and many internships were closed to women.[39]

The 1930s did not always mark constriction for women in the professions. Social work, for example, drew numbers of talented women. Many of this century's most prominent public women, such as Jane Addams, Florence Kelley, Julia Lathrop, and Lillian Wald, had been active in the settlement house movement in the early 1900s. By the 1920s, social work was undergoing important changes, with growing emphasis on graduate training, a group professional identity, and the casework method. During the 1930s, social workers provided crucial expertise for the expansion of federal, state, and local government services to meet the needs of the Depression. The New Deal could never have done as much as it did, or done it so quickly, without the expertise of the predominantly female field of social work. Women both of the older generation of social workers, the Progressive reformers, and those professionally trained in the 1920s found work in the expanding government services.[40]

In common with other women's fields like nursing or librarianship, pay and prestige for female social workers were low. Salaries declined as caseloads increased, and social workers bore the brunt of public hostility to the relief programs. Yet other people's misfortunes translated into more jobs for social workers, as settlement leader Lillian Wald wrote to a friend in 1932, "I think this is a good time for social workers; the only people who seem to be employed, —alas!" Women accounted for 68 percent of social workers in 1930 and 67 percent in 1940, numbering between 47,000 and 48,000 in the 1930s.[41]

In the field of business, women faced prejudice and discrimination. Most women in business were office workers, and this group made up a large proportion of the membership of the National Federation of Business and Professional Women. But the achievements of some business women took them beyond the secretarial pool. The census category of "Managers, Officials, and Proprietors" shows small increases for women between 1930 and 1940, while men stagnated (see Table 3-4). Women, however, were not equally represented at all levels in the business field. Paralleling the absence of women partners in Wall Street law firms, no women served on the New York Stock Exchange or the General Motors Board of Directors.[42]

A three-part series in *Fortune* in 1935 surveyed the status of women in business. *Fortune* singled out sixteen women executives of accomplishment, naming Josephine Roche, who ran a coal company in Colorado and served as Assistant Secretary of the Treasury in the New Deal, the most distinguished American businesswoman of the decade. *Fortune* could not resist stating: "There is no woman whose business achievement would properly rank with the first or the second or even the third line of male success. It is an ungallant statement. It is quite probably a statement of no lasting importance. But it is true." Only between 10,000 and 12,000 women earned more than $5,000 in 1929 (pre-Depression); most of these women were salaried employees, not captains of industry. Among the successful women *Fortune* cited were Elizabeth Arden and Helena Rubinstein, both of whom owned businesses that sold beauty products to women, and Mrs. Taube Coller Davis, who earned $100,000 a year for her syndicated advice to department stores.[43]

One profession that seemed to hold many opportunities for women in the 1930s was the field of journalism. Eleanor Roosevelt's press conferences gave women journalists status and prestige. Hollywood films like *Mr. Deeds Goes to Town* (1936) and *His Girl Friday* (1940) made the girl reporter a favorite female lead. Women editors and reporters numbered 7,105 in 1920, 14,786 in 1930, 15,890 in 1940, and 28,595 in 1950. While more progress was made numerically in the decades immediately preceding and following the 1930s, this was an exciting period for women journalists covering both domestic issues and international affairs.[44]

One thing that all newspaperwomen had in common was the strong prejudice they met from male coworkers and editors. By the 1930s, women journalists had invaded all branches of the newspa-

TABLE 3-4.
Female Managers, Officials, Proprietors
(Except Farm)

YEAR	NUMBER	PERCENT OF TOTAL	DECENNIAL INCREASE (PERCENT)	MALE DECENNIAL INCREASE (PERCENT)
1900	77,214	4.5	—	—
1910	216,537	8.6	180	43
1920	220,797	7.8	2	13
1930	304,969	8.4	38	27
1940	414,472	11.0	36	1
1950	699,807	13.6	69	33

Source: Frank Stricker, "Cookbooks and Law Books: The Hidden History of Career Women in Twentieth Century America," *Journal of Social History* 10 (Fall 1976):5.

per field, but they were underrepresented on the front-page, by-line assignments that made a reporter's reputation. Women had to battle their way out of the society pages and rewrite desks to get jobs in straight political reportage. The metropolitan or city beat was often the hardest to crack; the *New York Times* did not even allow a woman reporter in the city room until 1934. Women were banned from the National Press Club and its annual Gridiron dinner. (With Eleanor Roosevelt's help, women journalists organized an annual Gridiron Widow's party at the White House.) Women journalists excelled in the feature field and dominated the syndicates.

Ishbel Ross, herself a newspaperwoman, offered a breezy introduction to women journalists, past and present, in her 1936 *Ladies of the Press*. Ross singled out women who met the "front-page test" of the "successful front-page girl" in the 1930s. Lorena Hickok wrote lead stories on national issues for the Associated Press from the 1920s through 1933. Genevieve Forbes Herrick of the *Chicago*

Tribune, Marjorie Driscoll of the *Los Angeles Examiner*, Grace Robinson of the *New York Daily News*, and Elenore Kellogg of the *New York World* earned by-lines and wrote lead stories throughout this period. So did Ruth Finney of the Scripps-Howard chain, who was probably the leading woman political writer in Washington in the 1930s; Finney concentrated on the Congress and constitutional issues. These women were all living proof (as if any were needed) that women made just as good reporters as men.[45]

Eleanor Roosevelt gave a huge boost to the status of women reporters when she joined her husband in the White House in 1933. Ross observed, "Never was there such a gift from heaven for the working press." Bess Furman, who covered Eleanor Roosevelt for the Associated Press (her counterpart at the United Press was Ruby Black), seconded that: "No newspaperwoman could have asked for better luck." Eleanor Roosevelt understood the needs of these journalists, trusted them, and granted them unprecedented access to her activities and thoughts. One innovation was her press conferences for women only. Although the press conferences were supposed to be on nonpolitical subjects only, politics inevitably entered in with the First Lady's wide-ranging interests. About seventy-five women journalists attended the first press conference, and steady attendance hovered around thirty or forty. A front-page scoop for women reporters was Eleanor Roosevelt's announcement that the White House would start serving beer at official receptions in 1933.[46]

Since the press conferences were so informal, the reporters got to know Eleanor Roosevelt personally. Soon they found her visiting their homes, knitting baby blankets for their children, and having them to lunch at the White House. The women reporters who were closest to Eleanor Roosevelt were Lorena Hickok, Emma Bugbee of the *New York Herald Tribune*, Genevieve Forbes Herrick, Bess Furman of AP, and Ruby Black of UP. Lorena Hickok had been an Associated Press star in the late 1920s and early 1930s, but had resigned from the AP in 1933 because she could no longer write objectively about her good friend Eleanor Roosevelt. (A recent book, Doris Faber's *The Life of Lorena Hickok, E.R.'s Friend*, suggests the attraction went much deeper.) Hickok was part of the circle of newspaperwomen who formed Eleanor Roosevelt's closest personal friends in the 1930s. Often they would combine business with pleasure, as in a 1934 trip to Puerto Rico, where Eleanor Roosevelt was accompanied by Hickok, Bugbee, Black, and Dorothy Ducas. Another friend, Rose Schneiderman of the NRA Labor Advisory Board, also came along on the working vacation.[47]

It was not just on the domestic scene that women gained new recognition—international affairs also provided a new forum for women journalist's talents. Anne O'Hare McCormick of the *New York Times* made her name in the 1920s and 1930s with her penetrating coverage of European developments, especially her chronicling of Mussolini's rise to power in Italy. By 1936, McCormick was turning her attention to American politics as well, and that year she became the first woman to serve on the editorial board of the *New York Times*. In 1937 McCormick won the Pulitzer Prize for foreign correspondence, the first woman to do so. She also wrote extensively for the Sunday magazine section, an area of the *Times* less hostile to women's talents than the rest of the paper.[48]

Probably the preeminent female foreign correspondent of the 1930s was Dorothy Thompson. Thompson had won her reputation in Europe in the 1920s with her daring coverage of revolutions and wars, and her exclusive interviews with European leaders. In Vienna, she once left her home in evening clothes in a rush to cover a revolution in Poland. In 1928, she married novelist Sinclair Lewis. In 1931, she was back in Europe, interviewing Adolf Hitler; three years later, she was expelled from Germany for her articles criticizing the Nazi regime. She returned to America, where she became a highly successful newspaper columnist and radio commentator, speaking out against Hitler and calling for American intervention to stop the spread of fascism.[49]

Some women, like Freda Kirchwey, moved through the ranks of journalism to become editors and publishers in their own right. Daughter of the dean of the Columbia Law School, Kirchwey graduated from Barnard in 1915, where she was a militant activist for various causes. After graduation, she was a reporter for the *Morning Telegraph* and then the *New York Tribune*. In 1918, she began her lifelong association with the *Nation*, rising from foreign editor to managing editor to editor and publisher by 1937. Like many other women in journalism (Ruby Black and Bess Furman are two ready examples), she combined marriage, motherhood, and career. During the 1930s, as she gained a growing audience for her views, Kirchwey's attention switched to foreign affairs, where she was a strong interventionist.[50]

Like journalism, the academic field also had its share of successful professional women. Sophonisba Breckinridge, Grace Abbott, and Edith Abbott were all members of the faculty of the School of Social Service Administration at the University of Chicago. Mirra Komarovsky began her distinguished career in sociology at Barnard. Ruth Benedict and Margaret Mead pioneered in the new field of anthropology. Other prominent women scholars included Caroline Ware, distinguished economist, Constance Rourke, expert on American humor, and Persia Campbell, noted for her work on consumers. Dr. Alice Hamilton retired in 1935 from the faculty of the Harvard Medical School, the only Assistant Professor Emeritus in Harvard's history. Working with their husbands, but without institutional affiliations, Helen Merrill Lynd and Mary Beard had a strong impact on the fields of sociology and history. The contributions of these individual women show the continued vitality of scholarly life for women in the 1930s.

Women's roles in academic life are intimately connected with graduate education, an area where women have seen significant declines since the 1920s. In 1920, women received one out of seven Ph.D.'s granted; by 1956, the percentage had fallen to one out of ten. The percentage began to drop in the 1930s (see Table 3-5). Not until 1970 would women's share of doctorates again approach the levels of the 1920s.[51]

While women were declining as a proportion of doctorate holders, the number of women receiving Ph.D.'s continued to rise: up from 311 in 1930 to 419 in 1940. Women's proportion of total doctorates is the product of two factors—the rise and fall of the number of women receiving doctorates and the rise and fall of the total number of doctorates given to men and women. Since the 1920s, the number of women receiving doctorates has grown dramatically, a factor independent of men's aspirations and options for the Ph.D. Also, as Barbara Miller Solomon suggests, the decline in doctorates varied from field to field.[52]

In other ways, women in the academic profession were holding their own in the 1930s: 19,930 women were classified as college presidents, professors, and instructors in 1930; the figure reached

TABLE 3-5.
Women Doctorates

YEAR	NUMBER AWARDED	WOMEN AS % OF TOTAL	% DECENNIAL INCREASE
1920	90	15.1	—
1930	311	15.4	245.5
1940	419	13.0	34.7
1950	613	9.2	46.3
1960	1,090	10.5	77.8

Source: Frank Stricker, "Cookbooks and Law Books," *Journal of Social History*, Fall 1976, p. 6.

20,124 in 1940, evidence of stagnation, but not necessarily of decline. Women made up 26 percent of college faculty in 1920, 27 percent in 1930, and 28 percent in 1940. (As of 1976, women faculty had not again reached the 1940 level.)[53]

The great majority of women faculty were concentrated in the private women's colleges. In 1940, women made up 72 percent of the faculties of the twenty-two largest private women's colleges, compared to only 3 percent of the faculties of twenty-one men's colleges of comparable size. Realistically the only place a woman scholar could hope to teach during this time was in a women's college. Since women's colleges were only a small minority of all collegiate institutions, they could absorb few new faculty members; private institutions in general, and women's colleges in particular, were hard hit by the Depression, further limiting potential jobs. Marjorie Nicholson, in 1941 the first woman named a full professor at Columbia, noted that graduate schools used the dismal academic market for women to justify limiting admissions of women to graduate programs in the 1930s.[54]

Women faculty faced other challenges in the 1930s, especially increased competition from men. The number of male faculty members employed at women's colleges began to rise in the 1930s (a trend that has continued to the present), threatening women's one safe haven. Presumably male academics looked at women's colleges as a last resort in the tight job market; conversely, women's colleges wanted to bolster their image by attracting male faculty. At the same time, the new emphasis on publications and scholarly research hurt female professors, who were generally perceived to take greater pride in their teaching than in research and publication.[55]

The fight over a successor to Mary Woolley as president of Mount Holyoke College in 1936 and 1937 adds another dimension to women's experiences in academe in the 1930s. Mary Woolley, a symbol to many of the success of women's education, had left Wellesley's Biblical Literature department in 1901 to become president of Mount Holyoke. In 1935, as Mount Holyoke's centennial approached, Woolley announced her intention to retire. In her place, the trustees chose Dr. Roswell Ham, a Yale English professor. Women like Frances Perkins, Secretary of Labor and a 1902 Holyoke graduate, were appalled that in one hundred years of existence Mount Holyoke had not produced a single woman qualified to run it. Many Holyoke alumnae saw the choice of Ham as a repudiation of the women pioneers who had worked to make women's colleges vital and strong institutions, and resented the suggestion that a male president conferred more status on a women's college. Even within the women's colleges of the 1930s, women's position was not secure. The change, however, was less a result of the Depression than of changing evaluations of the role that a women's college should play in the modern world.[56]

One hundred years earlier, astronomer Maria Mitchell had noted that successful women in the professions needed "'extraordinary persistency' and a good bit of luck."[57] Her advice was just as relevant in the 1930s as it had been then. Yet women in the professions were not crippled by the Depression. In spite of legislation restricting women's right to work, in spite of the heightened discrimination and competition for jobs in the 1930s, the decade between 1930 and 1940 did not see drastic declines for women. Contrary to commonly held views that women's careers went into a steep decline in the 1920s and that the discrimination of the Depression was the final blow to an already weakened women's movement, women held their own in the professions during the 1930s.

Notes and References

1. Maxine Davis, *The Lost Generation: A Portrait of American Youth Today* (New York, 1936), p. 4; Minehan, *Boy and Girl Tramps of America*; "The Youth Problem," *Life*, June 6, 1938.
2. Lynd and Lynd, *Middletown in Transition*, pp. 207, 211; Bird, *The Invisible Scar*, p. 244.
3. Cynthia Fuchs Epstein, *Woman's Place: Options and Limits in Professional Careers* (Berkeley, 1970), p. 57; Phyllis Blanchard and Carolyn Manasses, *New Girls for Old* (New York, 1930), p. 37.
4. Paula S. Fass, *The Damned and the Beautiful: American Youth in the 1920's* (New York, 1977); Westin, *Making Do*, p. 87; Bird, *Invisible Scar*, p. 243.
5. *Life*, June 6, 1938, pp. 56, 41–43; Mabel Newcomer, *A Century of Higher Education for American Women* (New York, 1959), p. 49.
6. Westin, *Making Do*, p. 84; Elaine M. Smith, "Mary McLeod Bethune and the National Youth Administration," in Mabel Deutrich and Virginia Purdy, *Clio Was a Woman*, pp. 150–51.
7. Westin, *Making Do*, pp. 110, 91–92; Bird, *Invisible Scar*, pp. 17, 114, 119.
8. "Youth in College," *Fortune*, June 1936, pp. 156–58; Davis, *Lost Generation*, p. 39.
9. Bird, *Invisible Scar*, pp. 114–15, 130.
10. Terkel, *Hard Times*, pp. 346–47.
11. Westin, *Making Do*, pp. 84–85.
12. Stephanie Twin, *Out of the Bleachers: Writings on Women and Sport* (Old Westbury, N.Y., 1979), p. xviii; Ellen Gerber, *The American Woman in Sport* (Reading, Mass., 1974), chapter 2.
13. Fass, *Damned and the Beautiful*, p. 179; Westin, *Making Do*, pp. 85, 117; "Youth in College," *Fortune*, June 1936, p. 102.
14. Westin, *Making Do*, pp. 105–109.
15. "Youth in College," *Fortune*, June 1936, p. 101; James R. McGovern, "The American Woman's Pre–World War I Freedom in Man-

ners and Morals," *Journal of American History* 55 (1968):315–33; Blanchard and Manasses, *New Girls for Old*, p. 13.

16. Dorothy Dunbar Bromley and Florence Haxton Britten, *Youth and Sex: A Study of 1300 College Students* (New York, 1938), pp. 3, 5.

17. Blanchard and Manasses, *New Girls for Old*, p. 235; Bromley and Britten, *Youth and Sex*, pp. 5, 21; "Youth in College," *Fortune*, June 1936, p. 155.

18. Westin, *Making Do*, p. 90; Bromley and Britten, *Youth and Sex*.

19. Katherine B. Davis, *Factors in the Sex Life of Twenty-Two Hundred Women* (New York, 1929), quoted in Bromley and Britten, *Youth and Sex*, p. 118.

20. Blanchard and Manasses, *New Girls for Old*, pp. 5, 111. For a group of women who did make such choices, see Vern Bullough and Bonnie Bullough, "Lesbianism in the 1920's and 1930's: A Newfound Study," *Signs* 2 (Summer 1977):895–904.

21. Ryan, *Womanhood in America*, p. 169; Carroll Smith-Rosenberg, "The Female World of Love and Ritual: Relations Between Women in Nineteenth-Century America," *Signs* 1 (August 1975):1–29.

22. Charlotte Perkins Gilman, "The New Generation of Women," *Current History* 18 (August 1923):736–37; Addams and Balch, quoted in Ryan, *Womanhood in America*, p. 153.

23. Linda Gordon, *Woman's Body, Woman's Right* (New York, 1976), pp. 193–94.

24. Ryan, *Womanhood in America*, pp. 163–67, 181.

25. "The Youth Problem," *Life*, June 6, 1938, pp. 56–57; Newcomer, *A Century of Higher Education*, p. 214; Peter Filene, *Him/Her/Self: Sex Roles in Modern America* (New York: Harcourt Brace Jovanovich, 1974), p. 24.

26. "Youth in College," *Fortune*, June 1936, p. 156; Harriet Bradley Fitt, "In Praise of Domesticity," in Herbert Elmer Mills and His Former Students, *College Women and the Social Sciences* (New York: John Day, 1934), p. 265; Blanchard and Manasses, *New Girls for Old*, p. 175.

27. John Willig, "Class of '34 (Female) Fifteen Years Later," *New York Times Magazine*, June 12, 1949, p. 10+.

28. Frank Stricker, "Cookbooks and Law Books: The Hidden History of Career Women in Twentieth Century America," *Journal of Social History* 10 (Fall 1976):8.

29. Barbara J. Harris, *Beyond the Sphere: Women and the Professions in American History* (Westport, Conn., 1978), p. 141; Chafe, *The American Woman*, pp. 91–92.

30. Stricker, "Cookbooks and Law Books," p. 10.

31. Ibid., pp. 5–6; Janet Hooks, "Women's Occupations Through Seven Decades," *Women's Bureau Bulletin #218* (Washington, D.C., 1951), p. 154.

32. Chafe, *The American Woman*, pp. 90–91, 61; *Women's Bureau Newsletter*, December 1, 1936; Susan Kingsbury, "Economic Status of University Women in the USA," *Women's Bureau Bulletin #170* (Washington, D.C., 1939).

33. *The Trained Woman and the Economic Crisis: Employment and Unemployment Among a Selected Group of Business and Professional Women in New York City* (New York, 1931).

34. Lorinne Pruette, *Women Workers Through the Depression: A Study of White Collar Employment Made by the American Women's Association* (New York, 1934), p. 21.

35. Harris, *Beyond the Sphere*, p. 142; Chafe, *The American Woman*, p. 59; Epstein, *Woman's Place*, p. 201; Pruette, *Woman Workers Through the Depression*, p. 104; Stricker, "Cookbooks and Law Books," p. 8.

36. Robert W. Smuts, *Women and Work in America* (New York, 1959), p. 103.

37. Ibid., pp. 103–104; Epstein, *Woman's Place*, p. 200.

38. Chafe, *The American Woman*, p. 60; Epstein, *Woman's Place*, pp. 200, 7. For Florence Allen's career, see her autobiography, *To Do Justly* (Cleveland: Western Reserve University Press, 1965). See also *NAW: The Modern Period*, pp. 11–13.

39. Epstein, *Woman's Place*, pp. 200–201; Mary Roth Walsh, *Doctors Wanted: No Women Need Apply, Sexual Barriers in the Medical Profession, 1835–1970* (New Haven, 1977), pp. 186, 224.

40. For background on the history of social work, see Roy Lubove, *The Professional Altruist: The Emergence of Social Work as a Career, 1880–1930* (Cambridge, Mass.: Harvard University Press, 1965); Frank Bruno, *Trends in Social Work, 1874–1956* (New York, 1957); Joanna Colcord, "Social Work and the First Federal Relief Programs," *Proceedings of the National Conference of Social Work* (New York: National Conference of Social Work, 1943), pp. 382–94; Chafe, *The American Woman*, pp. 39–44.

41. Clarke A. Chambers, *Seedtime of Reform: American Social Service and Social Action, 1918–1933* (Minneapolis, 1963), p. 184; Epstein, *Woman's Place*, pp. 200, 7.

42. Stricker, "Cookbooks and Law Books," p. 5.

43. "Women in Business," *Fortune*, July, August, September 1935. The feature on women executives is in the September issue, beginning on page 81.

44. Stricker, "Cookbooks and Law Books," p. 6; Epstein, *Woman's Place*, p. 200.

45. Ishbel Ross, *Ladies of the Press: The Story of Women in Journalism by an Insider* (New York, 1936).

46. Ibid., p. 311; Bess Furman, *Washington By-Line: The Personal History of a Newspaperwoman* (New York, 1949), p. 153.

47. Ross, *Ladies of the Press*, pp. 309–22; Ruby Black, "New Deal for Newswomen in Capital," *Editor and Publisher*, February 10, 1934, p. 11. For much information on the newspaperwomen of the 1930s, see Doris Faber, *The Life of Lorena Hickok: E.R.'s Friend* (New York, 1980).

48. Ross, *Ladies of the Press*, pp. 366–68, 150. See also *NAW: The Modern Period*, pp. 439–40.

49. Ross, *Ladies of the Press*, pp. 360–66. See also Marion K. Sanders,

Dorothy Thompson: A Legend in Her Time (Boston: Houghton, Mifflin, 1973); *NAW:The Modern Period*, pp. 683–86.

50. June Sochen, *Movers and Shakers: American Women Thinkers and Activists, 1900–1970* (New York: Quadrangle, 1973), pp. 134–40.

51. Patricia Albjerg Graham, "Expansion and Exclusion: A History of Women in American Higher Education," *Signs* 3 (Summer 1978):766.

52. Stricker, "Cookbooks and Law Books," p. 7; Barbara Miller Solomon, "Historical Determinants in Individual Life Experiences of Successful Professional Women," *Annals of the New York Academy of Sciences*, March 15, 1973, pp. 175–76. Jessie Bernard, *Academic Women* (New York, 1964), p. 71, shows doctorates awarded to women by fields from 1920 to 1961.

53. Stricker, "Cookbooks and Law Books," p. 6; Graham, "Expansion and Exclusion," p. 766; Bernard, *Academic Women*, p. 40.

54. Newcomer, *A Century of Higher Education*, p. 165; Solomon, "Historical Determinants," p. 176.

55. Graham, "Expansion and Exclusion," pp. 768–69.

56. George Martin, *Madam Secretary: Frances Perkins* (Boston, 1976), pp. 369–77, covers the battle over Mary Woolley's successor and Frances Perkins's primary role in opposing the choice of a man.

57. Quoted in Solomon, "Historical Determinants," p. 177.

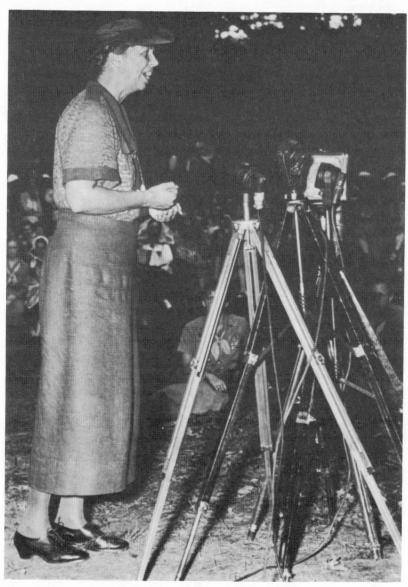

Eleanor Roosevelt addressing the Girl Scouts
Photograph courtesy the Franklin D. Roosevelt Library

Chapter Four
Feminism and Social Reform

Genevieve Parkhurst's 1935 *Harper's* article "Is Feminism Dead?" posed a question on the minds of public-spirited men and women in the 1930s. While Parkhurst concluded that feminism in fact was not dead, she did argue that working women were suffering cruelly from the Depression because the women's movement was crippled by lack of vision and uninspiring leadership. Parkhurst ended with a challenge to women in public life: "Are the women of America going to realize the destiny marked out for them when they began their long march of emancipation? Or are they, like the women of Germany, to stand accused of having betrayed themselves?"[1]

Parkhurst's article was one of many speculations about the fate of the women's movement after the passage of the suffrage amendment in 1920. Sophonisba Breckinridge likened the letdown to demobilization after a war. Once the goal of suffrage had been achieved, there was little agreement about what the next step should be. In 1919, suffrage leader Anna Howard Shaw had warned Emily Newell Blair, "I am sorry for you young women who have to carry on the work in the next ten years, for suffrage was a symbol, and now you have lost your symbol. There is nothing for the women to rally around." In 1919, Blair was too flushed with victory to understand Shaw's perceptive remarks; by

1930, after trying without much success to carve out a place for women in politics, she was only too aware of their meaning.[2]

Historians traditionally have thought that the women's movement fell apart after the vote was won, but many now believe that feminist activity continued in the 1920s. Instead of being united behind the single goal of suffrage, the movement splintered into a variety of causes: pacifism, professional politics, business and the professions. The women's movement had its greatest success in the period from 1920 to 1925, when politicians still feared that women might vote as a bloc. After 1925, the influence of the organized women's movement declined. J Stanley Lemons, who has chronicled the activities of women reformers during the 1920s, concluded: "It has been argued that American feminism was a failure and that the 1920's was when it collapsed and died. I believe that the major current of American feminism, 'social feminism,' was slowed in the 1920's, but it neither failed nor was destroyed. If, indeed, feminism 'failed,' the tombstone will have to bear another date, perhaps the 1930's or 1940's."[3]

If feminism died, however, it is wrong to place the blame on the 1930s. To paraphrase Lemons, some other decade will have to bear the tombstone. While women's issues may not have enjoyed much popular support in the Depression, the 1930s produced significant feminist accomplishments nonetheless. Some of these initiatives came from women's organizations; many were from individual women. Taken together, they show wide and varied roles for women in public affairs and a consciousness of women's contributions to broader movements for social reform. Feminism did survive in the depression decade of the 1930s, in a healthier state than is usually recognized.

In many ways, the 1930s were a time when active feminism would be expected. Many historians have noted that agitation for women's rights is usually most successful in times of generalized reform. The interconnections between the antislavery movement and the early women's rights movement in the 1840s, between woman suffrage and progressivism from the 1890s through 1920, and between the civil rights and antiwar movements of the 1960s and the reemergence of feminism in that decade all point to the complementary nature of women's issues and social reform.

After the Progressive era, the next period of social reform was the 1930s. While the New Deal did not produce revolutionary changes in the American system, it represented a time of questioning and economic readjustment. What effect did this have on women's rights? Most historians have suggested that women's issues were forced to take a back seat to the more pressing concerns of the Depression. June Sochen calls it "tragic" that when the president and his wife were both committed to women's rights, a serious economic depression prevented progress toward the goal of equality for women. Lois Scharf argues, "The massive economic dislocation, its causes and possible solutions, riveted the attention of Americans along the entire ideological spectrum. . . . The debate over the 'new woman' of the previous decade, who combined work and family, was completely subsumed by anxiety over the 'forgotten man' who combined no work with a possibly demoralized and disintegrating family."[4]

Yet the very concentration on economic issues in the Depression did lead to impressive gains for women in politics and government, achievements which just now are coming to light. In response to the emergency of the Depression, the federal government greatly expanded its social welfare services, an area where women have long predominated. Because of a unique set of circumstances, more women served in high administrative positions in the 1930s than ever before, a record not matched until the 1960s. These women in the New Deal, acting self-consciously as women reformers in government and working on behalf of less fortunate women hurt by the Depression, are perhaps the best example of the feminism in public life in the 1930s.

While women had served in appointive office at the federal level before the New Deal, their participation was hardly extensive. Julia Lathrop was chosen to head the newly established Children's Bureau in 1912, and she was succeeded by Grace Abbott in 1922. Mary Anderson ran the Women's Bureau from its inception in 1920; Helen Hamilton Gardener and Jessie Dell served on the Civil Service Commission in the 1920s; Louise Stanley headed the Bureau of Home Economics in the Department of Agriculture. These appointments were encouraging to feminists, but as New Deal politician and feminist Molly Dewson concluded, "Twelve appointments by five Presidents in 24 years was not an exhilarating record."[5]

The 1930s produced significantly more appointments of women to high positions. To quote Dewson again, "The change from women's status in government before Roosevelt is unbelievable." Some of the most prominent included Frances Perkins, Secretary of Labor; Ellen Sullivan Woodward, head of Women's and Professional Projects for the Works Progress Administration; Josephine Roche, Assistant Secretary of the Treasury; Marion Glass Banister, Assistant Treasurer of the United States; Nellie Tayloe Ross, Director of the Mint; Lucille Foster McMillin, Civil Service Commissioner. Two women broke new ground in the diplomatic field: Ruth Bryan Owen as the minister to Denmark from 1933 to 1936, and Florence Jaffray Harriman as minister to Norway from 1937 to 1941. Florence Allen was nominated to the U.S. Court of Appeals, the level just below the Supreme Court. The Labor Department under Perkins utilized the talents of such women as Clara Beyer (Division of Labor Standards), Katharine Lenroot (Children's Bureau), and Mary Anderson (Women's Bureau). Sue Shelton White, Emily Newell Blair, Mary Harriman Rumsey, and Rose Schneiderman all served in the National Recovery Administration. Hallie Flanagan headed the Federal Theater Project from 1935 to 1939. Many of these positions were "firsts" for women: first cabinet member, first director of the mint, first ambassador, first judge on the Court of Appeals. Such appointments brought credit to the individual women and reflected favorably on the efforts of women active in public life.[6]

Several factors came together in 1933 to bring about this progress for women in the New Deal. The expansion of government services to meet the urgent problems of the Depression created a demand for social workers to administer these new programs. Since women have traditionally dominated the fields of social work and public welfare administration, they were able to make important inroads here. At times, William Chafe observed, "Washington seemed like a perpetual convention of social workers as women from the Consumers' League, the Women's Trade Union League, and other reform groups came to Washington to take on government assignments." Moreover, barriers to women's participation are usually weaker when organizations or bureaucracies are in their formative stages. During the early 1930s, such a situation worked to the benefit of women, as they rose to power in the new and expanding social welfare programs. Later in the decade, the reverse was true.[7]

Another crucial factor was the election of Franklin Roosevelt to the presidency in 1932. In one of the greatest two-for-one package deals of the century, the country got Eleanor Roosevelt as well. This partnership had important implications for both social reform and feminism in the 1930s. Eleanor Roosevelt's crusading efforts on behalf of disadvantaged Americans, especially the poor and blacks, earned her a reputation as the conscience of the country. Throughout the 1930s Eleanor Roosevelt actively promoted women's issues as well, working to increase the number of women in prominent government positions. In addition, she participated in the innovative programs of the Women's Division of the Democratic party. Eleanor Roosevelt worked closely with all the women administrators, offering key support at crucial bureaucratic impasses. She also provided access to the president, as colleague Molly Dewson recalled: "When I wanted help on some definite point, Mrs. Roosevelt gave me the opportunity to sit by the President at dinner and the matter was settled before we finished our soup." Eleanor Roosevelt truly was, in Joseph Lash's words, "at the center of this growing New Deal political sisterhood."[8]

Even with Eleanor Roosevelt's active encouragement, the women's pleas might have fallen on deaf ears if Franklin Roosevelt had been unwilling to entrust women with major policymaking positions. But Roosevelt had a positive attitude about women in public service, which was nurtured in New York state government. There he often dealt with talented women in political and governmental circles, many of whom he met through Eleanor. Roosevelt also realized women's importance to the future of the Democratic party, and he actively courted their support through larger roles in the Democratic party and increased patronage.

Frances Perkins was another important supporter of women in government and politics in the 1930s, gathering around her in the Labor Department a circle of talented women who actively promoted women's issues. Perkins had been greatly influenced by the woman suffrage campaign and the Progressive reform movement, and she devoted the rest of her career to proving that women had important contributions to make in the fields of social welfare and public affairs. Of her appointment as Secretary of Labor, Perkins wrote to prominent feminist Carrie Chapman Catt: "The overwhelming argument and thought which made me do it in the end in spite of personal difficulties was the realization that the door might not be opened to a woman again for a long, long time, and that I had a kind of duty to other women to walk in and sit down on the chair that was offered, and so establish the right of others long hence and far-distant in geography to sit in the high seats." While publicly not identified as a feminist, behind the scenes Frances Perkins was a consistent force for women in Washington.[9]

The other main instigator of progress for women in politics and government in the 1930s was Molly Dewson. This dynamic woman, whose wry sense of humor added to her effectiveness as a reformer and politician, came to the New Deal by way of the Massachusetts Girls' Parole Department, the woman suffrage campaign, and the National Consumers' League. She was a social worker turned politician. Dewson worked on feminist as well as general reform questions, a pattern that characterized most women in the New Deal. During the 1930s, Molly Dewson was head of the Women's Division of the Democratic National Committee, where she used her position to increase women's roles in the party hierarchy and promote her issue-oriented approach to politics. She was also the main force behind the major appointments of women in the New Deal. A close friend of Eleanor and Franklin Roosevelt, Frances Perkins, and most of the other prominent women in government, Dewson acted as a gadfly on women's issues. While she rarely described herself as a feminist, she spent most of her time pushing women's causes.[10]

Almost all of the top women in politics and government in the New Deal were close friends as well as professional associates. These women looked to each other for support in their day-to-day work in government and their other wide-ranging interests. The one major exception to this pattern of cooperation was black educator Mary McLeod Bethune. As head of the Office of Minority Affairs in the National Youth Administration, Bethune held a more important job than many of the other women in government, but she was rarely if ever mentioned as an important "woman" in the New Deal. She saw herself, and others saw her, as a representative of black people. Yet Bethune was proud to be a pioneer for women as well. She accepted the NYA job because she felt "that if these talented white women were working at such responsible jobs at a time of national crisis I could do the same thing. I visualized dozens of Negro women coming after me, filling positions of high trust and strategic importance."[11] The fact that Bethune was not considered part of this group of leading women in the New Deal offers a revealing comment on the 1930s and the attitudes the other women brought to their government jobs.

What brought together most of the women in government, and excluded Mary McLeod Bethune, went beyond just their sex. These women had similar social backgrounds and career patterns, and had known each other from social welfare and reform activities dating back to the Progressive era and the woman suffrage campaign. They shared the excitement of setting up government programs that institutionalized goals for which they had been working over the last thirty years. To these old friendships were added new ones as other talented women gathered in Washington.

Eleanor Roosevelt, Frances Perkins, and Molly Dewson provided the focus for this maze of professional contact and personal friendship. Among the women in high positions in the New Deal, a network of cooperation and shared goals had emerged by 1933–34. Similar attitudes and concerns brought these women together in the midst of the male-dominated government bureaucracy. The women used their network as a major policy-influencing group within the New Deal on programs for social reform and women's issues. Under Molly Dewson, the network greatly expanded the roles of women in the Democratic party, increasing patronage, winning equal representation on many party committees, and generally revitalizing the Women's Division as an active segment of the party structure. The network's influence was just as striking in the field of social welfare. Many of the reforms enacted by the New Deal had been under discussion since the Progressive era, and women in the network supplied crucial expertise in drafting laws such as the Social Security Act of 1935, the Fair Labor Standards Act of 1938, and the NRA codes on minimum wages and maximum hours. Individual women made important contributions to the planning and implementation of these laws, but women's impact was heightened by working together as a group.[12]

The women's network also watched over women's interests in New Deal programs. These women realized that women's needs would be forgotten or overlooked unless the issue were continuously raised, a task the network took on. The women in the network lobbied for camps for unemployed women to match the CCC camps for men; they cooperated with WPA administrator Ellen Woodward to devise extensive programs for women on relief; they testified on women's behalf at NRA code hearings concerning hours and wages. The concerns of the network offer strong evidence of continued feminist agitation in the decade of the 1930s. While social reform ultimately took precedence over women's issues for many of these women, women in the New Deal still made important contributions to the feminist movement by advancing the cause of women in public life in the period beyond suffrage.

A unique set of circumstances which came together in the 1930s made possible these gains for women. Most important were the emergency nature of the New Deal, the contributions of Eleanor Roosevelt, Frances Perkins, and Molly Dewson, women's social welfare expertise, and women's larger roles in the Democratic party. By the late 1930s, many of these factors were on the wane. Once the sense of emergency receded, the social and economic programs in which women played the greatest part faced cutbacks. Moreover, the women began to be taken for granted politically: the second woman ambassador provided less political mileage than the first. By the late 1930s, the country's attention was increasingly focused on the question of American participation in the growing war in Europe. Unlike the Depression, when their roles as social workers and reformers had been indispensable, women's roles in the coming war were less clear.

Finally, women's participation in government declined because of the failure of their feminist vision. The women in the network fell into a trap: they believed that if they did a good job in government (which they did), the way would be easier for future generations of women. These women took few steps to recruit younger women and train them in what they had learned. As a result, when the women retired from government in the 1930s and 1940s, for the most part they were not replaced by like-minded women. In the 1930s women emerged as a strong force in establishing government policy, but they were unable to institutionalize these gains. Unlike laws on social security or labor relations, there are no laws to mandate that women be taken seriously in politics and government.

While unprecedented numbers of women served in appointive office in the 1930s, the decade saw a decline from the 1920s in the number of women elected to public office. Breaking into the male power structure of the traditional two-party system and winning nomination to run in a general election have continued to be more difficult than winning official appointments. The declining number of women elected to national and state office in the 1930s was of special concern to women in public life, who were keenly aware of developments in Europe, where women's public roles were under attack by fascism. Concern with the European situation was one reason why women in public life were so pleased with the important, yet limited, gains for women in the New Deal.

From 1918 to 1940, only twenty-eight women served in Congress. Emma Bugbee called political office on the national level a "widow's game" because most women who served were merely caretakers for the unexpired terms of their late husbands. Occasionally, stand-ins like Senator Hattie Caraway of Arkansas were reelected, but such women rarely exercised independent power in their own right. [13]

Hattie Caraway was the only woman to serve in the Senate in the 1930s. The House of Representatives had greater female representation, although usually no more than four or five women served during any given session. The Democrats were the majority power during most of the 1930s, and more Democratic women than Republican were elected. Ruth Bryan Owen, daughter of William Jennings Bryan, served two terms, but was defeated in 1932 because of her stand in favor of Prohibition. (In April 1933, Ruth Bryan Owen was nominated as Minister to Denmark, a very popular appointment in Congress.) In 1924, Mary T. Norton became the first Democratic woman elected to Congress, and she represented Jersey City, New Jersey, until her retirement in 1950. During the 1930s, she played an important role on the House Labor committee, especially during the fight over the Fair Labor Standards Act of 1938. Norton was quite active in the Women's Division of the Democratic National Committee, as was Caroline

O'Day, New York's congressional representative at large from 1934 to 1942. Caroline O'Day was a close friend of Eleanor Roosevelt, who campaigned for her in New York. Democrats Nan Wood Honeyman, another friend of Eleanor Roosevelt, and Virginia Jenckes both served for shorter terms.

On the Republican side, Edith Nourse Rogers of Massachusetts was the most distinguished representative; she served from 1925 to 1960. Other Republican members of Congress who served in the 1930s included Florence Prag Kahn of California, Mrs. Francis Bolton of Ohio, and Jessie Sumner of Illinois. Ruth Hanna McCormick, elected to the Congress from Illinois in 1928, was nominated as the Republican candidate for senator from Illinois in 1930, but was defeated in the general election. In 1938, Margaret Chase Smith of Maine was selected to complete her late husband's congressional term and then won election in her own right in 1940; in 1948, she was elected to the Senate from Maine. In 1940, Jeanette Rankin returned to the Congress as a Republican from Montana after a twenty-two-year absence: this historical coincidence allowed her to cast votes against the participation of the United States in both world wars. In all, the numbers and achievements of these women, Republican and Democratic, were neither outstanding nor disappointing.[14]

On the state level, 132 women were serving in thirty-four state legislatures in 1933, a small decline from the 149 women serving in state legislatures in thirty-eight states in 1929. While two women had served as governors in the 1920s (Ma Ferguson in Texas, and Nellie Tayloe Ross in Wyoming), no women won high elected office on the state level in the 1930s. Women found the greatest state opportunities in the areas of health, education, and welfare. Women also did much better in elected office the farther they moved down the scale from the national level. Many women held elected positions on various county boards and town councils, and women were well represented on school boards. The less prestige attached to the job, the more likely a woman would be picked to fill it.[15]

Women faced similar obstacles as they tried to break into the world of party politics. Commenting on the status of women in elected office, Emily Newell Blair observed, "Many women have entered but comparatively few have been able to secure place and power." In her 1933 survey of women's roles in the modern world, Sophonisba Breckinridge concluded "the door had opened a little" for women's participation in the political party process. A later survey of women's roles in the national party conventions through the 1944 election found a definite downward trend underway. For the Republicans the high point came in 1924; by 1936, only 6 percent of the Republican delegates were women.[16]

Women reached their peak of participation in Democratic national conventions in 1936, strong testimony to the determined efforts of Molly Dewson. In that year, women made up 14 percent of the total delegates. At the 1936 convention, women won representation on the platform committee, a major breakthrough and sweet victory indeed for the issue-oriented style that many women brought to politics in the 1930s. By 1940, a downward trend in participation in Democratic conventions was underway. As was true also at Republican conventions, Democratic women were much more likely to be alternates than delegates.[17]

Women's participation in appointive and elective office and participation in party conventions represent only part of their political activity in the 1930s. Eleanor Roosevelt, for one, claimed that women had had an important general effect on the tenor of public life since the passage of the suffrage amendment in 1920. Writing in 1940, she observed that one thing stood out in the twenty years that women had been voting: "namely, that on the whole, during the last twenty years, government has been taking increasing cognizance of humanitarian questions, things that deal with the happiness of human beings, such as health, education, security. There is nothing, of course, to prove that this is entirely because of the women's interest, and yet I think it is significant that this change has come about during the period when women have been exercising their franchise." To Eleanor Roosevelt's mind, women had made an important· contribution right there, strong rebuttal to critics who claimed that women had done nothing with their votes.[18]

Sophonisba Breckinridge suggested that another way to gauge women's political influence was in the area of lobbying. Breckinridge placed women's lobbying in a broad historical perspective dating back to the nineteenth-century abolitionists: "For to women, long denied the right to express their political convictions directly through their ballots, lobbying seemed to become a natural channel for exercising influence."[19] Women often found opportunities for strong leadership in lobbying organizations that attempted to influence public opinion and change public policy on the national and state levels. Groups such as the National Consumers' League, the Women's Trade Union League, and the Women's International League for Peace and Freedom offered especially large roles for women reformers.

One factor critical to the survival of feminism in the 1930s was the continued health and vitality of such women's organizations, which had been so important to the women's movement in the past. While the Depression made it difficult for the already financially strapped voluntary associations to work effectively, it did not cripple them entirely. In some cases, it actually opened up new opportunities. It is difficult to concede the demise of feminism when such groups continued to do good work in the decade of the 1930s.

During the 1920s, the most effective instrument of women's political power had been a lobbying group called the Women's Joint Congressional Committee. Charter organizations included the American Association of University Women, the General Federation of Women's Clubs, the National Consumers' League, the National Federation of Business and Professional Women, the National League of Women Voters, the Women's Christian Temperance Union, the National Women's Trade Union League, and others. The 1931 list of legislative priorities of the Women's Joint (as it was called) shows the major concerns of the women's bloc: support for the World Court, maternal and infancy programs along the lines of the 1921 Sheppard-Towner Act, a department of education, independent citizenship, adequate appropriations for the Children's and Women's Bureaus, and unemployment legislation. By the mid-1930s, however, the General Federation of Women's Clubs had withdrawn from the WJCC, as had the WCTU, perhaps signaling a general slackening of influence and interest in the Women's Lobby.[20]

Another prominent women's organization that redoubled its efforts in the 1930s was the Women's International League for Peace and Freedom, which celebrated its twentieth anniversary in 1935 as the world again began to move toward war. While the

WILPF's prime focus had always been disarmament and alternatives to war as an instrument of national policy, the WILPF also dedicated its efforts toward equal opportunity for women. During the 1930s, one of the most important contributions of the WILPF was Dorothy Detzer's role in instigating public sentiment for an investigation of the munitions industry during World War I. Senator Gerald Nye's investigation, which concluded that America had been pushed into the war by armaments industry profiteers, drummed up much popular opposition to war. The Women's International League for Peace and Freedom deserves major credit for the fact that the congressional hearings were held in the first place.

The Women's International League for Peace and Freedom demonstrates the international nature of feminism in the 1920s and 1930s. While no one national group dominated that organization, the United States section was always one of the strongest. Jane Addams served as president of the WILPF for many years until illness forced her to resign in the early 1930s. In 1931 Addams shared the Nobel Peace Prize with Dr. Nicholas Murray Butler, which brought great credit to the league. Addams was succeeded as WILPF president by another American, Emily Greene Balch, a former Wellesley professor fired for her radical views during World War I. She had been International Secretary of the organization since 1918. Balch's career paralleled Addams's in another respect: Balch won the 1946 Nobel Peace Prize.[21]

During the 1930s, the League of Women Voters continued to train women for citizenship, a task begun in 1920 in its role as heir apparent to the National American Woman Suffrage Association. While the orientation of the League of Women Voters was not specifically feminist, the national agenda did include issues of special interest to women, such as unemployment and old-age insurance, disarmament and peace initiatives, and support for appropriations for the Women's and Children's Bureaus.[22]

Probably more important than the national platform was the training for citizenship the league gave to thousands of women across the country. Mary Ann Page Guyol, who later spent twenty years as public relations director for the NLWV, first became interested in the league in the 1930s, when she and a friend organized a local chapter in Red Wing, Minnesota. Guyol remembered, "It filled a tremendous void in my life. . . . And I really did discover I could get things done. . . . I was right in the middle of the action, and I simply adored it." The league offered special rewards to women who had scaled down their aspirations because of the Depression: "You see, women rarely thought about going back to college or graduate school when the kids were gone. They couldn't afford it for one thing—and for another, it just wasn't done. So the league became our university, our graduate school—it was, well, just everything." Guyol believes that perhaps the most lasting contribution of the League of Women Voters to the 1930s was helping to shift the climate of public opinion from isolationism to internationalism.[23]

The League of Women Voters, a creation of the postsuffrage period, survived the Depression and has continued to flourish. Other women's organizations, especially those dating back to the Progressive era, often found it difficult to maintain their effectiveness and influence in the midst of the Depression. During the Progressive era, the settlement houses had been "the spearheads for reform," leading the good fight for municipal reform, labor rights, housing legislation, woman suffrage, child labor laws, and other Progressive causes. With the professionalization of social work and the changing social and political climate of the 1920s and 1930s, however, the settlement movement voluntarily relinquished its leadership role in social reform.

In the 1930s, settlement houses barely exceeded their numbers in the Progressive era, and they were concentrated predominantly in such large eastern cities as New York, Boston, and Philadelphia. By the 1930s, recreational and educational activities such as after school play groups and homemaking and citizenship classes had replaced social action. A recent study attributes this change to loss of financial autonomy as settlement houses became dependent on Community Chest organizations for their budgets. Since the professional and business elite usually controlled the purse strings of the Community Chests, settlements became more cautious about supporting unpopular causes which might jeopardize their financial backing. Spirit and commitment changed as well: residents saw settlements as a cheap place to live "rather than as a means of working more effectively with the poor." By the 1930s, women's impact on social reform through settlement houses was on the wane.[24]

The effect of the Depression on voluntary associations like the National Consumers' League and the Women's Trade Union League, also holdovers from the heyday of Progressive reform, was more ambiguous. These groups were only shadows of their former selves by the 1930s; declining membership and finances severely curtailed their impact. During the 1930s, all voluntary associations found it difficult to raise money. Molly Dewson described the 1930s as a "sad period" for the National Consumers' League because of its limited budget and lessened influence after Florence Kelley's death. During the same decade, the Women's Trade Union League could only afford one full-time organizer, and its budget dropped below $20,000. Ironically, the New Deal contributed to the financial troubles of such groups, because the public believed that New Deal reforms made agitation for hours and wages regulation and better working conditions less necessary. Molly Dewson protested such a short-sighted view to Eleanor Roosevelt: "We cannot leave it all to the government. Of course, the government is doing a better educational job than we could have done in a century, nevertheless, through this general education must run steel rods to hold together this new sentiment. Organizations like the Consumers' League and the Trade Union League are these steel rods."[25]

In spite of dwindling membership and precarious finances, groups like the Consumers' League and the Women's Trade Union League did have an impact in the 1930s, a strong one indeed. Many prominent members of the Roosevelt administration had received their training in these groups, and maintained their contacts once they took up their jobs in Washington. Actually, as Clarke Chambers notes, "The lines of influence, in these cases, worked both ways, from voluntary associations to public service and back." The women in government turned to their friends in voluntary associations for expert technical help or to obtain broader public support for specific proposals. Conversely, their friends in reform groups used the women in government as intermediaries to hasten federal action on social welfare policies. These voluntary agencies made vital contributions to the emerging New Deal social welfare policies: they supplied research and experience gathered over the last thirty years; they helped to write the laws and build public support for their passage; they often even furnished the personnel to run the programs. The New Deal "owed a profound debt" to these reform groups and their dedicated leaders.[26]

White women were not alone in organizing groups to improve conditions for their sex and their communities in the 1930s—black women were active as well. As Gerda Lerner has pointed out, black women and white women usually worked in "parallel but race-segregated" groups, rather than in interracial organizations. Mirroring the white women's club movement, which had begun in the 1890s, the National Association of Colored Women was formed in 1896. Like the General Federation of Women's Clubs, this organization was led by middle-class women, but it also attracted some working women who were concerned about issues of education, self-improvement, race pride, and the black community to the local clubs. An important step was taken in 1935 with the formation of the National Council of Negro Women with Mary McLeod Bethune, noted educator and New Deal administrator, as its first president. This organization served as a coordinating group for some twenty national and ninety-five local organizations, representing almost 850,000 organized black women.[27]

Some interracial cooperation between organized black and white women did occur in the 1930s. Spurred on by black activists like Eva Bowles and Anna Arnold Hedgeman, the predominantly white Young Women's Christian Association was encouraging interracial work on the antilynching crusade in the South by the 1930s. The YWCA added more black women to its staff, but they were usually assigned to black branches of the Y. Anna Arnold Hedgeman recalled her job in Brooklyn in 1938: "The Central YWCA of Brooklyn was located in a large, well-equipped building, while the Negro club, Ashland Place Branch, was in an unattractive, poorly maintained clubroom-residence operation in a former brownstone residence. Approximately four blocks separated these two buildings. There was no Negro neighborhood in the immediate vicinity of the Negro branch. It reminded me sharply of the big houses of Southern white folks and the shacks of Southern Negroes. . . ." While the YWCA still remained segregated, it was one of the few women's organizations open to both black and white women.[28]

Another attempt at interracial work occurred in the South concerning the issue of lynching. Tentative attempts at cooperation had begun in 1920 as black women sought the support of the white women's club movement in an attempt to end the lynchings which occurred each year in southern states. During the 1920s, black and white women worked together in the Women's Council of the Commission on Interracial Cooperation, which had 805 branches in the South by 1929. At the initiative of the Women's Council, the Association of Southern Women for the Prevention of Lynching (ASWPL) was founded in 1930 under the leadership of Jessie Daniel Ames, a white businessperson and former suffragist from Texas. Within this group black and white women worked tirelessly to challenge the myth that lynchings were done to protect white womanhood. Jessie Ames declared, "The women traced lynching directly to its roots in white supremacy." Moreover, Ames noted that racial violence against blacks and the repression of women through the pedestal concept of white womanhood kept both groups oppressed.

Working through established church groups and missionary societies, and drawing solidarity as Christian women, the ASWPL collected 40,000 signatures on an antilynching petition. This effort represented women in almost every county of the South. While attempts to secure antilynching legislation were unsuccessful in the 1930s, black and white women were far ahead of their communities in sensitivity to the plight of blacks in American society, a problem which only came to national attention in the 1950s and 1960s.[29]

Such activities testify to the continued vitality of women's organizations, both black and white, in the midst of the Depression. Yet many of these organizations came under attack in the 1930s. Interracial groups were obvious targets, because they challenged the twin prejudices of racial discrimination and sexual oppression, but Elizabeth Dilling's 1934 *The Red Network* shows that few women's groups escaped the red-baiting in the decade. *The Red Network* provided descriptions of more than "460 Communist, Anarchist, Socialist, I.W.W., or radical-pacifist controlled or infiltrated organizations and other agencies." Dilling's paranoia with respect to the red menace was wide ranging: she damned the Amalgamated Clothing Workers of America, the American Association for Labor Legislation, the American Birth Control League, and the American Civil Liberties Union (a special enemy). And that was only the beginning of her alphabetical list. All unions, even the conservative American Federation of Labor, were suspect; women's groups like the YWCA, the WILPF, the Women's Trade Union League, and even the League of Women Voters were not free from Communist infiltration. Among those 1,300 individuals singled out as suspect were Edith and Grace Abbott, Jane Addams, Sophonisba Breckinridge, Daisy Harriman, Florence Kelley, Margaret Dreier Robins, Eleanor Roosevelt, Rose Schneiderman, Mary Woolley, and Mary Van Kleeck.[30]

The Red Network typifies the accusations which reformers and feminists faced in the 1930s. In the midst of overcrowded schedules and strained budgets, women's groups had to take time off to answer absurd charges like Dilling's. Clearly some people were ready to believe what she had to say. In many ways, it is ironic that Dilling tagged major women's organizations as radical, because the women's movement as a whole had lost most of its radical associations by the 1930s. Feminists in the 1930s rarely concentrated their attention on broad questions of women's emancipation or proposed radical restructurings of the American economic and social structure. Instead, feminism turned inward in the 1930s, focusing on narrower issues such as restrictions on married women's right to work and the meaning of equality as embodied in the proposed Equal Rights Amendment.

The birth control movement illustrates the decline of radical contributions to feminism by the 1930s. During the 1910s, birth control had been closely linked with socialism, radical labor groups like the Industrial Workers of the World, women's emancipation, and the sexual experimentation of Greenwich Village. After World War I, the movement became more professional, concentrating on legal strategies such as opening clinics and lobbying for legislation. Gone was the inquiry into the ways in which birth control could improve working-class life or encourage a freer sexual standard for women. Birth control was becoming a medical issue, with doctors and health care professionals taking control.

The Depression hastened public acceptance of birth control because many American couples were forced to limit their families for financial reasons. During the 1930s many of the legal restrictions against birth control were finally removed. A 1936 federal court decision, *U.S.* v. *One Package of Japanese Pessaries*, struck down all federal bans on the sale and dissemination of contraceptive information, giving the medical profession wide discretion in prescribing contraceptives. During the 1930s the birth control movement consolidated its gains and reorganized its leadership, emerging in 1942 as Planned Parenthood. Birth control's respectability grew as it put more distance between its growing family orientation and its radical past.[31]

Other issues of interest to organized women in the 1930s similarly lacked radical rhetoric or concern. Women's groups organized to protest discriminatory federal legislation like Section 213 or the "married persons clauses" suggested by various states which restricted women's right to work. As Lois Scharf observed, "The apprehensions aroused by the intensified assault on married working women created a unity among women's organizations and institutions unmatched since the passage of the Nineteenth Amendment. Like the suffrage movement twenty years earlier, however, opposition to this distinct form of economic discrimination proved a narrow issue around which women of disparate views could unite, and the extent of their concern was shallow."[32]

The debate over the married persons clause is symptomatic of a problem that feminism faced in the 1930s. So much of the country's attention was focused on the problems of the Depression that women's issues, which were perceived as having little relation to the broader problems of the Depression, were ignored. Feminism was forced on the defensive in the 1930s: it aimed to stabilize women's current tenuous position rather than open new horizons for women in the economic and political world. At best, women were mobilizing to preserve the status quo. To do this, feminists switched to politically expedient arguments: instead of asserting the absolute right of women to work, they stressed that married women had to work to support floundering families in the midst of the Depression. Women's work was justified as an extension of their responsibilities in the home and family, a fairly traditional view. In the short run, it was probably necessary to downgrade the feminist aspects of the debate over married women's work in the Depression, but this had the unfortunate long-term effect of confirming traditional stereotypes about women's primary roles in the family.[33]

Women in public life did take the offensive in the late 1930s with the Woman's Charter, but the results of this campaign were disappointing. Drafted in late 1936 and circulated in 1937, this document represented an attempt to unify the women's movement in the 1930s behind a common cause. Prime movers behind the Woman's Charter were Mary Anderson of the Women's Bureau and social researcher and reformer Mary Van Kleeck. A broad coalition of women's organizations, ranging from traditional women's groups like the National Women's Trade Union League, the National League of Women Voters, the General Federation of Women's Clubs, the National Consumers' League, the American Association of University Women, and the Young Women's Christian Association to the Communist-dominated American League against War and Fascism, collaborated on the drafting of the charter. Concerted action was especially important in the late 1930s because "reactionary forces everywhere" were trying to deprive women of the political and social gains of the last fifty years.

The Woman's Charter is an interesting compendium of the goals and attitudes of women in public life in the 1930s. It was conceived as "a unique basis for unity, in which women in industry, in the professions and in business, on farms, in domestic service and in household management will take part in achieving the objectives." In keeping with the general tenor of feminism at that time, the Woman's Charter concentrated on women's roles in the public sphere and made no mention of women's family responsibilities. The second paragraph of the charter contained the best description of these goals:

> Women shall have full political and civil rights; full opportunity for education; full opportunity for work according to their individual abilities, with safeguards against physically harmful conditions of employment and economic exploitation; they shall receive compensation, without discrimination because of sex. They shall be assured security of livelihood, including the safeguarding of motherhood. The provisions necessary for the establishment of these standards, shall be guaranteed by government, which shall insure also the right of united action toward the attainment of these aims.[34]

While there was basic agreement on those general goals, the last paragraph of the Woman's Charter provoked controversy. It read, "Where special exploitation of women workers exists, such as low wages which provide less than the living standards attainable, unhealthful working conditions, or long hours of work which result in physical exhaustion and denial of the right to leisure, such conditions shall be corrected through social and labor legislation, which the world's experience shows to be necessary." Instead of unifying the women's movement, this clause of the Woman's Charter merely widened a basic split in the feminist movement. Disagreement over the Woman's Charter was one skirmish in the larger battle over the Equal Rights Amendment that dominated the ranks of feminists in the 1930s. Struggling to hold their own against the forces of the Depression, feminists were also engaged in an internal battle over the meaning of equality for women. One casualty was the Woman's Charter, which, in Mary Anderson's words, was "a complete flop."[35]

Actually, the divisiveness of the ERA issue dated to the 1920s. The National Woman's Party introduced the ERA in 1923 as the next logical step after the suffrage amendment. Soon after, the potential impact of the ERA on protective labor legislation for women began to split the women's movement. Attempts to compromise and build a common feminist platform failed. By the mid-1920s, the battle lines had been drawn, and emotions were running high.[36]

Women who supported the ERA, usually members of the National Woman's Party, argued that protective legislation had done more harm than good for women workers: restrictions on the hours that women could work, minimum wage standards, and limits on night work impeded rather than improved women's opportunities in the work force. ERA advocates objected that women were singled out as a group for special treatment: they wanted men and women treated alike in the work force and in all aspects of American life. Protective legislation for women struck them as paternalistic and patronizing.

The opponents of the ERA held entirely different views. They were unalterably opposed to an amendment which would remove the hard-fought gains of protective laws for women merely for the abstract notion of equality. In addition, opponents of the ERA strongly believed that the positive aspects of protective legislation (especially its impact on actual working conditions) far outweighed whatever discriminatory features the laws might contain. Both sides agreed that men and women alike deserved protection by the government, but ERA opponents feared that if the women's laws were struck down, regulatory legislation covering men and women would be difficult, if not impossible, to secure. In their eyes, this meant that everybody lost. For many women in public life, continuing support for protective legislation became a question around which there could be no compromise.

The ERA provoked other disagreements. Proponents of the ERA pointed to the thousands of discriminatory laws left unaffected by the passage of the nineteenth amendment. Georgia, Virginia, and Vermont laws allowed a husband to collect his wife's wages, but not vice versa; other states denied married women the right to enter into contracts. Husbands could divorce their wives if they had been unchaste before marriage in Maryland, and in Minnesota a man whose wife was guilty of adultery could collect damages from her lover, but the wife did not have the same recourse. Community property laws in eight states worked to the benefit of the husband, who was considered the head of the household. Laws in twenty-six states prohibited women from serving on juries, and several states even prohibited women from running for elected office. Faced with such blatant discrimination, the National Woman's Party offered the ERA as a solution. Opponents of the ERA, while admitting the laws were discriminatory, feared legal chaos if all laws that treated men and women differently were suddenly overturned.[37]

While much of the battle over the ERA was argued in terms of state versus federal rights or piecemeal change versus a blanket amendment, at base the two sides were working with two entirely disparate conceptions of women's nature. The National Woman's Party wanted women and men treated exactly the same: any special attention to women automatically made them second-class citizens. To the ERA advocates, the similarities between the sexes far outweighed the differences.

Opponents of the ERA, on the other hand, believed that men and women were fundamentally different. The two sexes had much in common, yet women had special needs. These needs were especially apparent in the workplace, where women, because they were physically weaker and entrusted with the responsibility of bearing children, needed special attention and protection. As William Chafe concludes, "the division of opinion could hardly have been greater."[38]

During the 1920s and 1930s, the issue became increasingly emotional. Opponents portrayed the NWP members as upper-class professional women who had no understanding of the conditions under which the masses of American women worked. Molly Dewson said that she did not want "our unfortunate sisters who work for a pittance in factories" to forego all protection so that certain women could reiterate a principle: "Some of these hard-boiled females seem to forget the virtues of generosity and sympathy for the underprivileged." Frances Perkins seconded this view: "There is one whole group of women who is always greatly excited about the work 'equality.' You make them equal and that suits them splendidly."[39] Rational discussion of the relative merits of the ERA was often lost in bitter personal recriminations.

At first, the social feminists who opposed the Equal Rights Amendment had the momentum. Only the National Woman's Party supported the ERA on its introduction in 1923, with almost all the major women's organizations arrayed against it. But in the 1930s, the ERA supporters began to pick up strength. The Business and Professional Women endorsed the ERA in 1937, a major breakthrough; by 1938, the amendment had been endorsed by the American Alliance of Civil Service Women, the National Association of Women Lawyers, the American Medical Women's Association, the Osteopathic Women's National Association, the Women's National Relief Corps, and locals of the Bindery Women's union. The NWP was no longer the ERA's lone supporter.

The Equal Rights Amendment also gained support from politicians and the major political parties. While Emma Guffey Miller tried unsuccessfully to have the Democratic convention in 1936 endorse the amendment, the Republicans supported the ERA in 1940 and the Democrats followed suit in 1944. The ERA was given a favorable report by the House and Senate Judiciary Committees in 1936–37, only to be recommitted by the full Congress. Although a setback, the congressional action also showed progress, since it represented the first time that the amendment had come up for congressional debate since its introduction in 1923. In response, opponents of the ERA formed a Committee of Five Hundred against the ERA, headed by New York lawyer Dorothy Straus. The ERA opponents were now clearly on the defensive.

While both sides mobilized their forces, the New Deal was

introducing fundamental changes which would shape the debate in years to come. The passage of the NRA codes, the Social Security Act, and the 1938 Fair Labor Standards Act diminished the old rationale for protective legislation for women. When the government protected both men and women alike with minimum wage standards, unemployment insurance, and a forty-hour week, women no longer needed to be singled out for special treatment.

In hindsight, it would appear that the passage of this New Deal legislation should have ended the rift on the ERA: now that protective laws were no longer necessary, reformers concerned with women's issues could reunite. Things were not so simple. First of all, opponents of the ERA pointed out that many women workers remained outside the protection of laws like the Fair Labor Standards Act, and therefore still needed special state laws to cover their working conditions. The main obstacle, however, was that the debate had long passed beyond rational discussion. By 1938, women opposed to the ERA had spent fifteen years trying to protect their gains from the "selfish" NWP members, and they could not change their views overnight. Even though the government continued to take on more responsibility for regulating working conditions, these veterans of the battle from the 1920s and 1930s rarely changed their minds later in their careers. Labor women like Mary Anderson and Rose Schneiderman remained firm in their opposition to the ERA long after the schism that had divided them in the 1930s should have been resolved. Eleanor Roosevelt, who changed her mind and embraced the Equal Rights Amendment in the 1940s, was the rare exception.[40]

The divisiveness on this issue no doubt diverted attention from other causes more worthy of women's support in the 1930s. But the battle over the ERA did not halt social action for women in the 1930s. While concerns for women did not enjoy popular mass-based support, feminism survived in the 1930s, even grew in some areas like the New Deal. Women's activity in the decade seems substantial enough to refute William Chafe's pessimistic conclusion that by the end of the decade, the women's rights movement had "reached a nadir" and "had ceased to exist as a powerful force in American society."[41]

While feminism was not dead, the women's movement was undergoing a period of transition in the 1930s, an evolutionary stage which had little to do with the economic contraction that was diverting everyone else's attention. During the 1930s, the old-guard feminists, those women who had first pioneered in education, the professions, and public life, passed from the scene. Jane Addams died in 1935, Florence Kelley in 1932, Grace Abbott in 1939. Charlotte Perkins Gilman committed suicide in 1935 when cancer made it impossible for her to lead a full and active life. Emma Goldman died alone in exile in 1940.

By the 1930s, leadership in the women's movement transferred to the next generation of women, who had had the benefit of attending college and entering the professions without confronting the epic struggles the earlier generation had faced. Since the battle had been so recently won, the women of this next generation retained a high consciousness of their special roles in public life as women reformers. These were the women who supplied most of the administrators for the New Deal, who kept the women's organizations and voluntary associations alive in the Depression, who rallied to protest laws that discriminated against women on the federal and state level. Their feminism had been so deeply ingrained during the Progressive era and the woman suffrage movement that it was natural, almost second nature, for them to continue such agitation into the 1930s.

But this second generation of women, the ones who kept feminism alive in the 1930s, were also growing older. As they neared retirement, they found that the next generation of women, those raised in the 1920s and 1930s, had different attitudes toward feminism and careers. These younger women took for granted the right to a college education, their ability to enter whatever professions they chose, their right to vote and hold office, their free choice between marriage and career (at least in theory). So much progress had occurred that younger women believed they no longer had to fight for their basic rights. Lillian Hellman, writing about the 1920s from the perspective of the late 1960s, typifies the attitudes of this third generation:

> By the time I grew up the fight for the emancipation of women, their rights under the law, in the office, in bed, was stale stuff. My generation didn't think much about the place or the problems of women, were not conscious that the designs we saw around us had so recently been formed that we were still part of the formation. (Five or ten years' difference in age was a greater separation between people in

the 1920's, perhaps because the older generation had gone through the war.) The shock of Fitzgerald's flappers was not for us: by the time we were nineteen or twenty we had either slept with a man or pretended that we had. And we were suspicious of the words of love. . . .

Hellman concluded, "I was too young to be grateful for how much I owed them in the battle of something-or-other in the war for equality."[42]

At few times in women's history have the gaps between generations been so clear as the great divide between the presuffrage pioneers and their postsuffrage sisters. Yet it is not fair to blame the younger generation for the failure of feminism in the postsuffrage period. While the media at the time carried article after article about the demise of the women's movement, individual women and various women's organizations struggled successfully to keep feminism alive in the midst of the Great Depression.

Notes and References

1. Genevieve Parkhurst, "Is Feminism Dead?", pp. 735–45.

2. Breckinridge, *Women in the Twentieth Century*, p. 255; Emily Newell Blair, "Wanted: A New Feminism," *Independent Woman* 10 (December 1930):499.

3. For a general discussion of women in the 1920s, see Lois W. Banner, *Women in Modern America: A Brief History* (New York, 1974), chapter 4; J. Stanley Lemons, *The Woman Citizen: Social Feminism in the 1920s* (Urbana, Ill., 1973). The quotation from Lemons is from page vii.

4. Sochen, *Movers and Shakers*, p. 163; Ann and Andrew Scott, *One Half the People: The Fight for Woman Suffrage* (Philadelphia: J.B. Lippincott, 1975), pp. 49–50; Lois Scharf, *To Work and To Wed* (Westport, Conn., 1980), p. 137.

5. Mary W. Dewson, "An Aid to the End" (unpublished autobiography, 1949), 1:139–40, found in Dewson papers, Schlesinger Library, Radcliffe College.

6. Ibid., pp. 124–41, covers women's jobs in the New Deal in great detail. See also Emily Newell Blair, "A Who's Who of Women in Washington," *Good Housekeeping*, January 1936, pp. 38–39, and *NAW: The Modern Period*.

7. Chafe, *The American Woman*, p. 42.

8. Dewson, "An Aid to the End," 1:2; Joseph P. Lash, *Eleanor and Franklin: The Story of Their Relationship, Based on Eleanor Roosevelt's Private Papers* (New York, 1971), p. 512. Lash's book is a good compilation of Eleanor Roosevelt's many activities in the 1930s.

9. For material on Perkins, see Martin, *Madam Secretary: Frances Perkins*; Mary Anderson, *Woman at Work: The Autobiography of Mary Anderson, as told to Mary N. Winslow* (Minneapolis, 1951). The letter, Frances Perkins to Carrie Chapman Catt, June 11, 1945, is quoted in Ware, *Beyond Suffrage*, p. 47.

10. Much information on Dewson can be found in Ware, *Beyond Suffrage*. See also Elsie George, "The Women Appointees of the Roosevelt and Truman Administrations: A Study of Their Impact and Effectiveness" (unpublished Ph.D. dissertation, American University, 1972); *NAW:The Modern Period*, pp. 188–91.

11. Mary McLeod Bethune, "My Secret Talks with F.D.R.," *Ebony* 4 (April 1949):42–51, reprinted in Bernard Sternsher, ed., *The Negro in Depression and War: Prelude to Revolution, 1930–1945* (Chicago: Quadrangle, 1969), p. 58. See also Elaine M. Smith, "Mary McLeod Bethune and the National Youth Administration," in Deutrich and Purdy, *Clio Was a Woman*, pp. 149–77.

12. Ware, *Beyond Suffrage*. The material in this section is drawn from this earlier work.

13. Emma Bugbee quoted in Chafe, *The American Woman*, p. 39.

14. For material on women in Congress, see Lorena Hickok and Eleanor Roosevelt, *Ladies of Courage* (New York, 1954); Martin Gruberg, *Women in American Politics: An Assessment and Sourcebook* (Oshkosh, 1968); Breckinridge, *Women in the Twentieth Century*, p. 300; individual biographies in *NAW:The Modern Period*.

15. For material on women in state and local offices through 1933, see "A Survey of Women in Public Office," National League of Women Voters (January 1933), found in National League of Women Voters papers, Schlesinger.

16. Emily Newell Blair, "Women in the Political Parties," in *Annals of the American Academy of Political and Social Science* (Philadelphia, 1929), p. 229; Breckinridge, *Women in the Twentieth Century*, p. 257; Marguerite J.

Fisher and Betty Whitehead, "Women and National Party Organization," *American Political Science Review* 38 (October 1944):898–99.

17. Fisher and Whitehead, "Women and National Party Organization," pp. 896–98, 903.

18. Eleanor Roosevelt, "Women in Politics," *Good Housekeeping* 110 (March 1940):45.

19. Breckinridge, *Women in the Twentieth Century*, p. 257.

20. Ibid., pp. 269–72. For background on the Women's Joint Congressional Committee, see Lemons, *The. Woman Citizen*, pp. 41–63.

21. Gertrude Bussey and Margaret Tims, *Women's International League for Peace and Freedom, 1915–1965* (London, 1965), p. 73; Banner, *Women in Modern America*, p. 172. See also Dorothy Detzer, *Appointment on the Hill* (New York, 1948). For material on Addams and Balch, see *NAW*.

22. Appendix 2 of Breckinridge, *Women in the Twentieth Century*, contains the 1932 National League of Women Voters platform.

23. Jeane Westin, *Making Do*, pp. 280–82.

24. Allen F. Davis, *Spearheads for Reform: The Social Settlements and the Progressive Movement, 1890–1914* (New York:Oxford, 1967); Judith Ann Trolander, *Settlement Houses and the Great Depression* (Detroit, 1975), p. 45.

25. Molly Dewson to Elizabeth Magee, February 7, 1954, National Consumers' League papers, Library of Congress; Molly Dewson to Eleanor Roosevelt, April 10, 1935, Eleanor Roosevelt papers, Franklin D. Roosevelt Library. Both are cited in Susan Ware, "Political Sisterhood in the New Deal:Women in Politics and Government" (Ph.D. dissertation, Harvard University, 1978).

26. Chambers, *Seedtime of Reform*, pp. 267–68.

27. Gerda Lerner, ed., *Black Women in White America* (New York, 1972), pp. 458, 493; Mary S. Sims, *The Natural History of a Social Institution: The Young Women's Christian Association* (New York:The Women's Press, 1936).

28. Lerner, *Black Women in White America*, pp. 458, 517.

29. Jacquelyn Hall, "Women and Lynching," *Southern Exposure* 4 (Winter 1977):54; Lerner, *Black Women in White America*, p. 472. See also Jacquelyn Dowd Hall, *Revolt Against Chivalry: Jessie Daniel Ames and the Women's Campaign Against Lynching* (New York, 1979).

30. Elizabeth Dilling, *The Red Network: A "Who's Who" of Radicalism for Patriots* (Kenilworth, Ill., 1934).

31. Gordon, *Woman's Body, Woman's Right*, especially chapters 10 and 11.

32. Scharf, *To. Work and To Wed*, pp. 59–60.

33. Ibid., pp. 59–65, 138.

34. For material on the Woman's Charter, see Anderson, *Woman at Work*, pp. 210–14. The quotation comes from Mary Van Kleeck, head of the Joint Conference Group for the Woman's Charter, in a January 19, 1937, letter to Eleanor Roosevelt, found in the Eleanor Roosevelt papers, FDRL. Van Kleeck also enclosed "The Woman's Charter: What and Why," a publicity flyer which had a full text of the Woman's Charter.

35. Anderson, *Woman at Work*, p. 212.

36. A good introduction to the ERA battle on which I have relied heavily is chapter 5 of Chafe, *The American Woman*, pp. 112–132.

37. Ibid., p. 121.

38. Ibid., p. 129.

39. Molly Dewson and Frances Perkins, quoted in Ware, *Beyond Suffrage*, p. 77.

40. For an interesting discussion of opponents of the ERA in the 1920s and 1930s, and why they rarely changed their views on the issue, see Barbara Miller Solomon, "Women Reformers and Labor Women Against the ERA: Attitudes, Responses, and Legacies," paper presented to the Organization of American Historians, San Francisco, April 1980.

41. Chafe, *The American Woman*, p. 132.

42. Lillian Hellman, *An Unfinished Woman: A Memoir* (Boston, 1969), pp. 29–30.

Women textile strikers, Greensboro, Georgia, 1934
Courtesy of Library of Congress

Chapter Five

Women on the Left: The Communist Party and Its Allies

During the 1960s, the rise of the New Left dominated American protest. (The term was used to differentiate it from the "Old Left" movement of the 1930s.) The civil rights and antiwar movements, and later the countercultural revolt, challenged the established American order. While groups such as the Students for a Democratic Society proposed radical political and economic alternatives to the prevailing system, their members often held fairly traditional ideas about women's roles in society. As a result, women who were active in these movements in the 1960s faced frustration and discrimination which limited their full participation.

At first, activist women ignored or internalized such patterns of sexism as being expected to get coffee, take notes at meetings, and run the mimeograph machines. They saw women's issues as secondary to broader goals of social change, and as yet they lacked the ideological framework to see their personal experiences as part of a general pattern of women's oppression. By 1967, however, when their tentative attempts to raise women's issues within the New Left had been met with jeers and hostility, women banded together to form a radical women's movement separate from the New Left. The revival of feminism as a national concern in the late

1960s, in which these women played a leading role, has been one of the most enduring contributions of that turbulent decade.[1]

Women had been active in the Old Left as well, but their participation took different forms. During the 1930s, most activity on the left was centered around the Communist Party, where women had prominent roles. These women, however, never seriously contemplated the formation of a separate women's movement. To their minds, an independent feminist movement was unnecessary: their concerns as women were part of the general struggle for revolution and a better world that their vision of communism embodied in the 1930s. Women in the New Left shared a similar attitude in the 1960s, but radical women thirty years earlier had a significant advantage: the Communist Party and the left in general were quite responsive to the issues that women raised. On the whole, the Old Left provided a far more sympathetic climate for the aspirations of women than did the New Left in the 1960s.[2]

When talking about the left in the 1930s, and women's roles therein, the Communist Party looms large. For all practical purposes, the CP *was* the left in the decade. The 1930s witnessed the Communist Party's greatest influence in the United States. No longer a small, sectarian group on the fringes of American society, the Communist Party played a vital and active part in the political life in the decade. During the 1930s, the CP was at the center of almost all progressive action and concern. Many men and women were drawn to the party because of the economic devastation of the Depression: while America floundered, the Soviet experiment seemed vital and alive. Daniel Aaron observed of intellectuals in the 1930s, "It was the times, not the party, that made them radicals. The party attracted them because it alone seemed to have a correct diagnosis of America's social sickness and a remedy for it." In interviews with present and former members of the Communist Party, Vivian Gornick repeatedly found that the Depression was the "clarifying experience" that propelled them toward radicalism.[3]

Mary McCarthy recalled the general fascination and respect that intellectuals like herself had for the members of the Communist Party in the 1930s. She admired their dedication and commitment to the cause, and she recalled, "For me, the Communist Party was *the* party, and even though I did not join it, I prided myself on knowing that it was the pinnacle." (Only later did she see the snobbery behind such attitudes.) The New York world in which Mary McCarthy traveled was laced with radical causes and personalities in the 1930s, a life-style McCarthy later satirized in *The Company She Keeps* (1942). Everyone went to dances for good causes at Webster Hall and attended parties to raise money for the Theater Union or the *New Masses*. McCarthy pointed out wickedly, "It was not difficult, after all, to be the prettiest girl at a party for the sharecroppers." If friends called up to ask if she were free for the evening, she never knew if "they wanted you to picket a movie house, attend a lecture at the New School, buy tickets for a party for Spain, or go and dance at a new night club." Everyone read the *Daily Worker*, belonged to the American League against War and Fascism, marched on picket lines, and paraded on May Day. It was hard to escape contact, as Mary McCarthy remembered, with this "left-wing life to which we felt superior, which we laughed at, but which nevertheless was influencing us without being aware of it."[4]

Women's participation in the Communist Party in America during the 1930s turned on the fortunes and priorities of the international Communist movement. In the end, the CP-USA always followed the party line from Moscow. The American Communist Party had been born during the repression that surrounded American participation in World War I, drawing much of its strength from the old Socialist movement. During the 1920s, harassed by authorities and generally out of step with the concerns of the superficially prosperous decade, the Communist Party had little impact. At the beginning of the 1930s, the party claimed just over 10,000 members.

During the 1930s, important shifts in Communist Party policy affected the CP-USA's relation to radical reform in the decade. From 1929 to 1935, the CP concentrated its attention on industrial workers and the unemployed; it also courted the support of black Americans, whom the CP identified as a colonized nation within the South. Such concern lay behind the CP's involvement in the Scottsboro case in Alabama in the early 1930s. The main organizing thrust, however, was the asserted need to replace the ailing capitalist system with Soviet-style socialism.

This policy underwent a dramatic change from 1935 to 1939 during the popular front phase of the CP. Identifying fascism as the most likely threat to the future of socialism, the Communist

Party now sought alliances with any liberal organization that made antifascism a prime concern. Eleanor Roosevelt, who prior to 1935 had been seen as a captive of the ruling class, became a model for emulation; the entire New Deal was seen as progressive. This period, which lasted until 1939, witnessed perhaps the CP's broadest participation in movements of concern to women, and in American reform in general. Then suddenly in 1939, with the signing of the Nazi-Soviet Pact,·the pendulum swung back, and popular front cooperation was out. This is the general time frame within which to consider women's roles in the Communist Party in the 1930s.[5]

Women made up a substantial part of the membership of the Communist Party in the 1930s. One study estimated that of the 20,000 members in 1933, 3,300 (or 16 percent) were women, equally divided between housewives and workers. Of these women members, 300 were black. By the end of the 1930s, a period of growth and expansion for the CP-USA, women made up between 30 and 40 percent of CP membership. This increase is clearly related to the shift during the popular front period to policies with more appeal to women. Peggy Dennis, who spent fifty years in the Communist Party herself, estimated that in 1943 46 percent of the 83,000 members of the CP were women. Yet women's representation at the grass roots level was never matched by leadership positions of a commensurate number, and many CP women felt they were not treated as equals by their male comrades.[6]

On the other hand, the Communist Party offered leadership opportunities for certain exceptional women. Anna Damon and Margaret Cowl headed the CP's Women's Commission during the 1930s. Anna Burlak played a large role in the textile-organizing efforts of the Trade Union Unity League. Grace Hutchins, author of the influential *Women Who Work* (1934), was active in the CP. Elizabeth Gurley Flynn joined the Communist Party in 1936 and immediately became a leading public speaker for communism in this country. She was elected to the party's national committee in 1938, and served on the CP's Women's Commission, writing a column for the *Daily Worker* covering political issues from her feminist viewpoint.[7]

Elizabeth Gurley Flynn came to the Communist Party by way of pre–World War I socialism and the International Workers of the World (the "Wobblies"), a radical labor organization that had its greatest influence in the period around 1912. Anita Whitney, leading California CP figure, also came out of prewar socialism, although she had joined the Communist Party in the immediate aftermath of the Bolshevik revolution. Several times during the 1930s, Whitney ran on the CP ticket in California, and in her race for state comptroller in 1936 she received nearly 100,000 votes.[8]

Probably the most widely known Communist woman in the 1930s was Ella Reeve ("Mother") Bloor. Although she was in her seventies in the 1930s, she was still quite active in party and public affairs. Native born, Bloor began as a Socialist and had been greatly influenced by Eugene Debs and Florence Kelley. Her early causes ranged from birth control in Connecticut (where she worked with Katharine Hepburn's mother), to organizing the coal mines with Mother Jones, and working for woman suffrage. When the Socialist party split in the wake of the Bolshevik revolution, Bloor sided with the Communist Labor Party, for whom she became a national organizer. During the 1920s and 1930s, Mother Bloor was active in most of the major strikes—Lawrence, Passaic, southern textiles. She organized protests against the executions of Sacco and Vanzetti and initiated hunger marches among unemployed groups once the Depression hit. During the mid-1930s, she participated in antifascism campaigns, CIO unionizing drives, and efforts to organize farmers. Although Bloor was never chosen as a candidate for the national Communist Party ticket, she served on the CP central committee throughout the decade. Equally important was the inspiration that Mother Bloor provided for other women in the party. Admiration for her dots many memoirs.[9]

While women who rose to the top of the CP hierarchy were more concerned with issues of socialism than feminism, all high-ranking women had some consciousness of women's special oppression. Anita Whitney took an interest in women and their roles in the Communist Party, as did Mother Bloor. Often such female leaders realized that prejudice in the larger movement limited women's effectiveness. Mother Bloor wrote in 1940:

> I do not minimize what our Party has done toward bringing about true equality, admitting no discrimination of race, color, or creed in our ranks. But I have often felt, earlier indeed, more than today, that there has been some hesitancy in giving women full equal responsibil-

ity with men. As for myself, I have no complaints. I have been honored with great responsibilities. But the power of all our women must be used to the full—especially today! We women must take our place consciously by the side of men, dropping any sense of inferiority. We must speak up without waiting to be asked, *and we must have something to say.*

Margaret Cowl, head of the Women's Commission in the 1930s and a leading party spokesperson on women, concluded in 1974 that while the leadership paid lip service to women's roles, "male supremacy" played a part in keeping women down: "There was indifference to the mass women's movements and they were not really accepted as part of the working-class movement of the United States."[10]

While certain women's talents were realized at the national level, other women met increased sexism further down the ranks. Vivian Gornick concluded, "Women who were 'the brilliant exception' often rose higher in the Party than they could in any other part of American life, but women who were simply ordinary beings were often more subjugated in the Party than they were in ordinary American life." Many Communist men held fairly traditional attitudes about women's proper roles. One young woman complained to the *Daily Worker*: "Apparently meetings, parades, dances and picnics and other Party activities are reserved only for the male sex, while mother and daughter are supposed to sit quietly at home and knit. Observers can notice these men beaming and approving the work of other girls or women when they see them selling *Daily Workers*, distributing leaflets, or carrying on the work of the Party. But it is different, should they confront their own wife or daughter mingling with others and helping the Party."[11]

Vivian Gornick uncovered many "unliberated" Communist marriages in her study of American communism. Interviewing Arnold and Bea Richman, Gornick found that during the 1930s Arnold Richman was the party activist, while his wife, Bea, was expected to host meetings, put up unexpected guests, and take care of the house. When Bea became involved in women's liberation in the 1970s, the Richmans' roles were reversed. This experience opened Bea Richman's eyes to what she had lived through in the 1930s: "What I want to know is how come so many people were thrown out for white chauvinism [racism] but not one goddamned

Communist was ever thrown out for male chauvinism?" Another woman recalled her Communist marriage: "Three nights out of five when we weren't having a meeting or throwing a party he'd show up at eleven at night with a mob of people, and guess who has to feed them and keep trotting out the drinks? 'Who the hell does all the goddam work?' I'd yell. 'While you sit on your ass making the revolution, *I'm* out there in the kitchen like a slavey. What we need is a revolution in this *house*.' But, of course, he simply ignored me, and of course I simply went on doing it."[12]

Peggy Dennis, herself a Communist and married to a fellow Communist for thirty-five years (although the union was never formalized), was quite sensitive to the potential conflict between women's public and private roles within the party. Dennis realized that most of the women who held leadership positions in the Communist Party did not have concurrent home responsibilities: Mother Bloor was divorced and her children full grown by the time she became an active organizer; Elizabeth Gurley Flynn never entered into any sustained personal relationships, and her child was full grown (raised by her sister) when she joined the CP. But Peggy Dennis wanted to have children, a personal life, and still retain her political activism. Her desire led to inevitable conflict and compromise.[13]

Peggy Dennis had joined the Communist Party in 1925 at age sixteen, having grown up in a self-contained, radical, foreign-born community on the West Coast. After she entered into her lifelong relationship with CP activist Gene Dennis (one of his many aliases), she became pregnant, mainly at his insistence. Peggy Dennis remembered that Gene had been regaling her "with visions of our travelling with babe on our backs from barricade to barricade, wherever the Revolution called." Her mother was closer to the mark: "The pity of it is it will change your life, not his." The Dennis baby was the first child among their activist friends, and their situation became a test case: could revolution be combined with motherhood? Dennis soon noted a strong reverse prejudice among many of their friends and CP activists—either one had a child and stayed home, or one remained free of domestic responsibilities and was an activist. "I was being told I had to choose between being a housewife at the beck and call of her man or becoming a classic version of an unencumbered male." Later she stated, "I did not want to do battle for women's rights. In my perverse way I was still defending my right to be Gene's wife *and* a Party activist." By the 1930s, Peggy Dennis had settled into what became a lifelong pattern, "that of being Gene's unofficial assistant; although he carefully called me 'my co-worker.' As the years passed, I sometimes lamented my lost individual public identity. But by then I no longer seemed able or willing to master the stamina to rebuild a different relationship with Gene, with the Party, or to restructure my own priorities."[14]

The difficulties of devoting one's whole life to the revolution while at the same time maintaining personal commitments affected men and women alike. In the case of domestic responsibilities, however, the burden fell completely on the woman. Collective responsibility for childrearing, either between parents or by the community, was never mentioned. Moreover, women had to make difficult personal decisions never faced by men. Peggy Dennis underwent several abortions when children would have interfered with her or her husband's work, and she knew other women who had had abortions on orders from the CP hierarchy.[15]

While the Communist Party can be taken to task for the sexism cited by women activists, few other groups in American society held more enlightened views about women's roles in the 1930s, and many held considerably worse. The Communist Party was one of the few to encourage public discussion of women's issues during this decade. Activity occurred on two levels: theoretical discussions of women's place under communism, and concrete action on issues of concern to women.

Marxist theory was clear about women's roles in the revolution. Working-class women shared the same interests as working-class men, because they faced the same problems of unemployment, imperialism, monopoly, and exploitation. Women's main task was to fight the capitalist system "side by side" or "shoulder to shoulder" with their men. Once the revolution had occurred, the working class as a whole would fight to eliminate whatever lingering discrimination remained against women. Women in the Communist Party tried to make the party live up to its professed ideals about equality for women and men.[16]

Mary Inman's *In Woman's Defense* provides a cogent and far-reaching analysis of women's place in Communist theory, and the interplay between feminism and the class struggle. Inman's treatise, serialized in the *Daily People's World* in Los Angeles in 1939, was published in book form in 1940. Inman summarized her purpose in writing the book: "Women must be activized in the interests of the people, and the people must be activized in the interests of women." Inman stressed that while women shared problems in common with men, "Women have general problems as women, such as 'the necessity to struggle against the ideology of female bondage,' and against the subservient doctrines preached to them through most of the women's magazines and the general press."[17]

Throughout *In Woman's Defense*, Inman often likened women's secondary status in society with that of black people, and showed how women were oppressed both by their sex and their class. All women were exposed to the same socialization process, which taught them to be passive and subservient. Inman decried the marriage institution because in it women were totally dependent on men: "She is dependent upon another for the very bread she needs to sustain life. Her life is not her own. Her time belongs to him. He is thought to have conferred a great favor upon her by making it possible for her to devote herself exclusively to him." Showing her awareness that women's oppression goes beyond just class, Inman noted that working-class men had the same power over their wives as the rich. The dependent wife of a rich man was no better than a glorified servant to her husband: "Her wifely task, besides being mate, is to exude charm and serve as a tail to his kite. And while, according to some standards, the kite may fly high, she always occupies a posterior position."[18]

Inman's analysis of the economic basis of marriage bore a strong resemblance to that of Charlotte Perkins Gilman, whom she cited approvingly at several points in the book. But Inman's most original contribution was her attempt to place women's work in the home within the broader economic system: "The housewife must be given credit for performing, in the home, work that is indispensable to the present method of machine production. . . . Recognition of the housewife's importance will raise her estimation in her own eyes and in the eyes of society. It will permit her to actively join the ranks of socially useful workers, where she rightfully belongs, swelling their numbers and releasing her political energies to the people." As Inman pointed out, the cook in a logging camp was a vital part of the lumber production. The same rationale applied to cooks in the homes of individual productive workers: "the labor of a woman, who cooks for her husband, who is making tires in the Firestone plant in Southgate, California, is essentially as much a part of the production of automobile tires as the cooks and waitresses in the cafes where Firestone workers eat." The housewife's unpaid domestic labor in the home was, in Inman's words, "the pivot of the system."[19]

Instead of glorifying women's labor in the home, Inman went to great lengths to show that housework was being performed with outmoded techniques. Here her acknowledged debt to Charlotte Perkins Gilman was greatest. "In the case of the housewife, more than any other group, there has been a lag in the method of performing socially useful work in isolated household units, by outmoded hand methods, which is a distinct handicap in a machine age, besides making her problems relating to the economic crisis more difficult of solution." The chores that women performed in the home, such as cooking, laundering, child care, and household cleaning, had lagged far behind in progressive machine methods. What a waste of time for 26 million households to perform such chores individually when the work could be accomplished far more efficiently under a collective system, and women's energies freed for social and political pursuits. Inman envisioned a household system along the lines proposed by Charlotte Perkins Gilman in *The Home* (1903).[20]

Inman's ideas did not sit well in the Communist Party hierarchy. In response to Inman, Avram Landy left few roles open for housewives in hastening the revolution (he believed that the only effective organizations for social change were trade unions) and would not admit any possible divergence of interest between working-class husbands and their wives. Inman's attempt to reconcile feminism and the CP line, and to analyze women's oppression within a Marxist perspective, brought her into conflict with the male leadership. The chilly reception to her work forced Inman to leave the Communist Party, and the implications of her analysis were put aside.[21]

The Communist Party was more successful in dealing with women's issues through mass action than on the theoretical level. Robert Shaffer, who has studied women's participation in the

Communist Party in the 1930s, admits that "work among women and against women's oppression had a relatively low priority in the concerns of the CP during the thirties." The lack of an independent mass women's movement to compel attention to these issues (such as the autonomous Socialist-feminist movement in the 1910s, with its ties to the Socialist party, birth control, woman suffrage, and other radical causes) made it easier to slight women's issues; the overwhelming impact of the economic crisis and the growing need to combat fascism contributed to the neglect. Yet women found encouragement for participation in "progressive collective activities," including ones which looked at the special oppression of women. Shaffer concluded, "Despite its important weaknesses, the CP's work among women in the 1930's was sufficiently extensive, consistent, and theoretically valuable to be considered an important part of the struggle for women's liberation in the United States."[22]

The Communist Party addressed women's issues in several ways. It offered a magazine specifically directed toward women. Called *Working Woman*, and later *Woman Today*, it was published by the Women's Commission; monthly circulation was estimated at 8,000 during the 1930s. This magazine, staffed and written almost entirely by women, illustrates the concerns and attitudes of CP women in the decade.

Another feature geared toward women was the women's column in the *Daily Worker*, the main CP paper. Written by Ann Barton and Helen Luke in the 1930s, the column covered a multitude of topics, ranging from sewing patterns and inexpensive recipes to discussions of bourgeois feminism, sexism in the Communist Party, and quotations from Marx and Lenin on women's roles. In one issue, Luke tentatively raised the question of sharing housework, which provoked sympathetic responses from women and sarcasm and hostility from men. *Working Woman* and the women's column in the *Daily Worker* provided a forum for women to discuss (and occasionally complain about) women's treatment in the Communist Party.[23]

The main voice raising women's issues in the CP in the 1930s was the Women's Commission, headed first by Anna Damon and then by Margaret Cowl. The Women's Commission was a national organization composed of representatives from local CP units from throughout the country; it also had its own director and staff. Although very active in the 1930s, the Women's Commission was dissolved in 1940 in the retrenchment following the Nazi-Soviet Pact. It was reestablished in 1945 under Elizabeth Gurley Flynn, with Claudia Jones, a young black woman, as her assistant.[24]

During the 1930s, the Women's Commission had responsibility for most of the CP's initiatives directed toward women. The Women's Commission launched recruitment drives to attract more women to the party, often timed to coincide with parades in honor of International Women's Day (March 8). There were even all-female party cadres. Usually these were composed of housewives who could only meet during the day, but occasionally such units operated in industry. Single-sex or not, women in local groups supported strikes, raised money for Spanish Loyalists, worked for the Woman's Charter, and organized protests at relief bureaus. One women's unit from Harlem organized a sit-in at the Italian consulate to protest Fascist aid to Franco; when several women leaders were beaten, the party press widely circulated accounts of the women's courage.[25]

During the 1930s, the Communist Party not only recruited women but also worked closely with women who, while not members, shared common goals. The CP focused first on issues of interest to working-class women and then reached out to middle-class women as well during the popular front period. Major initiatives included organizing the unemployed, union organizing, and working with middle-class women's organizations for feminist goals and in the fight against fascism.[26]

In the early 1930s, the Communist Party had its greatest appeal to women when it touched issues directly affecting their everyday lives. The CP was instrumental in setting up local community groups to combat high prices, which then demanded free milk for children, and prevented evictions for nonpayment of rent. The CP usually provided the leadership for these groups, but most of the members were not official party members. Reflecting the CP commitment to combat racism, these groups often included both black and white women. One such group, the New York Women's Council, began a housewife's boycott to protest high meat prices which mushroomed into a nationwide consumer's movement demanding lower prices; 20,000 people signed a petition calling for lower meat prices. Margaret Cowl stated that "the leading role of Communists in this victory was widely recognized." In general, some of the most successful Communist initiatives in the early 1930s involved working on bread-and-butter issues with housewives whose husbands were unemployed.[27]

Christine Ellis, one of the labor women interviewed in Staughton and Alice Lynd's *Rank and File*, described organizing such groups for the Communist Party in the 1930s. Ellis had first been drawn to the CP because the Communists were the most cultured and educated people in her Croatian community: "The thing that impressed me the most was the stress on education, culture, respect for others, devotion to a movement that would by its example win the masses to the cause of communism." One of her first assignments was organizing the unemployed in a black neighborhood on the West Side of Chicago in 1931. If local marshals evicted a family from their dwelling, the unemployed council just moved all their possessions back in from the street and took up a collection to pay the rent. Such actions won them the support of the local people.[28]

After her successful work in Chicago, Christine Ellis became an organizer for the rest of the Midwest, traveling from state to state setting up unemployed councils. In the Midwest, the problem was more likely farm foreclosures than rent evictions, and Ellis organized groups which bid ridiculously low prices at the auctions of the farm implements and land: fifteen cents for a tractor, five cents for a stove. The possessions were then returned to the family that had been foreclosed. Everywhere she went, Ellis found the women more militant than the men: "The women were usually the most outspoken because they had the children to feed and they had to provide the food for the family."[29]

Women also benefited from the CP's active involvement in the fight for unionization of the labor force. Vivian Gornick emphasized, "Throughout the Thirties and Forties, wherever major struggles were taking place between American labor and American capital, it was almost a given that CP organizers were involved." According to Mother Bloor, the Trade Union Unity League, a Communist-dominated organization, was involved in every major strike between 1929 and 1933. Some of the bitterest TUUL battles were fought in southern textile mills, which traditional labor groups like the AFL had completely ignored. TUUL organizer Anna Burlak led many of the textile battles and watched helplessly as martyrs like Ella May Wiggins lost their lives in the bitter Gastonia strike in 1929. Later in the decade, the CP worked closely with the emerging CIO. The Trade Union Unity League also pioneered the technique of organizing the wives, sisters, and mothers of strikers in predominantly male industries like steel and mining. This tactic was effectively used in the Flint auto strikes in 1937.[30]

Organizing farm workers in California put the Communist Party up against similar obstacles as it had faced in southern textiles. Marion Moran was one of many radicals who became Communists because of the party's work in the fields. The CP organizing drive provoked six years of bloody clashes, but it also offered participants, pickers and radical activists alike, a vision of what the cooperative future might hold. Marion Moran remembered, "It was my dream of socialism come true. . . . Of all the emotions I've known in life, nothing compares with the emotion and total comradeship I knew among the fruit pickers in the Thirties, nothing else has ever made me feel as alive, as coherent."[31]

Vivian Gornick found that for many old radicals, trade unionism was synonymous with their communism, because they spent their lives working in factories in order to organize coworkers. Some were deliberate "colonizers" sent in to provoke action; others sought out the CP simply because their working conditions were so terrible. Stella Nowicki became a colonizer in the Chicago meatpacking industry in the 1930s. Brought up in a farm family whose background in the coal mines made it sympathetic to socialism, Nowicki ran away from home in 1933 at age seventeen because her family did not have enough money to pay for food. She became involved in the Young Communist League, and then was sent to work in the stockyards. Union organizing was risky business in the early days, Nowicki remembered: "When I look back now, I really think we had a lot of guts. But I didn't even stop to think about it at the time. It was something that had to be done. We had a goal. That's what we felt had to be done and we did it."[32]

In addition to organizing the unemployed and supporting unionization drives, after 1935 the Communist Party reached out to middle-class organizations. The main reason behind this strategy was to unite liberal elements in America against fascism, and women's support was crucial to these efforts. Mother Bloor led a delegation of fifty American women to a 1934 international meeting in Paris for the initial anti-Fascist women's conference. Out of this grew the American League against War and Fascism, widely recognized as heavily Communist influenced. (Mary McCarthy recalled in 1949, "it was part of our metropolitan sophistication to know the truth about Communist fronts," and she specifically cited that anti-Fascist group.) The league engaged in publicity work to acquaint Americans with the dangers of fascism; it published pamphlets like Dorothy McConnell's 1936 "Women, War, and Fascism," which rallied women against the growing threat. The American League spearheaded the boycott of silk stockings made with Japanese silk, and worked diligently to raise money for the Spanish Loyalists.[33]

The drive against fascism was just one aspect of this broadened women's initiative after 1935. One group warmly welcomed in the popular front was writers, of whom women were some of the most prominent converts. Although the Communist Party supplied the critique of American capitalism fashionable among intellectuals in the 1930s, only a small number of writers actually joined the CP. Many more were fellow travelers: "those who were in the 'movement,' who sympathized with the objectives of the Party, wrote for the Party press, or knowingly affiliated with associations sponsored by the Party."[34]

The 1935 American Writers' Congress symbolized the influence of the Communist Party on writers in the decade. Among the signers of the call for the conference were prominent women novelists and journalists Fielding Burke, Josephine Herbst, Tillie Lerner, Meridel LeSueur, Grace Lumpkin, Myra Page, Genevieve Taggard, and Ella Winters, all known sympathizers or allies of the CP in the 1930s. Nelson Algren, Theodore Dreiser, Granville Hicks, Langston Hughes, Nathanael West, and Richard Wright also signed the call. The heady excitement surrounding the American Writers' Congress marked the peak of writers' involvement in the party. After 1936, disillusionment over the Moscow Trials and unresolved tensions between artistic expression and political ideology had significantly depleted the earlier solidarity. By the time of the 1939 Nazi-Soviet Pact, most writers had split from the Communist Party.[35]

During the heyday of the popular front, the CP also reached out to traditional women's organizations. Margaret Cowl stated, "While the Party places central importance on the role played by working class women, it does not ignore the importance of other sectors of the women's movement. . . . A central feature of the work of the National Women's Commission in the thirties was its success in influencing middle-class women in tying certain of their activities with those of working class women." In the mid-1930s, Ella Reeve Bloor thanked Eleanor Roosevelt and groups like the YWCA and the WTUL for their contributions to the cause of working women. Margaret Sanger, whose birth control plans had previously been seen as contrary to the interests of working women, now became an ally. Even the New Deal was praised.[36]

Especially important in bridging the gap between middle- and working-class women was the drive for the Woman's Charter, which the Communist Party endorsed and actively supported. The Woman's Charter had been put forth by a group of women led by Mary van Kleeck in 1936 and had the support of many women's organizations, including the National Consumers' League, the YWCA, and the League of Women Voters. The Communist Party was in complete agreement with the Woman's Charter's call for full political and civil rights for women and gave approval of the Woman's Charter a prominent place on its agenda of women's issues in the 1930s. The Communist Party was especially pleased with the provisions for equal pay for equal work.[37]

On issues such as the Woman's Charter and the Equal Rights Amendment, the Women's Commission aligned itself with social feminists like Eleanor Roosevelt and Frances Perkins. Their largest area of common ground was the Communist Party's strong support for protective legislation for women workers in the 1930s. Mary Inman wrote in *In Woman's Defense*, "In a society where workers bid against one another in a competitive labor market, the most oppressed need special legislation to protect them from employers who would exact from them so great a toll, because of their weak position, as to be a drag even on capitalism." Margaret Cowl attacked the "so-called Equal Rights Amendment" as reactionary and completely contrary to the interests of working women. Mary Inman spoke out against the "phony equality" that professional women from the National Woman's Party were promoting. If that was feminism, the Communist Party wanted nothing to do with it.[38]

The cooperation of the Communist Party with bourgeois feminists ended abruptly with the signing of the Nazi-Soviet Pact in 1939. In the general retrenchment following the pact, women's activities were drastically curtailed. The legacy of the Communist Party's activity on behalf of women in the 1930s is mixed. Certain women played prominent roles, and the Women's Commission raised women's issues within the party and in the society as a whole. Margaret Cowl claimed that middle-class women's organizations greatly profited from CP involvement: "These and other movements of women thrived because they had the benefit of the fund of political and organizational experiences of the U.S. Communist Party." On the other hand, women in the Communist Party faced consistent sexism from their male colleagues, which led to under-utilization of their talents. Women's issues were never given top priority by the predominantly male leadership. In the end, the experience of women in the Communist Party in the 1930s represents an important if incomplete step toward liberation.[39]

While the Communist Party attracted many women on the left in the 1930s, there were some notable exceptions. The life of Dorothy Day, founder of the Catholic Worker movement, exhibited strong similarities to the lives of those dedicated idealists who joined the Communist Party in the 1930s, but her path diverged at several crucial points. Dorothy Day's background, like that of Elizabeth Gurley Flynn and Mother Bloor, was in socialism and journalism. She worked on the *New York Call* (the Socialist daily paper) and the *Masses*, where she became acquainted with anarchism, communism, and the radical labor movement of the International Workers of the World. During the last stages of the woman suffrage campaign, she was jailed for picketing and went on a hunger strike. When the Communists split from the Socialists after the Russian revolution, Day did not join the Communist Party, although she admitted that she greatly admired their dedication.

At that point in her life, Dorothy Day was drifting. She continued her career in journalism, and wrote a novel, but only found stability in 1927, when she joined the Catholic Church. Day's autobiography, *The Long Loneliness*, shows how drawn she still was to the radical left: "If I could have felt that communism was the answer to my desire for a cause, a motive, a way to walk in, I would have remained as I was. But I felt that only faith in Christ could give the answer." After her conversion to Catholicism, Day spent the rest of her life trying to reconcile her long-standing radicalism with the dictates of the Catholic Church.[40]

In 1932, Dorothy Day went tò Washington to cover the Communist-led Hunger March. When she returned to New York, she found the French poet, philosopher, and peasant Peter Maurin on her doorstep. Maurin greatly influenced her life, and together they founded the Catholic Worker Movement. One of their first acts was to establish a newspaper, which Day named the *Catholic Worker*, reflecting her background in left-wing causes. The first edition of the *Catholic Worker* came out on May Day 1933 and sold for a penny a copy; by 1936, the circulation had grown to 150,000. As a journalist, Day brought considerable skills to the paper: she chose the news, edited copy, and wrote a column for the paper. The *Catholic Worker* was also noted for the exceptional artwork and graphics by Ada Bethune. The newspaper is still in existence today, and the price has remained the same: one penny.

The philosophy of the Catholic Worker Movement as developed by Dorothy Day and Peter Maurin stressed personal responsibility and the need for commitment in modern life. As such, it attempted to bridge the separation between the secular and heavenly aspects of the Christian life. During the Depression, Day and Maurin concentrated most of their efforts on setting up hospices, or houses of hospitality, where men and women could find a place to stay and a free meal. (There were separate hospices for women.) Maurin was also instrumental in establishing several collective farms.

So far these acts fall within traditional Christian charity. What made the Catholic Worker Movement so radical, and what set it apart so decisively from the conservatism of the Church, was its strong emphasis on the poor, the dispossessed, and the exploited. It aimed not just to pity the poor, but to improve their conditions. According to Day, supporting a strike or exposing injustice was just as much an act of mercy as praying for someone's soul. Given this philosophy, supporters of Day and Maurin often found themselves working on the same issues and causes as the Communist Party. The *Catholic Worker* supported the Scottsboro boys and protested Negro exploitation in the South; it printed exposés of conditions for women and children in factories; it gave support to strikes of all kinds, especially among farmers and steel and textile workers. Dorothy Day covered the emerging CIO with journalist Mary Heaton Vorse and climbed through a window in Flint to show her solidarity with the sit-down strikers at General Motors in 1937. When accused of being "communists in disguise," Dorothy Day would reply that "recognition of injustice by Communists should not automatically blind Catholics to injustice."[41]

The philosophy that Day and Maurin developed to explain their vision also bore strong similarities to the Communist view of the future. Adapting the old IWW slogan, Day hoped "to build a new society within the shell of the old." Day supported workers' ownership of the means of production, and hoped to abolish the assembly line and decentralize factories. She foresaw ownership of property by all classes, not just the privileged. At the same time, she was a strong pacifist, bucking the general Catholic trend toward supporting Franco: the *Catholic Worker* remained neutral in the Spanish Civil War.

In the end, however, even Day's break with the Catholic Church over Spain could not overcome the Communist Party's strong suspicion of Dorothy Day and the *Catholic Worker*. Organized religion, especially the Catholic Church, was portrayed as the enemy of the working classes; radicals who lacked Day's all-abiding faith in God and Catholicism saw a basic contradiction in being both a radical and a Catholic.[42] Yet Dorothy Day made important contributions to the radical causes of the 1930s, and in many respects her story is consistent with what the Communist Party was trying to accomplish in the decade.

One final question remains about women's activities on the left in the 1930s. How much of their motivation was fueled by feminist consciousness? To perhaps a greater degree than might be expected, these activists were aware of women's concerns and made deliberate efforts to reach out to other women. They did this through the Women's Commission of the Communist Party, through magazines and articles of special interest to women, and through fiction and poetry especially sensitive to women's concerns (Meridel LeSueur's work, for example). Yet unlike their

1960s counterparts, women on the left in the 1930s never felt their discrimination acutely enough to make women's concerns a major priority. Perhaps their participation in the radical movements of the 1930s allowed them more scope than did the New Left in the 1960s. More likely, they were unwilling or unable to generalize from their own experiences to a full-scale critique of women's roles in society. For them, the major commitment was to revolutionary socialism, which subsumed their hopes for a feminist future. This is a positive, if limited, contribution.

Surveying the history of women on the left in the context of the 1930s, it is not difficult to understand why so many women (and men) were drawn to groups like the Communist Party. The watchwords of the decade were *social significance*: solutions would be economic, not personal. The individual mattered less when the whole system was out of kilter. During the 1930s, groups on the left often offered the most cogent answers to America's pressing needs; such messages rang especially true to younger generations coming of age in the Depression. Perhaps the younger generation of women, those whom the old feminists of the 1930s feared they had lost, chose a commitment to a radical cause like the Communist Party instead of traditional feminism, which was seen, rightly or wrongly, as selfish, personal, and totally divorced from economic issues. Given the times, such a choice was not unjustified.

Notes and References

1. For background on the revival of feminism in the 1960s, and the links to the New Left, see Jo Freeman, *The Politics of Women's Liberation* (New York: David McKay, 1975), and Sara Evans, *Personal Politics: The Roots of Women's Liberation in the Civil Rights Movement and the New Left* (New York: Knopf, 1979).

2. The comparison between the Old and New Left was suggested by Jayne Loader, "Women on the Left, 1906–1941: Bibliography of Primary Sources," *University of Michigan Papers in Women's Studies* 2 (February 1974):9–82; Ellen Kay Trimberger, "Women in the Old and New Left: The Evolution of a Politics of Personal Life," *Feminist Studies* 5 (Fall 1979):432–50. Robert Shaffer, "Women and the Communist Party, USA 1930–1940," *Socialist Review* 45 (May–June 1979):73–118, suggests in a note on pages 111–12 that women's treatment in the present-day Communist Party is much less favorable than in the 1930s.

3. Daniel Aaron, *Writers on the Left* (New York, 1961), p. 160; Vivian Gornick, *The Romance of American Communism* (New York, 1977), pp. 95–96.

4. Mary McCarthy, "My Confession: One Writer's Encounter with Communism," *Reporter* 9 (December 22, 1953):31, 33; Mary McCarthy, *The Company She Keeps* (New York, 1942), pp. 112, 138.

5. Shaffer, "Women and the Communist Party," pp. 75–76.

6. Shaffer, "Women and the Communist Party," p. 90; Peggy Dennis, *The Autobiography of an American Communist: A Personal View of a Political Life, 1925–1975* (Westport, Conn., 1977), p. 159.

7. Shaffer, "Women and the Communist Party," pp. 90–92; *NAW: The Modern Period*, pp. 242–46. In 1940, Elizabeth Gurley Flynn was expelled from the American Civil Liberties Union because she belonged to the Communist Party. See Corliss Lamont, ed., *The Trial of Elizabeth Gurley Flynn by the American Civil Liberties Union* (New York:Horizon Press, 1968).

8. Al Richmond, *Native Daughter: The Story of Anita Whitney* (San Francisco, 1942), p. 171.

9. Ella Reeve Bloor, *We Are Many* (New York, 1940). Elizabeth Gurley Flynn wrote a warm introduction to the book, testimony to the impact Bloor had on other women in the Communist Party in the 1930s.

10. Richmond, *Native Daughter*, p. 194; Bloor, *We Are Many*, p. 308; Margaret Cowl, "Women's Struggles for Equality," *Political Affairs* 53 (May 1974):44. Cowl was preparing the article when she died. Born in 1897 of Lithuanian descent, she first became a member of the Women's Commission of the Communist Party in 1922 and was its secretary for many years. Cowl was the widow of Charles Krumbein, a CP activist in Chicago and New York. See her obituary in *Political Affairs*, April 1974, p. 1.

11. Gornick, *Romance of American Communism*, p. 207; Daily Worker letter quoted in Shaffer, "Women and the Communist Party," p. 94.

12. Gornick, *Romance of American Communism*, pp. 217, 133.

13. Peggy Dennis, "A Response to Ellen Kay Timberger's Essay, 'Women in the Old and New Left,'" *Feminist Studies* 5 (Fall 1979):453.

14. Dennis, *Autobiography of an American Communist*, pp. 35, 37, 56, 89, 130–31.

15. Dennis, "Response to Trimberger," p. 456. For another example of the trauma of an illegal abortion in Communist circles, see Vera Buch Weisbrod, *A Radical Life* (Bloomington, 1977), p. 167. Weisbrod's botched abortion adversely affected her health for the rest of her life.

16. Shaffer, "Women and the Communist Party," p. 79.

17. Mary Inman, *In Woman's Defense* (Los Angeles, 1940), pp. 8, 170.

18. Ibid., pp. 102–103.

19. Ibid., pp. 170–71, 142.

20. Ibid., pp. 34, 152.

21. For discussions of Inman's ideas and impact, see Loader, "Women on the Left," and Shaffer, "Women and the Communist Party," pp. 83–86.

22. Shaffer, "Women and the Communist Party," pp. 78, 74, 110. The Shaffer article has provided much of the information for this chapter, and my analysis was strongly shaped by his arguments.

23. Ibid., pp. 93–96.

24. Cowl, "Women's Struggles for Equality," p. 41.

25. Shaffer, "Women and the Communist Party," pp. 96–97.

26. Ibid., p. 98.

27. Cowl, "Women's Struggles for Equality," pp. 42–43. For material on CP organizing of unemployed councils, see Frances Fox Piven and Richard A. Cloward, *Poor People's Movements: Why They Succeed, How They Fail* (New York: Pantheon, 1977), pp. 41–95.

28. Lynd and Lynd, *Rank and File*, p. 24. For a colorful account of how one Chicago community foiled these eviction attempts time after time, see Mrs. Willye Jeffries in Terkel, *Hard Times*, pp. 397–402.

29. Lynd and Lynd, *Rank and File*, pp. 30, 32.

30. Gornick, *Romance of American Communism*, p. 146; Bloor, *We Are Many*, p. 243; Shaffer, "Women and the Communist Party," p. 99.

31. Gornick, *Romance of American Communism*, p. 101.

32. Lynd and Lynd, *Rank and File*, pp. 67–88; the quotation is from page 76.

33. Bloor, *We Are Many*, p. 250; McCarthy, "My Confession," p. 31; Dorothy McConnell, *Women, War, and Fascism* (New York, 1936).

34. Aaron, *Writers on the Left*, p. xvii.

35. For background on writers and the Communist Party in the 1930s, see Aaron, *Writers on the Left*. The list of writers who signed the 1935 call for a "Congress of American Revolutionary Writers" is found in Joseph North, ed., *New Masses: An Anthology of the Rebel Thirties* (New York: International Publishers, 1969), pp. 347–49; see also Chapter 6.

36. Cowl, "Women's Struggles for Equality," pp. 43–44; Shaffer, "Women and the Communist Party," p. 102; Loader, "Women on the Left," p. 52.

37. Cowl, "Women's Struggles for Equality," p. 41.

38. Ibid., pp. 41–42; Loader, "Women on the Left," pp. 52, 54–55, 60; Inman, *In Woman's Defense*, pp. 117–20.

39. Cowl, "Women's Struggles for Equality," pp. 43–44; Shaffer, "Women and the Communist Party," pp. 110–11.

40. Dorothy Day, *The Long Loneliness: The Autobiography of Dorothy Day* (New York, 1952), p. 141; see also William D. Miller, *A Harsh and Dreadful Love: Dorothy Day and the Catholic Worker Movement* (New York, 1973).

41. Day, *Long Loneliness*, p. 188; Miller, *Harsh and Dreadful Love*, p. 94.

42. Day, *Long Loneliness*, p. 196.

IF WE WOULD GUIDE BY THE
LIGHT OF REASON WE MUST
LET OUR MINDS BE BOLD

Federal Art Project mural, George Biddle,
installed in the Justice Department Building, Washington, D.C.
Courtesy of Franklin D. Roosevelt Library

Chapter Six
Literature and Fine Arts

The 1930s were a time of renewed creativity and vitality for artists in America, and women were in the mainstream of these cultural endeavors. The revival was fueled in part by the unique experiment in government patronage of the arts undertaken by the New Deal in the 1930s. Realizing that writers and artists were as hungry for work as construction workers and factory operatives, relief administrators established programs to provide work for unemployed writers, artists, actors, and musicians. While their immediate purpose was to give artists enough money to subsist on during the Depression rather than to embark on a permanent program of government support for the arts, these innovative government programs added an exciting note to the arts in the 1930s. Never before or since has the federal government played such a role; only the drastic dislocations of the Depression broke down old patterns of private patronage and allowed this cooperative experiment to take place.

The underlying conception behind the New Deal programs was a quest for cultural democracy: "to integrate the artist into the mainstream of American life and make the arts both expressive of the spirit of a nation and accessible to its people." Artists and administrators alike were committed to breaking down old notions that art was supported and consumed only by the elite. "Art for the millions," a popular New Deal phrase, expressed the philosophy that art was not a luxury, but a basic part of day-to-day existence. By making available to the public plays, classical music, murals, and sculpture, the artist was expected to become a more vital part of American life. This integration would encourage a revitalization of American art, drawing on the sources of uniquely American cultural expression being rediscovered in the 1930s.[1]

Throughout the 1930s, government patronage of the arts was concentrated in the section of the Works Progress Administration known as Federal One. WPA administrator Ellen Sullivan Woodward, and her successor Florence Kerr, had general responsibility for supervising the program, but the real policy decisions were made by the directors of individual projects: Holger Cahill of the Federal Art Project, Henry Alsberg of the Federal Writers Project, Nicholas Sokoloff of the Federal Music Project, and Hallie Flanagan of the Federal Theater Project. In addition, state and local directors shaped and molded individual units. Their combined output contributed significantly to American artistic expression in the 1930s.

These government programs offered unprecedented roles to women, both as administrators and as creative artists. The New Deal art projects, for example, provided unparalleled opportunities for women painters. In their pathbreaking book, *Women Artists, 1550–1950*, Ann S. Harris and Linda Nochlin describe the New Deal programs as uniquely sensitive to the needs of women artists. Commenting on the "remarkable efflorescense of women artists" in the 1930s, they claim only early twentieth-century Russia rivaled depression America in providing a setting so liberating for women's artistic creativity.[2]

Sponsorship of the arts took several forms. New York state, with its heavy concentration of unemployed artists, had provided work relief for unemployed artists in New York City as early as 1933, a forerunner of later national programs. After 1934, federal programs were initiated, concentrated in two areas of the bureaucracy: the Section of Painting and Fine Arts of the Treasury Department, under the direction of Edward Bruce, and the Federal Art Project (FAP) of the Works Progress Administration, directed by Holger Cahill. Their aims were similar: to put artists to work, to make art a larger part of everyday life in America, and to foster a "permanent revival of the aspirations and achievements of the American people."[3]

Over the course of its eight-year existence, the FAP produced 2,500 murals, 17,000 sculptures, and 18,000 easels for public buildings and institutions across the country. In addition, the FAP staffed and ran 100 community art centers. Its Index of American Design produced 22,000 watercolor renderings of objects, textiles, costumes, and furniture from the American past. A crafts section encouraged native American Indian crafts. Unfortunately many of these works of art, especially the large-scale murals in public buildings, have been either destroyed or painted over, victims of neglect or changing popular taste.[4]

Although the Federal Art Project was a national program, its operation was tied to regional quotas. Much of its impact, therefore, was felt in the large cultural centers with the largest number of unemployed artists—the New York City project, for example, accounted for almost half of the entire FAP's payroll in December 1937. At its peak it employed 2,323 artists. Between 75 and 90 percent of the personnel for each art project had to be drawn directly from the relief rolls, with the remainder available for supervisory and administrative positions.[5]

As leaders in the federal art programs, women made important contributions to arts administration in the 1930s. The muralist Ruth Reeves was the original national coordinator of the Index of American Design. Audrey McMahon of New York City, one of the earliest backers of relief for artists, was approached to head the Federal Art Project when it was set up in late 1935, but decided against going to Washington; instead she became head of the New York City project, the "flagship" of the Federal Art Project. Juliana Force of the Whitney Museum was associated with the New York City project throughout its existence; like McMahon, her influence extended far beyond New York. Other women who worked as administrators on the New York project included Olive Gavert, Berenice Abbott, Gwendolyn Bennett, and Constance Rourke.[6]

While the New Deal programs created unprecedented opportunities for women artists, they cannot be credited for all the gains. Rather, the artistic projects confirmed and cemented the progress women artists had been making over the past century. Women were no longer denied access to training, although they still had to fight for the objective assessment of their work in the eyes of judges and the public. On the eve of the Depression, according to K. A. Marling, "Women constituted an established artistic minority to be reckoned with." In the 1930 census, women made up 40 percent of the art professionals, almost twice the percentage of women's general participation in the work force at that time. Consistent with that figure, 41% of artists on relief were women, twice their general representation on relief in the 1930s.[7]

An important aspect of the federal art projects was the chance they gave women artists to have their work judged on an equal plane with the work of male artists. The Treasury Department, for example, held regional competitions for art projects in which the participants were asked to submit their plans anonymously. This proved a great boon to women artists, whose projects could now be treated on their artistic and creative merit rather than according to stereotypes in male judge's minds as to what works should be produced by women artists.[8]

The New Deal programs also fostered a spirit which seemed to transcend sexual divisions and barriers. Women artists remembered that in the excitement of creating socially relevant art during the Depression, men and women marched "shoulder to shoulder through hard times." This "fiercely egalitarian spirit" had radical implications for women artists: women considered themselves the equals of men, and felt no discrimination based on their sex. Perhaps this represented the arts project's greatest contribution to feminism and the arts in the 1930s.[9]

The list of artists, male and female, participating in the Federal Art Project in the 1930s reads like a *Who's Who* of American Art. In retrospect, some of the best-spent money supported struggling female artists such as Louise Nevelson, Alice Neel, and Lee Krassner, who were just starting their careers. Krassner, later married to painter Jackson Pollack, was thankful that the FAP allowed her to continue painting; beyond that, Krassner remembered, "There was the camaraderie instead of isolation, and that led eventually to other feelings. But basically, it was a living for us all." Louise Nevelson, perhaps the greatest twentieth-century American woman sculptor, worked in poverty and isolation in the 1930s, and much of her early work was lost; only a brief spell on the WPA helped her get by. Alice Neel, noted portrait painter, supported herself throughout the 1930s on the WPA, as did Rice Periera.[10]

These women, fledgling artists in the 1930s, later participated in the modernist movement that dominated the American art scene in the 1940s and after. In general, abstract art, which was picking up supporters in the 1930s, found little encouragement in the federal arts projects, which were still concentrating on documenting American subjects in a socially realistic style. Very few abstract works won approval for inclusion on the federal projects.[11]

While abstract art was downplayed, other styles won recognition in the 1930s. The mural was the showcase for much of this creative expression. It was uniquely suited to the times, portraying socially relevant themes and documenting the ordinary American at work and play. The American fascination with the mural had been fueled by Diego Rivera's murals glorifying the Mexican revolution commissioned by the Mexican government in the 1920s. In 1932 Rivera's success in Mexico City brought him a commission to do a mural for the Rockefeller Center, then under construction. He worked on the mural for two years, aided by a team of artists including Lucienne Bloch and Marion Greenwood, but the finished product was too inflammatory for the Rockefellers. The dispute centered on one fresco which contained a portrait of Lenin. Lucienne Bloch concealed a tiny Leica camera in her clothing, and in defiance of the guards took a picture of the offending panel. The Rivera mural was covered over in 1934, and later destroyed.[12]

Murals became staples on the arts projects because they were so readily accessible to the public. Rosalind Bengelsdorf worked on the Mural Division of the FAP from 1936 to 1939 and taught in a FAP art center. Agnes Tait, primarily an easel painter, was introduced to mural painting as part of a cooperative effort at New York's Bellevue Hospital in 1937. Lee Krassner remembered that working on murals under social realist artist Max Spivack had a positive impact on her style, introducing her to scale.[13]

Lucienne Bloch, daughter of the composer Ernst Bloch, spent four years on the FAP mural project. Her most ambitious work was a projected *Cycle of a Woman's Life* for the New York House of Detention for Women, which she aimed to make a creative and inspirational model for the women inmates. Bloch consulted both the inmates and the staff of the institution: at the prisoners' request, she included in the mural a flower-vendor familiar in the area as well as the prison's stray cat, Coconita. Although Bloch had hoped to trace the entire female life cycle, she completed only the "Childhood" panel.[14]

The Federal Art Project employed many other prominent women artists over the course of its existence. Agnes Tait was an easel painter for the Public Works of Art Project in New York from 1933 to 1934; her *Skating in Central Park* (1934) was chosen by Frances Perkins to hang in the Department of Labor building in Washington. Marion Greenwood worked on murals and other projects for the Treasury Art Project from 1936 to 1939, and Doris Lee undertook commissioned work for the Post Office. Printmaker Elizabeth Olds worked in the FAP Graphics section from 1935 to 1940, and in 1938 she was one of the founders of its Silk Screen section. (The silk screen technique was well suited to the democratization of art so desired by many intellectuals and left-wing artists in the 1930s.) Concetta Scaravaglione produced sculpture on a massive scale for the Treasury Section; one of her most widely known works was *Woman with Mountain Sheep*, done for the Garden Court of the Federal Building at the 1939 New York World's Fair. Other women who worked on federal art projects at various points in the 1930s included Helen Lundeberg, Isabel Bishop, Minna Citron, and Elizabeth Logan. In addition, while she was never officially associated with the WPA arts projects, Florence Stettheimer's work represented many of the same themes seen in the WPA murals and paintings, especially her *Cathedrals of Wall Street* (1939), which featured small cameos of Eleanor Roosevelt and Fiorello LaGuardia.[15]

In the end, one of the most significant aspects of the Federal Art Project was that artists were able to continue their creative work, rather than having to look for jobs in nonartistic areas. Helen Lundeberg, who painted italianate murals on Los Angeles buildings, acknowledged her debt to the projects: "It gave me enough to live on, and also made just being an artist okay." The Great Depression forced the government to assume responsibility for arts patronage for almost an entire decade, giving a critical boost to the aspirations of many women artists. According to K. A. Marling, "the art projects sanctioned and consolidated the gains of a century of women's struggles for access to training, and for professional recognition, by coming to the rescue of artists to whose skills and cultural contributions sexual labels were no longer germane." Women's collective contribution to the decade's artistic endeavors "confirms their centrality to an understanding of what American art of the '30s was really all about."[16]

The Federal Writers Project (FWP) paralleled the Federal Art Project in its innovative approach to employment of writers generally and its treatment of women specifically. The Federal Writers Project employed between 4,500 and 5,000 creative writers, researchers, and administrators at its height. Like the FAP, the project was concentrated in places where writers were likely to be found: California, Massachusetts, and especially the New York City area. In all, the FWP produced more than a thousand publications, the most famous being the WPA state guides, which combined tourism, folklore, and history. Other projects included regional guides such as *U.S. One, Maine to Florida*; ethnic and folklore studies; and collections of slave narratives in the South.[17]

The Federal Writers Project provided valuable opportunities both for women administrators and writers. Katherine Kellock developed the concept behind the WPA state guidebooks and oversaw their editing and publication. Carita Corse was state director of the FWP in Florida, and Eudora Richardson in Virginia. Miriam Allen DeFord worked with the California unit doing research into San Francisco's past. Prominent black women who were associated with the FWP included Margaret Walker, who later wrote the novel *Jubilee*, and Katherine Dunham, who researched black Chicago cults (including the forerunner of the Black Muslims) under sociologist Horace Clayton. Zora Neale Hurston was an editor for the Federal Writers Project in Florida in the late 1930s. While on the project she produced three books in rapid succession.[18]

Often, writers' association with the FWP was for only a short period of time, until they could again support themselves without relief. Meridel LeSueur worked briefly on the Minnesota unit, which gave her time to finish a novel while raising two small children. Tillie Olsen spent a short time on the California project, where she recorded the life stories, songs, and dreams of Slavs, Filipinos, and Mexicans in California. During this time, Olsen also worked on the novel *Yonnondio: From the Thirties*, which she published in 1974. (She discovered the unfinished manuscript after it had been lost for more than thirty years.) Tillie Olsen realized how much a book of the 1930s it remained: "Unfinished, it yet bespeaks the consciousness and roots of that decade, if not its events."[19]

Unlike the Federal Art Project, which touched many prominent artists during the 1930s, the Federal Writers Project drew few famous writers. In 1938, FWP director Henry Alsberg admitted that only 82 of the 4,500 employees of the project were nationally recognized as writers; the rest were journalists, editors, free-lance publicists, and the like. A few, like John Cheever and Richard Wright, launched their literary careers on the Writers Project. Wright's "Uncle Tom's Children" won the *Story* magazine prize as the best story by a FWP writer in 1938.[20]

Occasionally writers needed help toward the end of their careers, not at the beginning. Novelist Anzia Yezierska's powerful descriptions of immigrant life, particularly *Hungry Hearts* (1920) and *Bread Givers* (1925), had brought her fame, fortune, and a Hollywood movie contract in the 1920s, but she found herself penniless once the Depression hit. The Federal Writers Project was her salvation. She described the experience in her autobiography, *Red Ribbon on a White Horse*: "A new world was being born. A world where artists were no longer outcasts, hangers-on of the rich, but backed by the government, encouraged to produce their best work. The President said so." Yezierska was eager to join.[21]

But first Yezierska had to qualify for relief, since the Writers Project drew between 75 and 90 percent of its members from the relief rolls. Yezierska's friends prepared her for the questions she would face at the relief office: "Just remember the rules. Two years' residence in the city. No relatives. No friends, no insurance. No money. No nothing—you've got to be starving to death." After several weeks of red tape, Yezierska finally obtained relief certification, whereupon she joined the Writers Project in New York City. "The savior of art!" she laughed. "At the bargain price of $23.86 per artist."[22]

Yezierska's experiences on the Writers Project show both its potential and its problems. At first she was assigned to the creative unit, where she was encouraged to work on an autobiographical piece about the WPA. After her poverty and isolation in the 1920s and 1930s, the WPA offered a supportive atmosphere for creativity: "Each morning I walked to the Project as light-hearted as if I were going to a party. The huge barracks-like Writers' Hall roared with the laughter and greetings of hundreds of voices. . . . There was a hectic camaraderie among us, although we were as ill-assorted as a crowd in a subway express." When the writers received their first paychecks, "we were as hilarious as slum children around a Christmas tree."[23]

For a while, the project fulfilled Yezierska's dreams: she was able to do some work at home, choose her own subjects, and benefit from the feedback of fellow writers like Richard Wright, then on the New York project. But the Writers Project, indeed all the arts projects, increasingly came under congressional attack. It was suggested that they were havens for subversives and allowed writers to loaf on government time. After a public scandal in New York, bureaucratic controls replaced the earlier freedom. The creative project was abolished, and Anzia Yezierska was assigned to do research for the New York City Guide. Although she protested she was not a journalist, Yezierska was now obliged to turn in at least 2,000 words a day on such subjects as the trees in Central Park and the animals in the Bronx Zoo. If she failed to meet her daily quota, it was doubled the next day. The previous warm, supportive atmosphere evaporated under such bureaucratic constraints: "Every day it became harder to blind ourselves to the cold fact that we, like the privy-builders and road-makers of other public projects, were being paid not for what we did, but to put money into circulation." Though disillusioned when she finally severed herself from the Writers Project in the late 1930s, Yezierska remained grateful for her association with this unique government experiment in patronage of the arts.[24]

Art and literature were not alone in securing federal support in the 1930s: music also received government assistance. Yet, in contrast to the other federal arts projects, the Federal Music Project displayed little interest in encouraging women musicians or composers in the 1930s. Of the approximately 15,000 musicians employed on the Federal Music Project under national director Nicholas Sokoloff in 1937, only 2,253 were women. Among the federally supported orchestras that toured the country, women made up only a small proportion of the musicians, although an all-women's orchestra called the Commonwealth Symphony, partially supported by the WPA, performed in Boston in the 1930s under the direction of Solomon Branslavsky. The Federal Music Project encouraged the work of American composers and on occasion performed compositions by women. On the whole, however, the Federal Music Project had nowhere near the impact on women's musical aspirations and creative development as the writers and art projects did on their respective members.[25]

Women found greater opportunities in the Federal Theater Project. The 1930s witnessed the only federally funded national theater in American history. Like other areas of artistic expression in the 1930s, the theater had been hurt by the Depression: the lights of Broadway literally went dark for weeks at a time during the winter of 1932–33. Widespread unemployment in the theater industry was a major reason behind the establishment of the Federal Theater Project in late 1935. Hallie Flanagan, head of Vassar's Experimental Theater and an old Grinnell classmate of WPA director Harry Hopkins, was the happy choice to run this innovative program.

Hallie Flanagan's whole professional life had been devoted to the theater. A 1911 graduate of Grinnell College in Iowa, she studied drama, voice, and playwriting while teaching high school there. A play called *The Curtain* won her a $100 prize and gained her entry into George Pierce Baker's famed 47 Workshop for playwrights at Harvard in 1923. After receiving the master's degree at Harvard, Flanagan joined the Vassar faculty in 1925. The next year she won a coveted Guggenheim Foundation traveling fellowship. She used it to study drama in Europe, where she was greatly impressed by the tradition of government sponsorship of the arts.

When she returned to this country, Flanagan became head of the Vassar Experimental Theater, eager to try out some of the innovative ideas for directing and staging plays she had learned in Europe. *Can You Hear Their Voices?* (1931), adapted from a play by Whittaker Chambers, presaged the documentary techniques later employed successfully by the Federal Theater. Flanagan was a natural choice for the 1935 position to head the Federal Theater Project. Although many saw the program as a stopgap measure to ease the theater industry through hard times, Flanagan envisioned more—a great national theater bringing arts to the people on an unprecedented scale. Flanagan hoped the Theater Project would be part "of a tremendous re-thinking, re-building, and re-dreaming of America."[26]

During the four years of its existence, the Federal Theater Project played to more than 25 million people across the country. For many Americans, it was their first contact with live theater. Some of its most successful plays were T. S. Eliot's *Murder in the Cathedral*, Sinclair Lewis's *It Can't Happen Here* (staged simultaneously in eighteen cities), *Macbeth* with an all-black cast, and the *Swing Mikado*, a jazz rendition of the Gilbert and Sullivan opera. Equally popular were the "Living Newspapers," which staged major issues of the day such as farm problems ("Triple A Plowed Under") or the Tennessee Valley Authority ("Power"). Under Flanagan's direction, the Federal Theater became a "daring, innovative national network of regional theaters dedicated to education, social comment, and entertainment."[27]

But such innovative ideas came under attack in the late 1930s. Congress grew tired of the proliferation of New Deal agencies, and, as the sense of emergency from the early depression passed, conservatives began looking for convenient scapegoats. The Federal Theater, which was suspected of radicalism, communism, and New Deal propaganda, was almost too easy a target. Ellen Woodward supported the arts projects before the House Un-American Activities Committee in 1938, and Hallie Flanagan made a spirited defense of the Theater Project before the committee. During Flanagan's testimony Congressman Joseph Starnes challenged her concerning Orson Welles's production of *Doctor Faustus*. "You are quoting from this Marlowe. Is he a Communist?" Flanagan replied, "Put in the record that he was the greatest dramatist in the period immediately preceding Shakespeare." Up against such ignorant opposition, Flanagan's fight was futile, and the Federal Theater Project was terminated abruptly on June 30, 1939. The other federal arts projects limped on under state sponsorship until 1943, when wartime priorities signaled their demise.[28]

Hallie Flanagan's innovative direction of the Federal Theater Project in the 1930s is symptomatic of the creativity unleashed by government patronage of the arts. In the end, however, all the arts projects failed to establish themselves on a permanent basis: they remained too tied to their original purpose—feeding needy artists and writers—and never built a national constituency willing to institutionalize federal support for the arts. Any hope that this might have happened was dashed by the country's intervention in World War II, which directed all government resources toward the war effort. Finally, with postwar prosperity, government sponsorship of the arts was a dead issue.[29]

The crisis of the Depression was no doubt the major reason for the establishment of government patronage of the arts in the 1930s. The impact of hard times on the arts went much further than the programs of Federal One, however, affecting both the subjects that artists chose and the forms they selected to express their ideas. Malcolm Cowley observed in 1939 that there never was a period "when literary events followed so closely on the flying coat-tails of social events." Daniel Aaron noted that the Depression "influenced, directly or indirectly, almost every American writer of any importance." Many artists sought to understand the forces that had produced the Depression and to document the country's response to the cataclysm. Out of this came the decade's strong impulse to make art socially relevant, a concern felt by artists in many fields. The Depression also encouraged an intensely nationalistic and patriotic search for American roots, as many intellectuals turned away from European concerns to subjects of their own country. In general, the Depression encouraged artists to view their society, and their own place in it, from a new perspective.[30]

The documentary, perhaps the decade's most distinctive genre, was the form many artists chose to convey their new concerns in the 1930s. Literature, art, film, music, dance, theater, radio, and nonfiction writing were all affected by the documentary impulse. This point of view is best represented by James Agee and Walker Evans's *Let Us Now Praise Famous Men*, the photography of Dorothea Lange, and movies such as Pare Lorentz's *The River* (1936). The artistic desire to examine in minute detail, either on film, canvas, or paper, the collective psyche of a nation was well suited to a country in the throes of self-examination brought on by the Depression. This orientation reflected the general attempt of artists to combine social consciousness with distinctively American subjects which characterized artistic expression in the 1930s.[31]

The camera was a favorite tool for documenting America in the 1930s. Perhaps the most widely known woman photographer of the 1930s was Margaret Bourke-White, whose picture of Fort Peck Dam in Montana graced *Life*'s first cover on November 23, 1936. Bourke-White's interest in photography had begun in college, and in 1929 she became a photographer for the new *Fortune* magazine. Although at first more interested in industrial and mechanical subjects, by the mid-1930s Bourke-White had begun to concentrate on human subjects; a 1934 *Fortune* piece on victims of the drought in the Midwest shows her developing interest. In 1936, she began collaborating with novelist Erskine Caldwell on *You Have Seen Their Faces*, a study of southern sharecropping. Published in 1937, with Caldwell's text illustrated by Bourke-White's photographs, the book provided a moving description of the physical and emotional devastation of the sharecropper's life, caught up in the never-ending cycle of poverty. The photographs and text of *You Have Seen Their Faces* stirred readers' emotion in a way similar to documentary movies such as Lorentz's *The River*.[32]

Throughout the 1930s, Margaret Bourke-White was employed by *Life* and *Fortune* or did free-lance work on her own. Other photographers joined the government in a far-reaching experiment in social documentation mounted by the Historical Section of the Resettlement Administration under Roy Stryker. The Resettlement Administration, and later the Farm Security Administration, sent talented photographers roaming the country to document the American scene; unlike the Federal Art Project, these photographers were not drawn from the relief rolls. Today Walker Evans is the best known of this group, but the Resettlement Administration also employed Dorothea Lange, Arthur Rothstein, Marion Post, and Russell Lee, who stayed with the project far longer than Evans. Their photographs remain the best visual introduction to American life in the 1930s.[33]

Dorothea Lange began her career as a portrait photographer in San Francisco, but as the Depression deepened, she began to photograph breadlines, the unemployed, and radical-led demonstrations. She was drawn to the subjects because "the discrepancy between what I was working on in the printing frames and what was going on in the street was more than I could assimilate." A 1934 exhibition of these photographs brought Lange into contact with University of California social economist Paul S. Taylor, who became her collaborator and husband. Their first project, documentation of the conditions of migrant laborers in California, brought Lange's work to the attention of Roy Stryker at the Resettlement Administration, and he put her on the staff in 1935. She remained associated with the government agency until 1939.[34]

Unlike FSA photographers Arthur Rothstein and Russell Lee, who were based in Washington, Dorothea Lange did most of her work from California. She called herself a photographer-investigator, and with her Rolleiflex camera and a 4 × 5 Graflex on a tripod, she documented the impact of the Depression on ordinary Americans. Lange needed only ten minutes in a pea-pickers camp to capture the despair and resignation of a young woman in a picture she titled "Migrant Mother." This 1936 photograph (see frontispiece) came to symbolize in many minds the concerns of the FSA in the 1930s. Throughout her years on the federal project, Lange devoted much of her time to documenting the migrant labor situation in the West.

From 1936 to 1938, Dorothea Lange and Paul Taylor spent their summers collaborating on a project illustrating the effects of drought and mechanization on farmers in the Dust Bowl and the South. *An American Exodus: A Record of Human Erosion* (1939) was similar to Bourke-White and Caldwell's *You Have Seen Their Faces*. (Another similarity was that in both cases, the writer-photographer team was also husband and wife.) Unfortunately, the impact of the Lange-Taylor book was lessened by America's increasing preoccupation with the widening war in Europe. During the 1940s, Lange again returned to work for the federal government, this time documenting the relocation of Japanese-Americans on the West Coast in 1942 and 1943.[35]

The photographs by Dorothea Lange and the Resettlement Administration were just one aspect of the federal government's attempt to document the American landscape in the 1930s. Various government agencies sent investigators into the field to do with words what Lange and Arthur Rothstein were doing with their cameras. Journalist Lorena Hickok was hired by Harry Hopkins of the Federal Emergency Relief Administration to travel around the country and report on the impact of New Deal programs on people's lives and hopes. Martha Gellhorn, sent on a similar mission, used the material she gathered to write a novel, *The Trouble I've Seen* (1936). Gellhorn poignantly described the despair and humiliation of people forced on relief, the excitement and futility of workers' strikes, and men's and women's painful resignation as their dreams of a better life crumbled and disappeared. Later in the 1930s, Gellhorn made journalism, especially the coverage of the Spanish Civil War, her primary commitment, and was married for a time to Ernest Hemingway.[36]

Gellhorn's blending of fiction, reportage, and documentary reflects the orientation of many writers in the 1930s. Writers wanted to participate in the great movements of the day, and to use their writing as a vehicle for social significance and social change. Whether the end result was a novel, a magazine article, a short story, or a documentary film was immaterial.

Agnes Smedley, author of the autobiographical novel *Daughter of Earth* (1929), was one such writer. By the 1930s, Smedley had become fascinated with the emerging Chinese revolution. Although she never joined the Communist Party, she was in sympathy with its aims and goals in China. After losing her journalism position because of her political leanings, Smedley wrote *Chinese Destinies* (1933), portraits of the Chinese way of life. Smedley's next book, *China's Red Army Marches* (1934), traced the rise to power of the Communist forces under Mao Tse-Tung, and in 1937 she was one of the first Westerners to be granted access to the Communist government. In 1940, ill health forced Smedley to cut back her reportage. Her retrospective *Battle Hymn of China* (1943) was well received in the United States, because this country and China were allied during the Second World War. With the onset of the Cold War in the late 1940s, however, Smedley's work was blacklisted due to her Communist associations. Coming full circle, by the 1970s Smedley's radicalism and feminism finally found an enthusiastic audience.[37]

Josephine Herbst, like Smedley, was a radical journalist, and she covered both domestic and international events. She grew up in Iowa, worked her way through the University of California, and then spent three years in Paris. Paralleling the literary trends of her generation, she replaced the Bohemian expatriate life of the 1920s with political activism in the 1930s. As a journalist, Herbst covered farmers' strikes in the Midwest, the Soviet experiment, and the Cuban uprising. Herbst's coverage of the Spanish Civil War marked a lessening of her radical commitments, as she grew disillusioned with political activism. Besides her journalistic work during the decade, Herbst also established a name for herself as a novelist. Her trilogy (*Pity Is Not Enough*, 1933; *The Executioner Waits*, 1934; *Rope of Gold*, 1939) traced one family's fortunes from Reconstruction through the 1930s. The trilogy was based on stories of Herbst's own family. The second volume took place amidst World War I and growing labor militancy; the third covered an attempt to organize farmers in Pennsylvania during the Depression and ended with the CIO strikes in the auto industry in 1937. Herbst's books blended reportage and fiction in a way characteristic of the decade, and showed the concerns that the Depression forced on the consciousness of writers. [38]

Mary Heaton Vorse, journalist and writer, actively participated in both fields in the 1930s. From a comfortable middle-class background, Vorse had been radicalized by the 1912 textile strike in Lowell, Massachusetts, and she devoted the rest of her life to political activism. Her articles in the *Nation, Harper's Magazine*, and the *New Republic* brought labor's cause to a wider audience. She also used the novel to convey her sympathies: *Strike!* (1930) is a thinly fictionalized account of the Gastonia textile strike in North Carolina, during which Vorse worked as an organizer for the Amalgamated Clothing Workers of America. During the CIO's Flint organizing campaign, Vorse collaborated with Josephine Herbst on a "Living Newspaper" which dramatized the demands of the sitdown strikers. Later that year, while covering a steel strike in Muncie, Indiana, Vorse was wounded. Soon after, while on a women's picket line in Youngstown, Ohio, she was wounded again, this time grazed by a bullet. Vorse's *Labor's New Millions* (1938), a history of the rise of the CIO, showed that the road to union organization was far from peaceful in the 1930s. [39]

Meridel LeSueur also typifies the committed radical journalist and occasional novelist found so often in the 1930s. As a journalist and a Communist, Meridel LeSueur traveled widely during the decade. She described life on midwestern farms, radical farmers' strikes, union organizing attempts, people on picket lines and on relief, women working in strike kitchens and waiting in unemployment offices. Whether short story or nonfiction, these pieces blended her politics, feminism, and artistic talent into one. During the 1930s LeSueur was on the staff of the *New Masses*, where many of her articles appeared; she also wrote for the *Daily Worker*, the *American Mercury*, *Partisan Review*, and the *Nation*. In 1935, Le-Sueur gave a speech on Proletarian Literature and the Midwest at the American Writers' Congress. Her 1940 anthology, *Salute to Spring*, includes her short story "I Was Marching," which describes the 1934 Minneapolis general strike and captures the camaraderie of working-class people uniting to improve their lives.[40]

Out of this effort to document the American experience and to use art for socially relevant purposes came the proletarian novel, one of the most distinctive genres of the decade. Relationships between classes, identification with the working class, and details of ordinary life were featured. This welding of political consciousness and artistic spirit had varying degrees of success, and very few of these novels have survived. Some of the best known are Jack Conroy's *The Disinherited* (1933), Robert Cantwell's *The Land of Plenty* (1934), Michael Gold's *Jews Without Money* (1930), and James T. Farrell's *Studs Lonigan* (1932).[41]

In the rediscovery of women's lost fiction, quite a few proletarian novels have surfaced. While it is perhaps too strong to say that women showed a special affinity for this form, women writers of the 1930s were attracted to the proletarian novel. Mary Heaton Vorse's novel *Strike!* fits this mold, as does much of Meridel LeSueur's work. Josephine Herbst's trilogy is usually classified as proletarian, although she herself disliked the term: "When I was writing my trilogy I never thought of it as 'proletarian'—in fact I hated the term, and thought it never comprehensive enough."[42]

Among the works dealing with proletarian themes are novels by Lauren Gilfallen, Catherine Brody, and Clara Weatherwax. Gilfallen's popular *I Went to Pit College* (1934) described a Smith College woman who went to Avella, Pennsylvania, to see how the miners lived. Brody's *Nobody Starves* (1932) told of working-class people facing the Depression—the strikes, the violence, but especially the fear and desperation of people struggling to survive. Clara Weatherwax's *Marching!Marching!*, a description of a lumber strike in the Pacific Northwest, consciously blended fact and fiction: one chapter consisted entirely of newspaper clippings, portraying the strike from the differing perspectives of labor and management. *Marching! Marching!* won the *New Masses*—John Day Company Award for the best novel on an American proletarian

theme in 1935, but literary critics have not been so kind. Daniel
Aaron described *Marching!Marching!* as a "pastiche of 'proletarian' clichés."[43]

Like Weatherwax's book, proletarian novels were often based on
real events. Strikes were popular themes, because they provided
drama, excitement, violence, and the opportunity for characters to
spout class-conscious radical rhetoric. The Gastonia, North Carolina, textile strike of 1929 proved an especially popular topic, inspiring no less than six novels in the 1930s. Mary Heaton Vorse's
Strike! (1930) fictionalized the event, as did Grace Lumpkin's *To
Make My Bread* (1932). Fielding Burke, Olive Tilford Dargon's
pseudonym, wrote *Call Home the Heart* (1932), also based on the
Gastonia strike. Burke's novel chronicled the life of Ishma Waycaster as she went from farm poverty to mill life, organizing for the
National Textile Workers Union and the Communist Party. In
Burke's sequel, *A Stone Came Rolling* (1935), Ishma Waycaster
returned to full-time organizing in the mill towns and coordinated
a regional textile strike. These novels highlight the problems and
frustrations faced by labor activists in the South in the 1930s.[44]

Women poets in the 1930s often looked at the world from a
similar radical perspective. A book of revolutionary verse called
Unrest 1931 featured poems by Sara Bard Field, Rosa Zagnoni
Mariononi, Lola Ridge, Lucia Rent, and Isobel Stone. Other
radical poets from the decade included Muriel Rukeyser, Ruth
Lechlitner, Edna St. Vincent Millay, and Genevieve Taggard.
Taggard's collection *Calling Western Union* (1936) reflected prole-
tarian themes. Strong identification with the masses and a concern
for radical causes shaped poems such as Lola Ridge's "Stone Face,"
about the Tom Mooney case; Edna St. Vincent Millay's "Say That
We Saw Spain Die"; and Muriel Rukeyser's "On Trial," about the
Scottsboro case.[45]

But not all women's novels from the 1930s portrayed the under-
side of American society. Tess Slesinger's *The Unpossessed* (1934)
described the radical-intellectual world of New York in this period
of activism. *The Unpossessed* follows a young Greenwich Village
couple, who are full of revolutionary fervor and sympathy for the
working classes but only manage to dabble in communism and
other causes. They have no more success in dealing with their
personal relationship, and the book centers around the woman's
decision to have an abortion, mainly because her husband is unable

to deal intellectually with the idea of pregnancy and children. The book ends with her abortion, which stands alone as the short story "Missis Flinders." In 1935, Slesinger published a collection of short stories entitled *On Being Told That Her Second Husband Has Taken His First Lover and Other Stories,* all told from a feminist perspective. Sadly, Tess Slesinger died of cancer in her thirties in 1945.[46]

Among black women writing in the 1930s, Zora Neale Hurston stands out. Like so many black writers of the 1920s and early 1930s, Hurston's career was shaped by the literary movement called the Harlem Renaissance. Led by Alain Locke, Claude Mc-Kay, and Langston Hughes, the Harlem Renaissance emphasized racial pride and the search for black roots and culture in a white society. Women were active in this literary movement, too, notably Nella Larsen, author of the 1929 novel *Passing,* Jessie Fauset, author of *Plum Bun* (1928) and *The Chinaberry Tree* (1931), and the poet Georgia Douglas Johnson. For the most part, the artistic spirit which had animated the Harlem Renaissance in the 1920s had burned itself out by the early 1930s. The one exception was Zora Neale Hurston, who in spirit and themes very much partook of the earlier movement. As "the most prolific black woman author of her day, and perhaps the most accomplished figure in Afro-American letters in the 1930s," Hurston brought dignity to her race and her sex.[47]

Zora Neale Hurston was born around 1901 in Florida, where she was a child of much spirit and independence. She studied at Howard University, and then went North, where she came under the influence of the Harlem Renaissance, then in full swing. In 1925, she won a fellowship to study anthropology at Columbia with Franz Boas. Under the sponsorship of a white patron, she traveled through the American South and the West Indies, gathering material for *Mules and Men* (1935) and *Tell My Horse* (1938), which Hurston wrote while on the Florida Writers Project. Her novels strongly reflect her interest in folklore, especially *Jonah's Gourd Vine* (1934) and *Their Eyes Were Watching God* (1937), probably Hurston's best novel. In 1942, Hurston published her autobiography, *Dust Tracks on a Road.*[48]

While federal sponsorship of the arts and a commitment to socially relevant expression characterized much of the literary and artistic output of the 1930s, not all creative work in the decade fits so neatly into those categories. Artists have always responded to their own special muses, which often pay more attention to the inner springs of creativity and vision than to the outside world. For these artists, the cataclysm of the Great Depression and the corresponding search for social significance were of lesser importance to their craft.

Although few artists had an easy time in the Depression, not everyone in the art world was associated with the federal relief projects. One artist who broke into the art world on her own in the late 1930s was not exactly a youngster. Anna Mary Robertson ("Grandma") Moses, whose work was first exhibited in 1939 at an Exhibition of Unknown Artists, had not painted until her late seventies. Her primitive style was in keeping with the American regionalism which dominated much of American painting in the 1930s. Grandma Moses had her first one-artist show in 1940, and has remained popular ever since.[49]

Georgia O'Keeffe, one of the twentieth century's most widely respected artists, had also achieved prominence by the 1930s. O'Keeffe, born in 1887, studied at the Art Institute of Chicago and the Art Student's League in New York. When her drawings were shown to Alfred Stieglitz in 1916, he was so impressed by O'Keeffe's work that he began exhibiting her art at his galleries. From 1923 to 1946, O'Keeffe had one-artist shows every year at his gallery. She also became his wife (in 1924), and the thousands of photographs Stieglitz took of her during their marriage are an enduring legacy of Georgia O'Keeffe's beauty and Alfred Stieglitz's talent. During the 1930s, O'Keeffe became fascinated with the Southwest, and she began painting the bones and skulls she is famous for. Her paintings of flowers also won special praise at the 1946 retrospective of her work at the Museum of Modern Art. After Stieglitz's death in 1946, Georgia O'Keeffe moved permanently to New Mexico, where she still lives.[50]

In the field of literature, women's interests were varied. Pearl Buck's *The Good Earth* led the fiction lists in 1931 and 1932; her Nobel Prize for Literature in 1939 was in large part recognition for this book. With *North to the Orient* (1935) and *Listen, the Wind* (1938), Anne Morrow Lindbergh won a devoted following for her graceful prose, going beyond public curiosity about the wife of aviator Charles Lindbergh. Margaret Mitchell's 1936 *Gone With the*

Wind was one of the most successful novels not only of the 1930s but of all times. Ten years in the making, this book sold 1 million copies in the first six months after publication and catapulted Mitchell to fame and fortune. Mitchell won the Pulitzer Prize for literature in 1937, and when *Gone With the Wind* was made into a motion picture in 1939, starring Clark Gable and Vivien Leigh, the story came alive to millions more. Undoubtedly these more traditional writers found greater favor with the general reading public than the writers of proletarian novels.[51]

The 1930s marked the end of the careers of several major American novelists who had achieved prominence earlier in the century. Edith Wharton died in 1937; her last book, the unfinished *The Buccaneers*, was published posthumously. Willa Cather, who lived until the 1940s, published a book of short stories (*Obscure Destinies*, 1932) and her last novel, *Sapphira and the Slave Girl* (1940). Ellen Glasgow published *Vein of Iron* (1935), one of her final portrayals of strong and independent pioneer women; Glasgow died in 1945. With Edna Ferber and Susan Glaspell, known for their strong heroines and feminist themes, nearing the end of their literary output, the old guard of women writers who had dominated American letters since the early twentieth century was passing from the scene.[52]

Gertrude Stein, an important if enigmatic influence on literary expression from her Paris apartment at 42 Rue de Fleurus, finally achieved public acclaim in her native country in 1932 with *The Autobiography of Alice B. Toklas*. Written in a far more accessible style than Stein's other works, the book became a bestseller. The success of the Alice B. Toklas book led to a triumphant American tour—which Gertrude Stein then described in her next book, *Everybody's Autobiography* (1937). "Alice B. Toklas did hers and now everybody will do theirs," the book opens.[53] Among the women who "did theirs" and reflected on their public careers through autobiography were Emma Goldman (*Living My Life*, 1931), Ellen Glasgow (*The Woman Within*, 1934), Margaret Sanger (*Autobiography*, 1938), and Eleanor Roosevelt (*This Is My Story*, 1937).

During the 1930s and early 1940s, a group of younger women began publishing their work. Katherine Anne Porter's *Pale Horse, Pale Rider* appeared in 1939, followed in the next year by Carson

McCullers's first novel, *The Heart Is a Lonely Hunter*. Mary Mc-
Carthy brought out *The Company She Keeps* in 1942. Djuna Barnes's
experimental *Nightwood* appeared in 1937. And May Sarton began
her career as a poet and novelist. These women would dominate
postwar American fiction.[54]

The theater also held opportunities for young playwrights like
Lillian Hellman, who came of age in the 1930s. Hellman's first
play, *The Children's Hour*, written when she was only twenty-
seven, was a smash hit on Broadway in 1934. The play concerned a
girl's accusations about lesbianism between two teachers in a
boarding school. Watching the rehearsal, theater owner Lee Shu-
bert said to Lillian Hellman, "This play could land us all in jail,"
but *The Children's Hour* ran for 691 performances. Flushed with
success, Hellman quickly went to work on a second play, *Days to
Come*, which was a complete flop. It was two years before Hellman
could write another play, "and when I did get to it I was so scared
that I wrote it nine times." That play was *The Little Foxes* (1939),
a turn-of-the-century tale of the Hubbards, a southern family tor-
mented by greed and material wealth. Hellman's next play, the
anti-Fascist *Watch on the Rhine*, won the New York Critics Circle
Award as the best play of 1941. In the 1960s and 1970s, Lillian
Hellman turned from playwriting to autobiography, and her
books, especially *Pentimento* (1973), give a captivating picture of
theater life in the 1930s.[55]

While the theater industry was not exactly thriving in the 1930s,
privately backed plays were being written and produced, including works by women. Edna Ferber and George S. Kaufman co-
authored the popular *Dinner at Eight* (1932); Rachel Crothers won
acclaim for *When Ladies Meet* (1932) and Zoe Akins for *The Old Maid*
(1934). One very popular play, later made into a successful movie,
was Clare Booth's 1936 *The Women*. Playwriting was but one of
Clare Booth's careers: she was an editor at *Vogue* and *Vanity Fair* in
the 1930s, a war correspondent, a member of Congress from 1943
to 1947, and ambassador to Italy. In addition, she was married to
Henry R. Luce, managing editor of *Time*.[56]

Women were also prominent in music in the 1930s, although in
general women's contributions to classical music reflected long-
term trends rather than a specific response to the Depression.
Paralleling their growing representation in the art world, women

increased their proportion in the world of music from the early twentieth century forward. The battle for access to formal training had been won; harder to crack was the prejudice which kept women musicians and women's compositions from being taken seriously.

During the 1930s, one of the country's most widely known women composers remained Amy (Mrs. H. H. A.) Beach, who was nearing the end of her long and productive career; she died in 1944. Marion Bauer was one of the most prolific composers of the decade, producing symphonic and chamber works as well as pieces for piano and voice. She had studied with Andre Gedalge and Nadia Boulanger in Paris. Gena Branscombe specialized in composing and conducting chorale works, and she founded the Branscombe Chorale in 1934, which performed annual Town Hall concerts throughout the 1930s. In addition to her composition activity, Mary Howe helped found the National Symphony Orchestra in 1930, assisting Elizabeth Sprague Coolidge, one of the greatest patrons of music this country has ever seen, in setting up the music foundation bearing her name at the Library of Congress. Florence Price became the first black woman to have a piece played by a major American orchestra when the Chicago Symphony performed one of Price's symphonies in 1933.[57]

Another important woman composer in the 1930s was Ruth Crawford Seeger, who in 1930 became the first woman to receive a Guggenheim fellowship in composition and is now considered an early leader of avant-garde twentieth-century music. Seeger's favorite medium was the chamber ensemble; her most highly regarded piece is her 1931 "String Quartet." Yet scholars who have rediscovered Ruth Crawford Seeger have been surprised by her relatively small output (thirty-one works) and the fact that she virtually ceased composing after her 1931 marriage to her teacher, Charles Seeger. Increasing domestic responsibilities (four children of their own, plus three from Seeger's former marriage) cut into her time for composition, but just as important was a shift in her own interests toward folk music. Her main contribution in the 1930s was the transcription and arrangement of more than a thousand folk songs in collaboration with her husband. Later in her life, Ruth Crawford Seeger returned to classical composition. Her first piece in twenty years, written in 1952, won critical acclaim, but she died, tragically, of cancer that same year. Ruth Crawford Seeger's was a rich and varied musical life, one which lives on in her daughter Peggy Seeger and her stepson Pete Seeger, both folk-singers.[58]

Women composers, like all women artists, have often faced prejudice in securing public recognition for their works. The same was true of women musicians in the 1930s, who faced blatant discrimination in many facets of their musical careers. While women could study and train on their chosen instruments, they were barred from almost all major orchestras. The first (and only) woman hired for an orchestra was usually a harpist, a position considered suitable for women's sensitivity and talents. Harpist Edna Phillips became the first woman member of the Philadelphia Orchestra in 1930. She was joined in 1936 by cellist Elsa Hilger. The number of women who broke into the major orchestras in the 1930s was minuscule—many institutions like the Boston Symphony Orchestra did not hire any women until after World War II. Orchestra positions were rarely opened to competitions or blind auditions, and under such an "old-boy" system women's talents were ignored. Women were told that their domestic duties precluded regular rehearsal attendance, and that travel was too difficult because facilities were lacking for women musicians on the road. (Such problems had not deterred ballet and theater companies from traveling with women. The difference seems to be that women were essential to those productions, while orchestras could function quite happily with no women at all.) In New York's active classical music scene in the 1930s, only 100 women held steady positions in the performing arts, compared to 17,000 men; the women's average wage of $30 to $35 a week was barely a third of what their male counterparts earned. Faced with such overwhelming odds, many women musicians chose teaching or performing in amateur musical groups.[59]

One alternative in the 1930s for women musicians barred from major orchestras was the women's orchestra. A 1936 report cited 522 women players in eight women's orchestras; *Time* magazine reported twelve women's orchestras in 1939. While such orchestras did quite well in the 1930s, they were by no means the result of any systematic program to put unemployed female musicians to work. In fact, women's orchestras dated to the late nineteenth century. The Los Angeles Women's Symphony, which claimed seventy members in the 1930s, had existed since 1894. In 1926, Ebba Sundstrom founded an all-women's orchestra in Chicago, which had 100 members in the 1930s. Ethel Leginska's National Women's Symphony Orchestra was started in Boston in 1932. Frederique Joanne Petrides founded the Orchestrette Classique in New York, and also published a newsletter, *Women in Music*, from 1935 to 1940.[60]

By far the most famous of the women's orchestras was founded by Antonia Brico in New York in 1935. Antonia Brico was one of the few American women to conduct major (male) orchestras in the 1930s. After studying conducting in Berlin from 1925 to 1930, Brico made her debut with the Berlin Philharmonic in 1930, conducting a program of Dvořak, Handel, and Schumann. In 1933, she returned to the United States, where she had her debut at the Metropolitan Opera House with the Musicians' Symphony Orchestra, the first of three scheduled concerts. The second concert took place as scheduled, but the third was canceled because the baritone soloist refused to work under a woman conductor.

Despite her well-received and well-publicized debut in the United States, Antonia Brico received few subsequent offers to conduct major orchestras. In response, Brico founded her women's orchestra, which opened in Carnegie Hall on February 18, 1935, with a program of Schumann, Handel, and Tchaikovsky. For several years, the orchestra flourished, and Brico believed that she had proven her point that women were as good musicians as men. In 1939, she admitted ten men to her orchestra, renaming the group the Brico Symphony. But without the novelty of the all-female orchestra, public support slowly waned. Like almost all the other women's orchestras, by the 1940s it had disbanded.[61]

Despite her success in New York with the Women's Orchestra and the backing of such influential musicians as Bruno Walter, Jean Sibelius, and Artur Rubinstein, Brico found that no major orchestra would hire a permanent woman conductor. Nor could Brico count on enough guest-conducting offers to make a living. Unlike musicians, who can continue to play their instruments in any setting, a conductor cannot exist without an orchestra. In 1942, Antonia Brico left New York to settle in Denver, where she became a teacher and led an amateur orchestra. She conducted an all-Sibelius program in Helsinki in 1946, but then the conducting offers ended. Only after a 1973 documentary entitled *Antonia: Portrait of a Woman* and the revival of the women's movement did Antonia Brico finally begin to receive the conducting offers that she had been awaiting since the 1930s.[62]

Antonia Brico's career provides a fitting summary of women's cultural roles in the 1930s. The decade contained both triumphs and disappointments. The prejudice that Brico faced is strong testimony to the barriers faced by women in the arts; her triumphs, both in the 1930s and in the present, give hope that such barriers can be overcome.

Notes and References

1. Jane DeHart Mathews, "Arts and the People: The New Deal Quest for a Cultural Democracy," *Journal of American History* 62 (September 1975):316; Francis V. O'Connor, ed., *New Deal Art Projects: An Anthology of Memoirs* (Washington, D.C.: Smithsonian Institution, 1973). For a general, somewhat encyclopedic introduction to the arts programs, see William F. McDonald, *Federal Relief Administration and the Arts* (Columbus, Ohio, 1969).

2. Ann Sutherland Harris and Linda Nochlin, *Women Artists, 1550–1950* (New York, 1977), pp. 62–63; Karal Ann Marling and Helen Harrison, *7 American Women: The Depression Decade* (Poughkeepsie, N.Y., 1976), p. 14.

3. Richard D. McKinzie, *The New Deal for Artists* (Princeton, N.J., 1973), pp. xi, 23.

4. For general background, see ibid.; Marlene Park and Gerald E.

Markowitz, *The New Deal for Art: The Government Art Projects of the 1930's with examples from New York City and State* (Hamilton, N.Y., 1977).

5. McKinzie, *New Deal for Artists*, p. 93; Francis V. O'Connor, *Federal Support for the Visual Arts: The New Deal and Now* (New York: New York Graphic Society, 1969), pp. 35–39.

6. McKinzie, *New Deal for Artists*, pp. 77, 135.

7. Marling and Harrison, *7 American Women*, pp. 11, 13.

8. Ibid., pp. 11, 14.

9. Ibid., pp. 5, 14.

10. Ibid., p. 13; McKinzie, *New Deal for Artists*, p. 178; Harris and Nochlin, *Women Artists*; Eleanor Munro, *Originals: American Women Artists* (New York, 1979), pp. 29–30, 108, 128, 174; Elsa Honig Fine, *Women and Art: A History of Women Painters and Sculptors from the Renaissance to the 20th Century* (Montclair, London, 1978), pp. 143–44.

11. McKinzie, *New Deal for Artists*, p. 54; Park and Markowitz, *New Deal for Art*, p. 27.

12. Park and Markowitz, *New Deal for Art*, p. 33; Marling and Harrison, *7 American Women*, p. 22.

13. Harris and Nochlin, *Women Artists*; Munro, *Originals*, p. 108.

14. Marling and Harrison, *7 American Women*, pp. 22–23. Bloch was one of the seven women chosen for the Vassar exhibit. The other six were Rosalind Bengelsdorf, Minna Citron, Marion Greenwood, Doris Lee, Elizabeth Olds, and Concetta Scaravaglione.

15. Marling and Harrison, *7 American Women*; Donna G. Bachmann and Sherry Piland, *Women Artists: An Historical, Contemporary, and Feminist Bibliography* (Metuchen, N.J., 1978).

16. Munro, *Originals*, p. 74; Marling and Harrison, *7 American Women*, pp. 6, 14.

17. Jerre Mangione, *The Dream and the Deal: The Federal Writers Project, 1935–1943* (Boston, 1972), pp. 123–24, 257; Monty Noam Penkower, *The Federal Writers Project: A Study in Government Patronage of the Arts* (Urbana, Ill., 1977).

18. Penkower, *Federal Writers Project*, pp. 22, 41, 49, 143–44, 169.

19. Tillie Olsen, *Yonnondio: From the Thirties* (New York, 1974), pp. 157–58; Penkower, *Federal Writers Project*, pp. 167, 169. Tillie Olsen was known by the name Tillie Lerner in the 1930s.

20. Penkower, *Federal Writers Project*, p. 73; Leuchtenberg, *Franklin D. Roosevelt and the New Deal*, p. 127. .

21. Anzia Yezierska, *Red Ribbon on a White Horse* (New York, 1950), p. 150. For more on Yezierska, see *NAW: The Modern Period*, pp. 753–54.

22. Yezierska, *Red Ribbon*, 156.

23. Ibid., p. 165.

24. Ibid., p. 198.

25. On the Federal Music Project, see Christine Ammen, *Unsung: A History of Women in American Music* (Westport, Conn., 1980), pp. 114, 266. See also *NAW: The Modern Period*, pp. 173–74.

26. For more on Hallie Flanagan, see her *Arena* (New York, 1940);

NAW: The Modern Period, pp. 237–39. The quotation is from *NAW*, p. 239.

27. Flanagan, *Arena; NAW: The Modern Period*, p. 238.

28. For excerpts of the 1938 hearings, see Eric Bentley, ed., *Thirty Years of Treason: Excerpts from Hearings before the House Un-American Activities Committee, 1938–1968* (New York: Viking, 1971). The quotation is from page 25.

29. McKinzie, *New Deal for Artists*, p. 179.

30. Malcolm Cowley, quoted in Jack Salzman, ed., *Years of Protest: A Collection of American Writings of the 1930s* (New York: Pegasus, 1967), p. 377; Aaron, *Writers on the Left*, pp. 391, xvii.

31. For an excellent survey of the documentary form in the context of the decade, see William Stott, *Documentary Expression and Thirties America* (New York, 1973).

32. *NAW: The Modern Period*, pp. 94–95; Stott, *Documentary Expression*, pp. 211, 214, 270.

33. See Stott, *Documentary Expression* for background on the New Deal program.

34. The material on Lange is drawn from Karin Becker Ohrn, *Dorothea Lange and the Documentary Tradition* (Baton Rouge, 1980), and *NAW: The Modern Period*, pp. 408–409. The quotation is from page 408.

35. Stott, *Documentary Expression*, p. 225.

36. *NAW: The Modern Period*, pp. 338–40; Martha Gellhorn, *The Trouble I've Seen* (New York: William Morrow, 1936). Lorena Hickok's reports have been published in Richard Lowitt and Maurine Beasley, eds., *One Third of a Nation: Lorena Hickok Reports on the Great Depression* (Urbana: University of Illinois Press, 1981).

37. Agnes Smedley, *Daughter of Earth* (New York, 1929). This book has been reprinted by the Feminist Press (1973), and the afterword by Paul Lauter is a good introduction to Smedley's life. See also Ronald Gottesman, "Agnes Smedley," in Edward T. James, ed., *Notable American ·Women: A Biographical Dictionary, 1607–1950* (Cambridge, 1971), 3:300–302.

38. Much of the information on women writers has been drawn from the excellent annotated bibliography by the Women and Literature Collective, *Women and Literature: An Annotated Bibliography of Women Writers* (Cambridge, 1976, 3rd edition). Material on Herbst is found on pages 32–33. See also *NAW: The Modern Period*, pp. 333–35.

39. *NAW: The Modern Period*, pp. 712–14.

40. *Women and Literature*, pp. 37–38; Meridel LeSueur, *Salute to Spring* (New York, 1940). More information about LeSueur is available in the introduction to her *The Girl* (Cambridge: West End Press, 1978). The novel was written in 1939, but no publisher was willing to bring it out. Parts of the manuscript were reprinted as short stories, but it was not until

1977 that the entire manuscript was accepted for publication. At that time, LeSueur extensively revised the manuscript.

41. Richard Pells, *Radical Visions and American Dreams: Culture and Social Thought in the Depression Years* (New York, 1973), pp. 169–80.

42. *Women and Literature*, p. 32.

43. Ibid., pp. 38–39, 46–47; Aaron, *Writers on the Left*, p. 300; Stott, *Documentary Expression*, p. 121.

44. Jayne Loader, "Women on the Left, 1906–1941: Bibliography of Primary Sources," *University of Michigan Papers in Women's Studies* 2 (February 1974):32; *Women and Literature*, pp. 19–20.

45. Joseph North, ed., *New Masses: An Anthology of the Rebel Thirties* (New York, 1969); Jack Conroy and Ralph Cheyney, *Unrest 1931* (New York: Henry Harrison, 1931); Salzman, *Years of Protest*, pp. 199, 366–67, 371.

46. *Women and Literature*, p. 44.

47. *NAW: The Modern Period*, p. 362; Margaret Perry, *Silence to the Drums: A Survey of the Literature of the Harlem Renaissance* (Westport, Conn., 1976), pp. 15, 73–77, 89.

48. Ibid., pp. 121–22; *Women and Literature*, pp. 34–35.

49. Harris and Nochlin, *Women Artists*, p. 64; Bachmann and Piland, *Women Artists*.

50. Material on O'Keeffe is found in Bachmann and Piland, *Women Artists*; Fine, *Women and Art*; Munro, *Originals*. The quotation is from Harris and Nochlin, *Women Artists*, p. 300.

51. Allen, *Since Yesterday*, pp. 173–74.

52. *Women and Literature*, pp. 48–49, 22–23, 28–31, 25–27.

53. Gertrude Stein, *Everybody's Autobiography* (New York: Random House, 1937), p. 3.

54. *Women and Literature*, pp. 27–28, 40, 72–73, 18.

55. Lillian Hellman, *Pentimento* (Boston, 1973), p. 134. See also Hellman, *An Unfinished Woman: A Memoir*.

56. Victoria Sullivan and James Hatch, eds., *Plays By and About Women* (New York: Random House, 1973).

57. This material is drawn from Jo Ann Skowronski, *Women in American Music: A Bibliography* (Metuchen, N.J., 1978); Adrienne Fried Block and Carol Neuls-Bates, eds., *Women in American Music: A Bibliography of Music and Literature* (Westport, Conn., 1978); Ammen, *Unsung*.

58. Barbara Jepson, "Ruth Crawford Seeger: A Study in Mixed Accents," *Feminist Art Journal*, Spring 1977, pp. 13–16.

59. Ammen, *Unsung*, pp. 200–202, 206; Block and Neuls-Bates, *Women in American Music*.

60. Ammen, *Unsung*, pp. 104–106, 111, 114–15.

61. For the Brico Orchestra, see Ammen, *Unsung*, pp. 112–13. See *Newsweek*, August 1, 1938, p. 21, *New York Times*, February 19, 1935, and January 4, 1939, for reviews of Antonia Brico's activities, cited in Block and Neuls-Bates, *Women in American Music*.

62. The film, by Judy Collins and Jill Godmilow, was entitled *Antonia: Portrait of a Woman* and was released in 1973. Folksinger Collins was a former music student of Brico in Denver.

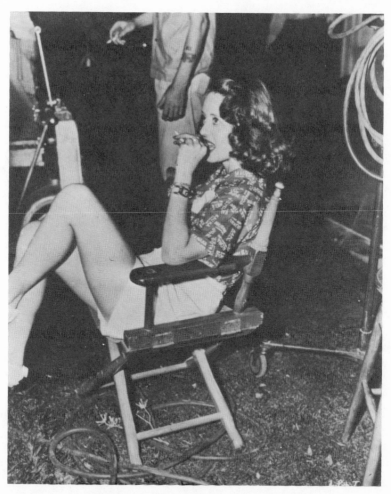

Bette Davis on the set
Courtesy of Harvard Theatre Collection

Chapter Seven
Popular Culture, Popular Heroines

Popular culture usually holds important clues to understanding the concerns of a decade, and the popular culture of the 1930s provides an especially abundant source. During the decade, fads, fashions, and celebrities offered welcome, necessary relief from the grim economic conditions all around. Radio, movies, and magazines helped to unify the country and raise American spirits to meet the challenge of the Great Depression.[1]

Unlike modes of cultural expression where contributions often prove timeless and enduring, the world of popular culture is by definition transitory and fleeting. The diversions that so engaged the attention of Americans in the 1930s will have little meaning to those who did not live through the contract bridge craze, the birth of the Dionne quintuplets, or the abdication of Edward VIII in 1936. Yet many aspects of popular culture are worthy of historical inquiry, because they reflect the values and interests of the mass culture which has dominated American life since the 1920s. Studying the popular heroines of the 1930s, women who were singled out by the media for fame, fortune, and admiration, provides valuable clues as to perceptions of women's roles in the society at large.

Eleanor Roosevelt was certainly the decade's most widely known, and probably its most greatly admired, woman. In 1938,

Life hailed her as the greatest American woman alive. Because of her wide-ranging interests and her broad conception of the First Lady's role, Eleanor Roosevelt entered people's daily lives far more than previous wives of presidents. Through her newspaper column "My Day," radio broadcasts, speeches, and wide travels, Eleanor Roosevelt became known as the conscience of the administration. As a result, she received thousands of letters from ordinary citizens who saw her as their own advocate within the complex New Deal bureaucracy.[2]

Eleanor Roosevelt made some of her most courageous statements in support of civil rights, well before the issue became one of national concern. At a 1939 meeting of the Southern Conference on Human Welfare, she challenged southern segregation by placing her chair so that it straddled the aisle of the black and white sections in the hall. In 1939, she publicly resigned from the Daughters of the American Revolution after the DAR refused to allow black vocalist Marian Anderson to sing in Constitution Hall. Eleanor Roosevelt was instrumental in securing permission from the Interior Department for Anderson to give a free concert at the Lincoln Memorial, which was attended by 75,000 people.

Eleanor Roosevelt's popular espousal of causes such as civil rights came at a price. Especially during her first several years in the White House, she often faced a hostile press. People complained that she was meddling in government affairs instead of staying at home like a good wife. Other people made fun of her appearance, especially her large teeth and rather stiff, upper-class demeanor. Despite such "Eleanor-haters," the First Lady built a devoted following who defended her right to hold her own ideas, even if they did not always agree with her views. In a January 1939 Gallup poll, 67 percent approved of the way Eleanor Roosevelt was handling herself as First Lady, a higher approval rate than the president was receiving at the time. Women in the sample approved of her activities by an even greater margin, 73 percent to 27 percent. Following her work for human rights at the United Nations in the 1940s and 1950s, Eleanor Roosevelt became one of America's most admired women of all time.[3]

While Eleanor Roosevelt's popularity grew in the 1930s, other women in the New Deal rarely received such widespread admiration from the press and public. Frances Perkins never enjoyed favorable publicity; Molly Dewson, while beloved to those who knew her in Democratic and social welfare circles, was not a nationally recognized figure. The women in the New Deal were not glorified by the press, partly because they shunned the limelight. Changing social concerns and values also caused the country to shift its attention from older women administrators to new popular heroines—women who were successful in the exciting and glamorous areas of mass culture. During the 1930s, such heroines included sports figures, aviators, and especially women film stars. Hollywood, not Hull House, guaranteed women's popularity in the decade.

The trend toward fashioning women into nationally known figures had begun in the 1920s with the extensive media coverage of such exploits as Gertrude Ederle's successful swim across the English Channel in 1926 and Amelia Earhart's flight across the Atlantic in 1928. These women set the stage for the emergence of the popular athletic heroine of the 1930s.

Life magazine, which boasted a circulation of 16 million in 1938, was fond of highlighting young and attractive female athletes. Sonja Henie, the Norwegian figure skater who did much to publicize the sport in this country in the 1930s, appeared regularly on *Life's* cover or in photo essays. Alice Marble, tennis star, and Patty Jane Berg, golfer, were also featured. Predictably, *Life* preferred to feature women in fairly traditional "feminine" sports like tennis, golf, riding, and skating, activities often associated with the leisured classes and compatible with ideals of feminine grace and demeanor.[4]

Sportswriter Paul Gallico, in a 1936 *Reader's Digest* article called "Women in Sports Should Look Beautiful," concluded that only in eight out of twenty-five sports did women live up to his standard. Ball games were out—they were too strenuous, and made women perspire. According to Gallico, women should concentrate on archery, shooting, fishing, riding, flying, and skating, because such sports taught women to move gracefully. Gallico also liked these sports because the women wore "some pretty cute costumes." During the 1930s, advertisers were discovering that the female body was a marketable commodity. Since athletes usually had attractive bodies (especially if they avoided "masculine" sports, which built muscles in the wrong places), they were prime candidates for mass exposure. New sports clothing, such as lighter, looser tennis dresses and even the introduction of tennis shorts by Alice Marble in 1937, revealed more of a woman's body. Women's basketball teams drew larger crowds when they appeared in orange satin shorts, a daring innovation. Hollywood scouts began to attend swim meets and tennis tournaments to look for attractive extras for films.[5]

It is difficult to determine whether wider public awareness of female sports figures increased female participation in athletic activities in the 1930s, but one recent historian has described the period between 1925 and 1935 as a "golden era" for women in sports. According to surveys, the most popular sports for women in the decade were basketball and swimming, traditional favorites. Bowling, tennis, golf, and ice-skating were also quite popular. With the exception of basketball and softball, these were all individual rather than team sports. Participation in individual sports often lessened the conflict between athletic endeavors and sexual stereotypes, a problem which male athletes rarely face.[6]

Yet, during the 1930s, women's softball and basketball teams flourished. Many of these teams were sponsored by industrial organizations for publicity purposes and given catchy names such as Slapsie Maxie's Curvacious Cuties, a softball team. In southern California alone, there were 1,000 women's softball teams in 1938. In some regions, women's softball games outdrew the men's. In basketball, amateur teams sponsored by industries, wealthy individuals, or businesses (as distinct from collegiate varsity teams) entered regional and national tournaments. One of the strongest teams of the early 1930s was the Golden Cyclones, made up of women from the Employer's Casualty Company of Dallas. Professional basketball made a tentative appearance in 1936 with the All American World's Champion Girls Basket Ball Club. Later known as the Red Heads (for the red wigs they wore while playing), this team toured the country playing exhibition games.[7]

Many individual women excelled in sports in the 1930s. Floretta McCutcheon dominated women's bowling; Eleanor Holm and Helen Madison set swimming records. Alice Marble and Helen Wills dominated women's tennis. A women's ski team entered the Olympics for the first time in 1936, and women became interested in speed skating, not yet an Olympic sport. Some women were even able to turn their sports prowess into careers: Sonja Henie had her own ice-skating review in the late 1930s, backstroke champion Eleanor Holm gave swimming exhibitions, and Esther Williams began her career as the star of Hollywood movies with aquatic themes.

By far the outstanding athlete of the 1930s was Mildred "Babe" Didrickson. Didrickson was obviously a gifted athlete, for she excelled in several different sports; a feat accomplished by few men or women. She began in women's basketball, leading the Golden Cyclones to several national tournament victories; in the 1931 tournament she scored 106 points in five games. In 1932, Didrickson won the National AAU Outdoor Championships in *five* events—hurdles, high jump, shot put, javelin, and basketball throws. She tied for first in a sixth event and finished fourth in a seventh, thus single-handedly winning the team championship. In the 1932 Olympic games, where she was only allowed to enter three events, she won gold medals in javelin and hurdles and a silver in high jump. (She actually had tied for first, but was given the silver because of her unorthodox form.) This phenomenal accomplishment won her the Associated Press's designation as woman athlete of the year. AP later voted her the outstanding woman athlete of the half-century.

Even with the publicity of her success in amateur athletics, Didrickson at first found it difficult to earn a living as a professional athlete. There were few women's professional teams at the time, so Didrickson made herself into the attraction. She toured for a season with a mixed basketball team called Babe Didrickson's All Americans and pitched for a baseball team for $1,500 a month. Didrickson then discovered golf, the sport with which her name is usually associated. Playing in a men's tournament in 1938, she met her husband, George Zaharias, who became her business manager. In 1947, she was one of the founders of the Ladies Professional Golf Association, where she dominated the women's professional golf tour just as she had basketball and track and field. Like Amelia Earhart in aviation, Babe Didrickson symbolized women's capabilities in new fields, and her popularity showed the public's receptivity to women as heroic figures during the decade of the 1930s.[8]

Life readers ranked the disappearance of Amelia Earhart as one of the top five news stories of 1937. Earhart, just forty years old at the time her plane was lost somewhere over the Pacific Ocean, symbolized the excitement of flying in its early years and the opportunities for women in this new field. Born in Kansas and raised in the Midwest, Earhart became fascinated with flying during World War I. In 1921, she took flying lessons from aviation pioneer Neta Snook, and gained her pilot's license. Earhart achieved national prominence in 1928, when she was the first woman to fly across the Atlantic. She was only a crew member (her job was to keep the log), but her exploit catapulted her into the spotlight. Because of her modesty and a strong physical resemblance to Charles A. Lindbergh, Earhart earned the nickname "Lady Lindy."[9]

Earhart's contributions to aviation and women's history went farther than being "baggage" (in her words) on a flight across the Atlantic. During the 1920s, she flew in barnstorming derbies and cross-country races; in 1929, she was a founder and the first president of the Ninety Nines, a group of women pilots. (There were hardly more than a hundred licensed women pilots in the entire country at that time.) Other prominent members of the Ninety Nines included Fay Gillia, Nena Paris, Louise Thaden, Blanche Noyes, and Frances Harrell Marsalis.

Throughout her career, Amelia Earhart struggled to expand opportunities for women in aviation. In 1932, she fulfilled her own personal dream of flying the Atlantic solo, the first woman to do so. The flight was a difficult one (her altimeter failed, and an exhaust manifold caught fire), but she displayed the level-headedness and courage characteristic of a crack pilot in the fifteen-hour flight. She also displayed her feminism, saying after this flight, "I shall be happy if my small exploit has drawn attention to the fact that women, too, are flying." In 1935, she was the first person to fly solo from Hawaii to the mainland, which won her a $10,000 prize. In that same year, she achieved another first: a nonstop flight from Mexico City to Newark.[10]

Earhart's exploits brought her fame, lecture and book contracts, a position as aviation editor for *Cosmopolitan* magazine and the vice presidency of Ludington (later National) Airlines. In 1931, she married George Putnam, who became her business manager. After her solo flight across the Atlantic, she was honored at a White House reception hosted by President Herbert Hoover. She felt even more at home there once the Roosevelts were in residence, and she became a good friend of Eleanor Roosevelt. In April 1933, Earhart and Roosevelt went for a late-night airplane ride from Washington to Baltimore—dressed in evening clothes. Eleanor Roosevelt shared Amelia Earhart's love of flying, and Earhart encouraged the First Lady to take lessons. While nothing ever came of this, Amelia Earhart realized what a boon Eleanor Roosevelt's staunch support was to the fledgling air industry.

Amelia Earhart was not the only female aviator to win recognition in the 1930s. Anne Morrow Lindbergh accompanied her husband on his test flights in the 1930s, sharing her experiences in *North to the Orient* (1935). In 1936, Louise Thaden won the Bendix cross-country race, beating out both male and female pilots; in 1938, Jacqueline Cochran won the $12,000 Bendix race.

While women excelled in cross-country barnstorming, they were unable to make inroads into commercial aviation. Helen Richey was hired as a copilot by Central Airlines but had to give up hopes of being a commercial pilot when the all-male pilots' union refused to let her join, and the Commerce Department ruled she could not fly passengers in bad weather. A harbinger of the future was the introduction of trained nurses (then called hostesses) to commercial flights in 1931. Stewardess, not pilot, soon became the accepted role for women in aviation, Amelia Earhart's brave example notwithstanding.[11]

Amelia Earhart became an appealing role model for several generations of American women. Her commitment to feminism (perhaps the guiding principle of her life, after her love of flying) and her modest and unselfish demeanor made her attractive to the older generation of women who had despaired at the antics of younger women during the 1920s and 1930s. Amelia Earhart's pioneering achievements, her pride in her sex, and her ease at adapting to modern life and mores, made her attractive to younger women, too. To reach out to some of these young women more immediately, the president of Purdue University asked Earhart in 1934 to join the University faculty as a counselor in careers.

The position at Purdue had an additional attraction for Earhart: the Purdue trustees gave her a fully equipped Lockheed Electra, which she called the "Flying Laboratory." Realizing that the plane made round-the-world air travel possible, Earhart gave in to her feeling that there was "just about one more good flight left in my system." The original departure was delayed by mechanical problems, but Amelia Earhart and navigator Fred Noonan eventually left Miami on June 1, 1937, heading east. On July 2, as they attempted the most difficult part of the trip (finding Howland Island, a tiny dot in the Pacific just two miles long, less than a mile wide, and only fifteen feet above sea level), they began to run low on fuel. Their last radio message was "Circling . . . Cannot see Island . . . Gas is running low." Although rumors about Amelia Earhart's survivial have persisted for years, it seems most likely that her plane went down and sank in the Pacific Ocean somewhere near Howland Island. She had prepared herself for death, leaving a farewell note to her husband, but her disappearance came as a shock to many Americans. With Amelia Earhart's passing, women had lost a most articulate and inspiring heroine.[12]

During the 1930s, Eleanor Roosevelt, Sonja Henie, Babe Didrickson, and Amelia Earhart shared the limelight with colorful figures from the world of entertainment. It was the era of hot jazz improvisation called swing music, and the country delighted in the singing of Bessie Smith (tragically killed in an auto accident in 1937) and Ethel Waters. Sally Rand wowed them at the 1933 Chicago World's Fair when she performed wearing large fluffy fans and nothing else. But the real stars of the 1930s were movie actresses, the new cultural standard-bearers of twentieth-century America. Movie stars had replaced figures in politics, business, and the arts as the most popular role models for American youth.[13]

The movies dominated American popular culture from the 1920s through the 1940s, but they played an especially large role during the 1930s. Movies provided diversion and escape from the grim economic news coming over the radio or in the daily newspaper; screwball comedies and Busby Berkeley extravaganzas took the public's mind off the Depression. Movies also reinforced traditional American mores and played an important role in propping up the collective spirit of the country during the hardship of the 1930s. Unlike other forms of entertainment, movies kept their audiences during the Depression; between 60 and 90 million Americans attended movies each week during the 1930s. For many families, the 10¢ for a weekly movie was as important an item in their budget as bread or milk.[14]

Movies had a growing impact on the nation's youth. Replacing the traditional institutions of family, church, and community, movies were now becoming the primary source of information on values and behavior for many young people. Young women were especially susceptible: according to one study during the 1920s, girls between the ages of eight and nineteen went to almost one movie a week. Increasingly, young women looked to the movies for guidance on the latest fashions and beauty tips. One girl described a Joan Crawford film: "I watch every little detail of how she's dressed, and her make-up, and also her hair." Another girl described Greta Garbo: "I'll bet every girl wishes she was the Greta Garbo type. I tried to imitate her walk, she walks so easy as if she had springs on her feet." With the popularity of blonde stars such as Jean Harlow and Mae West in the 1930s, nationwide sales of peroxide skyrocketed.[15]

Young men and women were also learning from the movies how to interact with members of the opposite sex. Clearly these young people were taking notes from their favorite screen performers: ". . . it was directly through the movies that I learned to kiss a girl on her ears, neck, and cheeks, as well as on the mouth." A sixteen-year-old girl wrote, "I know love pictures have made me more receptive to love-making because I always thought it rather silly until these pictures, where there is always so much love and everything turns out all right in the end, and I kiss and pet much more than I would otherwise." Another woman said, "No wonder girls of older days, before the movies, were so modest and bashful. They never saw Clara Bow and William Haines. . . . If we did not see such examples in the movies, where would we get the idea of being 'hot'? We wouldn't." Such films with their projection of the new sexual mores of the 1920s and 1930s signaled the demise of the restrictive Victorian norms that had governed women's behavior in the past.[16]

During the 1920s and 1930s, fascination with the private lives of movie stars swelled. Magazines like *Movie Screen* and *True Confessions* furnished intimate details of stars' lives off the screen and provided lavish pictures of the opulent life-style available to those who made it big in Hollywood. Many young girls noticed that movie stars were practically the only women who could be assertive and earn large amounts of money, yet still keep the respect (even adulation) of society. It is no wonder that young girls of the 1930s were more likely to aspire to be Bette Davis or Jean Harlow than public servants like Frances Perkins or Molly Dewson.

Then (as now) American women received conflicting and ambiguous messages from the silver screen. Film critic Molly Haskell suggests that the movie industry has been dedicated throughout its history to reinforcing what she tags the "big lie" of women's inferiority. Women figure more prominently in film than any other art, industry, or profession dominated by men, yet movies generally reflect traditional attitudes about women's roles. This conservative orientation prevailed in many films of the 1930s: women were told that their only acceptable roles lay in marriage, family, and deference to men. On the other hand, certain films of the 1930s gave audiences a cast of independent and powerful women, perhaps more than in any other decade in film history. Compared to the portrayal of women in the 1960s and early 1970s, the roles available to women in the 1930s made it a wonderfully liberated period for women in film. [17]

When describing images of women in film in the 1930s, indeed when talking at all about films of that decade, it is necessary to distinguish between movies made before and after the Production Code of 1934 went into effect. This code set standards of proper moral decorum on the screen: passionate embraces were discouraged, exposure of sex organs was forbidden (including animals like the chimp in Tarzan, who wore a body stocking), and revealing clothing for women was barred. Married couples slept in twin, never double, beds. The futility of crime and the sanctity of marriage were upheld. By declaring sex, passion, and crime off limits, movies cut themselves off from much of social reality. While not legally binding, this code ushered in an era of self-censorship by the film industry after 1934.

Before the adoption of the Production Code in 1934, however, Hollywood experienced one of the most creative periods in its history as it experimented with sound movies, which had been introduced in the late 1920s. Until the Production Code went into full force between 1933 and 1934, Molly Haskell observes, "women were conceived of as having sexual desire without being freaks, villains, or even necessarily European. . . . Women were entitled to initiate sexual encounters, to pursue men, even to embody certain 'male' characteristics without being stigmatized as 'unfeminine' or predatory." The stars of *Morocco* (where Marlene Dietrich calmly applied lipstick while facing a firing squad), *Blonde Venus* (where Dietrich appeared in top hat and tails), *She Done Him Wrong*, and *Design for Living*, all movies made between 1930 and 1933, were truly liberated heroines.[18]

A film like *Design for Living* (1933) probably would not have made it ⁺ the censors later in the decade. *Design for Living* containeu ..o explicit sex, but its subject matter, especially the acceptance of certain kinds of female behavior, would have been suspect after 1934. An adaptation of Noel Coward's play directed by Ernst Lubitsch, the film starred Miriam Hopkins, Fredric March, and Gary Cooper in a love triangle. Hopkins is an American in Paris who is in love with two men, one a playwright, the other a painter. Hopkins marries Cooper when March leaves town, but then spends the night with March while Cooper is away. In the end, instead of choosing between the two (a choice the director found irrelevant), she decides to live with them both. Hollywood censors would soon disallow such unconventional and nonjudgmental endings.[19]

During the early 1930s, several "fallen women" films served as vehicles for some of Hollywood's greatest stars. Marlene Dietrich in *The Blue Angel* (1930) plays a cabaret singer who seduces and destroys a stuffy professor, played by Emil Jannings. In *Blonde Venus* (1932) Dietrich sleeps with Cary Grant in order to get money for her husband, who is dying of radium poisoning. When her husband learns of this, Dietrich is kicked out and turns to prostitution. She uses her body to regain her power, and finally returns to give herself to her husband, now cured of illness. In *Susan Lenox, Her Fall and Rise* (1931), Greta Garbo plays a Swedish-American farm girl running away from a forced marriage who takes refuge in the cabin of construction engineer Clark Gable. Garbo and Gable sleep together, and plan to marry, but are separated inadvertently. When Garbo has an affair with a carnival owner, Gable will not forgive her. Garbo becomes the mistress of various rich men, but, as time passes, realizes how much she still loves Gable, and follows him around the world begging his forgiveness.[20]

Greta Garbo's *Queen Christina* (1933) is another example of the openness and experimentation that characterized pre-Code pictures. Garbo plays a seventeenth-century Swedish queen who rides around in men's clothing when she wants to escape the confines of court life. On one of these jaunts she meets the envoy of the Spanish king, who is bringing a marriage proposal to her. At a country inn, Garbo and the envoy are forced to share a room, where he discovers (to their mutual pleasure) that she is a woman. The envoy is still unaware that his lover is Queen Christina, and is flabbergasted when presented to her at court. She eventually abdicates her throne in order to marry him, only to have him die in her arms after a duel with one of her political and emotional rivals just as she and her lover were to leave for Spain. Garbo decides to sail anyway, and the movie ends with one long shot of Garbo on the prow of the ship. What was so absorbing about this movie (besides Greta Garbo's beauty) was its willingness to flaunt sexual customs: women masqueraded as men, women had sexual feelings and acted on them. Some critics, noting Queen Christina's close physical relations with women as well as men, have interpreted her heterosexual escapades as a cover for her true lesbian identity. Such open challenges to sexual mores would not appear again for many years.[21]

The early 1930s introduced Marlene Dietrich, Greta Garbo, Jean Harlow, Joan Crawford, and other talented actresses to the American film public. But the star whom everyone remembers best from this period is Mae West. She was the hit sensation of 1933. Her first starring role came in *She Done Him Wrong*, where she plays a Gay Nineties saloon keeper named Lady Lou who eventually marries a federal agent disguised as a minister (Cary Grant). Mae West quips when Cary Grant comes into her saloon, "You can be had," and later adds the famous line "Why don't you come up and see me sometime?" Grant asks West in the film, "Haven't you ever met a man who could make you happy?" and West replies, "Sure. Lots of times." Never before had a woman been so open about exploiting men for her own pleasure and playing the games of sex usually reserved for men. In fact, Mae West's explicit sexuality (specifically, a song in *She Done Him Wrong* called "A Guy What Takes His Time") was a major impetus behind the crackdown resulting in the Production Code of 1934.

In other Mae West films of this period, notably *I'm No Angel* (1933), she fired off the suggestive statements that became her trademark: "When a girl goes wrong, men go right after her." "Am I making myself clear, boys?" she leers seductively, adding under her breath, "Suckers." Mae West, though certainly not styling herself as a role model for womankind in general, does offer an example of a woman who controls her own destiny and lives life on her own terms. She openly flaunts society's expectations about manners, sex roles, and whatever else happens to be in the way. Even when she marries Cary Grant at the end of *She Done Him Wrong* (the conventional ending for all heroines), she does not give in completely. Grant, after slipping a wedding band on her finger, says to Lady Lou, "Surely you don't mind my holding your hand?" West replies, "It ain't heavy. I can hold it myself."[22]

In 1935 Mae West earned $480,833, the second highest income in the country, topped only by newspaper magnate William Randolph Hearst.[23] But by the mid-1930s, Mae West's unconventional screen presence had been effectively suppressed by the new Production Code. No longer could she act so independently when it came to women's roles and relationships between the sexes; no longer could she make the double entendres that delighted and shocked her audiences. Her bawdiness removed, she had to settle for the role of comedian. Yet audiences who remembered her bombshells from the early 1930s continued to respond to her swagger and suggestive style.

The Production Code dealt a blow to Mae West's ribald presence on the screen, but it worked to women's benefit in other ways. Its deemphasizing of sex and passion forced women out of the bedroom and into the working world. The movie industry now gave women careers, as typified by the large number of reporters and working girls who dot the films of the 1930s. Rosalind Russell was a reporter in *His Girl Friday* (1940), as was Jean Arthur in *Mr. Deeds Goes to Town* (1936). Ginger Rogers's *Kitty Foyle* (1940) told the story of a working girl who was forced to choose between marriage and career.

The gold diggers genre presents similar tales of working-girls' lives. As Molly Haskell has noted, the gold diggers were young women determined to make it on their own terms, but who often gladly gave in when the right man came along. Gold diggers were often chorus girls or models (which in Hollywood was sometimes synonymous with prostitute). Ginger Rogers starred in *Gold Diggers of 1933*, which featured the lavish production number "We're in the Money"; Ruby Keeler made her name in such movies as

Footlight Parade and *42nd Street*. *Gold Diggers of 1937*, starring Joan Blondell and Glenda Farrell, traced a group of young chorus girls (or chorines, as they were called) thrown out of work when their show fails. They discover that an insurance convention is in town and seek out the men as dates, sexual partners, and especially as potential husbands. In another movie, two women are forced to take jobs as process-servers in order to make do: "For a thousand dollars we'd make a sap out of any man." While many of these gold diggers were on the make for a husband, audiences also remembered the strong bonds of female solidarity that characterize these winning films.[24]

A variation on the gold diggers' theme was the backstage drama, such as *Stage Door* (1937). This movie starred Ginger Rogers, Katharine Hepburn, Andrea Leeds, and Lucille Ball as the inhabitants of a boardinghouse for aspiring actresses in New York called the Footlight Club. The theater district was hurt by the Depression, and the young women faced disappointments and setbacks as they struggled to break into show business. The plot concerns a newcomer to the Footlight Club, played by Katharine Hepburn, whose initial haughty behavior and beautiful clothes alienate the other women; in the end, Hepburn wins them over with a touching curtain speech eulogizing another Footlight member (Andrea Leeds) who has committed suicide when she lost out on a big part to Hepburn. Throughout *Stage Door*, men make only token—and negative—appearances: Adolphe Menjou plays a lecherous Broadway producer who tries to seduce young actresses in return for favorable treatment in casting. The women, on the other hand, dominate the film with their cheerful humor, friendship, loyalty, and solidarity.[25]

The snappy tone of *Stage Door* is in keeping with the self-confidence of the screwball comedies which flourished in the 1930s, bringing comic relief to their Depression-weary audiences. A forerunner of this genre was the runaway hit *It Happened One Night* (1934). Claudette Colbert plays a rich girl trying to escape her family and fiancé, aided by a newspaper reporter (Clark Gable) who gets drawn into her plans on a long bus ride from Florida to New York. Colbert and Gable fall in love, and after a series of comic misunderstandings and misadventures they are finally united in marriage at the end. Showing the power of films to affect consumer spending, undershirt sales plummeted when Clark Gable appeared without an undershirt in a famous scene.

Like *It Happened One' Night*, many of the screwball comedies featured a "battle of the sexes that was a battle of equals," according to Molly Haskell. She cited Katharine Hepburn and Cary Grant in *Bringing Up Baby* and *Holiday*, Rosalind Russell and Grant in *His Girl Friday*, Irene Dunne and Grant in *The Awful Truth*, and John Barrymore and Carole Lombard in *Twentieth Century*. In most of these comedies, the dialogue is so rapid and witty that one can barely keep up with it. Since women seem more autonomous the more they are allowed to talk on the screen, the heroines of these screwball comedies emerge as wonderful, if somewhat wacky, characters with brains of their own.[26]

Howard Hawks claimed that the dialogue in *His Girl Friday* was the fastest that had been written to date. This movie, which starred Cary Grant, Rosalind Russell, and Ralph Bellamy, concerns an ex-newspaperwoman named Hildy Johnson who is leaving the newspaper business to marry a tepid insurance salesman named Bruce. But she is obviously still attracted both to her profession and to her ex-boss, played by Cary Grant, who also happens to be her ex-husband. Grant is upset about losing his star reporter and connives to keep her from leaving, in part by overpraising the pleasures of simple married life she will enjoy with solid Bruce. In the end, Hildy Johnson sends her suitor back to his mother in Albany and returns to journalism; she and Grant also agree to try marriage again, this time on a more equal basis. *His Girl Friday* was a remake of the 1930 Ben Hecht film *The Front Page*, where the Hildy Johnson part was played by a man; when the movie was remade in the 1970s, both parts were again played by men. It was to Howard Hawks's credit that he saw the potential for casting a woman as the central character in the Ben Hecht play, a respect for women's capabilities well in keeping with their general treatment in the films of the 1930s.[27]

The 1930s gave motion picture fans many great actresses, gifted artists whose careers spanned more than the decade. Katharine Hepburn, who began her Hollywood career in 1932 with *A Bill of Divorcement*, won an Oscar for her portrayal of young actress Eva Lovelace in *Morning Glory* (1933). Her other 1930s roles included aristocratic, upper-class screwball heroines (*Holiday, Bringing Up*

Baby, The Philadelphia Story), small-town social climbers *(Alice Adams)*, and career women like an aviator in *Christopher Strong* and an actress in *Stage Door*. Hepburn was an independent and spirited character offscreen, and this quality came through in most of her films, no matter what the plot. She remained one of the few actresses who was ever allowed to sacrifice love for career, at least temporarily, as in *Woman of the Year* (1941).[28]

Bette Davis also began her career in the 1930s. She was such a strong actress that she could play unsavory roles (like Mildred in *Of Human Bondage*, 1934) without jeopardizing her career. In *Dangerous*, for which she won an Oscar in 1935, Davis plays a wife who deliberately causes an auto accident when her husband refuses to give her a divorce. At the end of the movie, Davis realizes the error of her ways and dedicates the rest of her life to her now-crippled husband.

Davis's portrayal of the heartless, selfish Southern belle *Jezebel* (1938) won her a second Oscar. *Jezebel* was Warner's low-budget answer to *Gone With the Wind*, then in production; the part of Julie Marsden was Bette Davis's consolation prize for having lost out on the part of Scarlett O'Hara. After an extensive talent search during which most of Hollywood's leading actresses auditioned for Scarlett's role, unknown Vivien Leigh was chosen for the part. (Clark Gable was always everybody's choice for Rhett Butler.) Scarlett O'Hara had the qualities of a spoiled Southern belle, but at the same time was a strong and independent woman who knew exactly what she wanted and went after it. Vivien Leigh's portrayal of Scarlett is yet another example of the strong women's roles offered by Hollywood films in the 1930s.[29]

Clark Gable's performance as Rhett Butler in *Gone With the Wind* made him the number-two box-office star in the late 1930s. Bette Davis also joined the elite group of ten top-grossing stars (male and female) in the 1930s, making the list from 1938 to 1941. Ginger Rogers (as part of the Rogers–Fred Astaire team), Joan Crawford, Claudette Colbert, Jeannette McDonald, Myrna Loy, and Sonja Henie also appeared at the top of the popularity chart during the decade. Judy Garland held the number-ten position in 1940 for her performance in *The Wizard of Oz*. Garland was one of the few child stars of the 1930s who remained a popular entertainer as an adult.[30]

The number-one box-office attraction between 1935 and 1938 was also a child: Shirley Temple. In many ways, this precocious and adorable little girl was perfect for post-Code Hollywood. As a prepubescent child, she was sexually innocent, although Graham Greene was sued by Temple's studio for writing about her allure to pedophiles. In many of Temple's film roles she is an orphan. With no parents to rule her life, she can join Her Majesty's troops in India and meet with a rival potentate, board an ocean liner to the Far East, and win radio contests and talent searches after running away from home. By 1940, Shirley Temple had starred in twenty-one films and had become a commercial product, with Shirley Temple dolls, books, and clothes flooding the market. Look-alike contests were held, and mothers wanted daughters to have ringlets exactly like Shirley Temple. Just as the blonde bombshells had sent peroxide sales skyrocketing and Gable had sent purchases of men's undershirts plummeting in the 1930s, Shirley Temple's influence also reached far beyond the silver screen.[31]

While Hollywood was quite open-minded in its treatment of women on film in the 1930s, it would be wrong to suggest that all heroines produced by Hollywood in the decade were uniformly independent, intelligent, and autonomous women. The conventional ending for most movies remained that of the woman's renouncing her independence for the fulfillment of marriage and family life. While a heroine might pursue her own career or run a business for the first eighty-nine minutes of a film, she was often married off at the end. The interesting question is whether audiences remembered the independence of the character she had played for most of the movie or the conventional ending that "resolved" the plot.

Film images of women were often unflattering and degrading. In some 1930s movies, almost every other word about women is "dames." An enduring scene is Jimmy Cagney's shoving a grapefruit into Mae Clark's face in *The Public Enemy* (1931). Busby Berkeley's fantasy extravaganzas, so beloved by Depression-wracked audiences, treated women literally as objects. In films such as *Fashions of 1934*, women are portrayed as harps, tied up with big bows. In other Berkeley films, women are typewriters, mechanical dolls wound up by male dancers, flowers, and water nymphs. Sexual undercurrents were unmistakable in the scene in *Footlight Parade* where a camera pans across a waterfall formation of women's thighs, spread open to reveal bead-covered crotches.[32]

Not all films which gave women leading roles cast them in a positive light. *The Women* (1939), written by Clare Booth (Luce), was described by one commentator as a "grotesque 1939 study in bitchery, pettiness, superficiality, and stupidity." *The Women* featured an array of MGM stars—Norma Shearer, Joan Fontaine, Joan Crawford, Paulette Goddard, Rosalind Russell, and a young Donna Reed. Not a single man appears on the screen, and supposedly all the film's animals were female, too. The plot concerns a group of society women who gleefully watch perfume salesgirl Joan Crawford wreck Norma Shearer's marriage. Meeting together at the manicurist's, at lunch, at a divorce ranch in Reno, the women are portrayed as nothing more than schemers and shallow, conniving gossips. On the other hand, the novelty of an all-woman film was exciting and original, even if it made men look like angels by omission.[33]

In addition to acting, women in the 1930s found opportunities in Hollywood as screenwriters, production assistants, management personnel, and even occasionally as directors. Significantly, most of the women prominent in these areas in the 1930s were holdovers from the 1910s and 1920s. Conforming to the dictum that women tend to do better in organizations or bureaucracies when they are in their infancy, women in Hollywood reached their peak of participation during the early years of the industry, when many independent production units competed with each other. Films were so new that the talents of any energetic newcomer were welcome, even those of women. Once production was centralized in larger and larger conglomerates, such as Metro-Goldwyn-Mayer or Twentieth Century–Fox, women's talents were easier to pass over.

The number of female screenwriters shows these declining fortunes. In 1928, fifty-two of the 239 scenarists and screenplay writers were women, or a little more than 20 percent. By 1935, after a substantial increase in the ranks of screenwriters paralleling the growth of the movie industry in the past seven years, women's percentage of the total had dropped to 15 percent. In 1940, women made up barely 10 percent of Hollywood's screenwriters.[34]

Screenwriters' names were not household words, to be sure, but when the movie industry could barely produce enough films to keep up with the ever-increasing public demand, successful writers could command high salaries. Some of the most prominent women screenwriters during the 1930s included Anita Loos, Frances Marion, Zoe Akins, Bess Meredyth (who was married to director Michael Curtiz), Sonya Levine, Dorothy Farnum, Lorna Moon, and Vicki Baum. Most of these women began their careers in the silent era and then switched to talkies. The only new female recruit in the 1930s was Frances Hackett, who was part of a male-female writing team.[35]

Anita Loos, for example, got her start with a 1928 silent screen adaptation of her 1925 novel, *Gentlemen Prefer Blondes.* (She later worked on Howard Hawks's 1953 version, starring Marilyn Monroe and Jane Russell.) After the stock-market crash, Anita Loos left New York to work for Irving Thalberg at MGM, eventually earning more than $2,500 a week there. She stayed at MGM for eighteen years. Her list of screenplays includes *Red Headed Woman*, with Jean Harlow (1932); *San Francisco* (1936), starring Clark Gable, Spencer Tracy, and Jeanette McDonald; *Saratoga* (1937), Jean Harlow's last film; and *The Women* (1939). *The Women*, adapted by Loos and Jane Murfin from Clare Booth's smash Broadway play, is a warning to those who suggest that women authors or screenwriters will automatically offset the male bias in film production.[36]

Anita Loos was brash enough to demand that she be taken seriously in ego-studded Hollywood. Frances Marion, the other major screenwriter from the decade, embodied similar traits. She had been a cub reporter and commercial artist, married and divorced, before she was bitten by the movie bug (as she described it) at age twenty-four. Her friend, the newspaper reporter Adela Rogers St. John sent her to Lois Weber, one of the few successful women directors in the early days of Hollywood. Weber offered Marion a job as an extra, with the chance to write dialogue on the side. She acted in several pictures (her screen test described her as the refined type) but concentrated on writing scenarios. She enjoyed writing, but also saw it as a better hedge for the future: she preferred to trust her brains rather than her looks for her long-term prospects.

When Frances Marion began working in Hollywood in 1914, things were hectic and loose. By the 1920s, she noticed that Hollywood was becoming more established; by the 1930s, acceler-

ating production schedules further standardized studio proce-
dures. The atmosphere was one of hard work rather than carefree
experimentation, almost like that of a factory. During the 1920s,
Marion wrote many scripts for her friend and benefactor Mary
Pickford, as well as the screenplays for the movies *Stella Dallas* and
Anna Karenina. In 1930, she wrote the script for *Anna Christie*,
where Greta Garbo made her debut in talkies with this line:
"Gimme a visky. Ginger ale on the side. And don' be stingy,
ba-bee." Other Frances Marion credits from the 1930s include *The
Champ* (1931), from her original story; *Dinner at Eight* (1933), with
Frank Mankiewicz; *Riffraff* (1935), written with her close friend
Anita Loos; and *Camille* (1937), with another woman screenwriter,
Zoe Akins.[37]

Screenwriters sometimes remained with their scripts during the
actual shooting to make revisions or supply additional dialogue.
Very rarely, however, did women like Frances Marion or Anita
Loos have the opportunity to work with a woman director. Lois
Weber, a pioneer here, made her last Hollywood picture in 1927.
She struggled to continue her filmmaking after that, but found
few who were interested in her ideas. She died in 1939.[38]

The outstanding woman director of the 1930s was Dorothy
Arzner. Arzner had grown up around actresses and the movie
industry (her father owned a Hollywood restaurant frequented by
the film community), and, after considering a career as a doctor,
she decided to try Hollywood. She recalled that because of the
influenza epidemic of 1917–18, the studios were willing to take on
anyone who seemed intelligent and eager to learn. She started at
the bottom typing scripts, and worked her way up to cutting,
editing, and then to the position of Chief Editor at Paramount. She
also began to do some shooting at this time. In 1927, she bargained
with Paramount for a long-term contract to write and direct, with
full control over production. Dorothy Arzner left Paramount in
1932 and, unlike Lois Weber, was able to direct major films on a
free-lance basis.

One of Arzner's most interesting films from the 1930s was *Christopher Strong* (1933). It starred Katharine Hepburn as an aviator
who has an affair with a married man and then kills herself (deliberately, in a plane, as she sets a new altitude record) because she is
pregnant. Arzner personally chose Hepburn for the role because

she was of the "very modern type" she wanted. The script was written by Zoe Akins, who worked closely with Arzner at RKO on the film.[39]

Arzner's direction of *Craig's Wife* (1936) for MGM, with unknown Rosalind Russell chosen for the unsympathetic part of Mrs. Craig, shows how Arzner brought to her work a perspective different from that of a man. Arzner interpreted Mr. Craig as a mother-dominated man who fell in love with a woman who was stronger than he. Arzner thought Mr. Craig should be grateful to Mrs. Craig for making a man out of him, an interpretation substantially different from the (male) playwright, who saw Mr. Craig as a nice guy with a shrewish wife. Arzner's interpretation won out. Other Arzner films include *The Bride Wore Red* (1937), with Joan Crawford, and *Dance, Girl, Dance* (1940). She left Hollywood for good in 1943.[40]

Two additional roles were open to women in Hollywood in the 1930s—studio management and gossip columnist. Ida Koverman, special assistant to Louis Mayer at MGM, was described by Frances Marion as "the only woman executive whose advice was respected by the male stars." Koverman's stature was also heightened by the fact that she "discovered" Judy Garland. Koverman was joined in the upper ranks of MGM management by Mabel Walker Willebrandt, who became chief in-house counsel for MGM after leaving the United States Attorney's Office in Washington, where she had been in charge of enforcing Prohibition. Willebrandt found her talents more suited to the growing movie business than the fruitless task of keeping the nation dry in the 1920s.[41]

Two women dominated the world of Hollywood gossip in the 1930s, Louella Parsons and Hedda Hopper. Parsons was the first on the scene—Hopper did not begin her column until late in the 1930s. Parsons controlled gossip, and Hollywood, from her impregnable position as a representative of William Randolph Hearst's chain of newspapers, then at their height. Parsons had begun as a scriptwriter, but soon switched to newspaper work, concentrating on the lives of movie stars. She invented the movie gossip column just at a time when public interest in the private lives of the stars was swelling. In the 1930s, Louella Parsons's column was carried by four hundred papers, with daily readership in the millions. Parsons was one of the few women (or men) to exercise power independently of the heads of the major studios. In the cutthroat world of Hollywood, Parsons made a career out of scoops and exclusive stories, although her columns were famous for their inaccuracy. She often confused names, marriages, and even a person's sex, but nobody seemed to care. She was queen.

Hedda Hopper came to Hollywood as the fifth wife of DeWolfe Hopper, not a very secure position as it turned out. When she divorced him, she tried to make it as an actress, model, and radio bit player. In the late 1930s, she was asked to write a gossip column to challenge Parsons's hegemony. Once syndicated by the *Los Angeles Times*, the most powerful paper in southern California, Hedda Hopper was assured of her audience. Like Parsons, Hopper fed the country's voracious appetite for gossip and rumors about Hollywood stars.[42]

Louella Parsons and Hedda Hopper were part of the glittering world of Hollywood in the 1930s, a world that simultaneously gave women independent roles on the screen and put them down, that slowly squeezed women out of leadership positions but still had room for survivors from the 1920s. On the whole, though, Hollywood in the 1930s supported women's aspirations to a degree unprecedented in decades before and since. The experimentation encouraged by the novelty of talkies, the pre Production Code freedom to challenge established norms, and the presence of a large group of talented women screenwriters and directors all contributed to this progress for women.

The liberated movie heroines could never have been sold to the American public without tacit public support for the attitudes embodied in the films. The positive record of Hollywood is in keeping with the general progress that women made in many areas of politics and culture in the 1930s. The decade produced a wide variety of heroines: the commitment of Eleanor Roosevelt, woman of conscience; the bravery and courage of Amelia Earhart, pioneer in flight; and the ambiguous yet in many ways liberating images of women on the silver screen.

Notes and References

1. The best introduction to popular culture in the 1930s is to look through back volumes of magazines like *Life*, the *Saturday Evening Post*, and women's magazines like the *Ladies Home Journal* and *Good Housekeeping*. For *Life* magazine, see also *The Best of Life* (New York: Time-Life, 1973), which contains material on the 1930s.

2. *Life*, April 4, 1938, p. 31. The well-known montage of Eleanor Roosevelt—her varied poses and moods—appeared in the December 7, 1936, issue of *Life*, pp. 18 19.

3. For Eleanor Roosevelt's life, see *NAW: The Modern Period*, pp. 596 601; and Lash, *Eleanor and Franklin*.

4. Banner, *Women in Modern America*, pp. 142, 160.

5. Gallico quoted in Twin, *Out of the Bleachers*, pp. xxxiv, xxix xxx.

6. Gerber, *The American Woman in Sport*, p. 6; Twin, *Out of the Bleachers*, p. xxviii. Twin quotes track and field star Willye B. White: "A female athlete is always two different people. A male athlete can be the same all the time" (p. 93).

7. Twin, *Out of the Bleachers*, p. xxx; Gerber, *The American Woman in Sport*, pp. 90 93, covers women in basketball.

8. Gerber, *The American Woman in Sport*, chapter 3, covers each sport and developments for women within it. The material on Babe Didrickson is found on pages 92, 108, 133. See also *NAW: The Modern Period*, pp. 756 57.

9. This material on Amelia Earhart is drawn from George Palmer Putnam, *Soaring Wings: A Biography of Amelia Earhart* (New York, 1939);

and Katherine A. Brick, "Amelia Earhart," in Edward T. James, ed., *Notable American Women: A Biographical Dictionary, 1607–1950* (Cambridge, Mass., 1971), 1:538–41.

10. Amelia Earhart quoted in Putman, *Soaring Wings*, p. 127.

11. Ibid., pp. 159–60, 232; Banner, *Women in Modern America*, pp. 160–62.

12. Putnam, *Soaring Wings*, p. 290. See also Amelia Earhart (arranged by George Palmer Putnam), *Last Flight* (New York, 1937).

13. Ryan, *Womanhood in America*, p. 367; Chris Albertson, *Bessie Smith: Empress of the Blues* (New York: Macmillan, 1975); interview with Sally Rand in Terkel, *Hard Times*, pp. 168–74.

14. For movies in the 1930s, see Robert Sklar, *Movie Made America* (New York, 1975). See also *Life Goes to the Movies* (New York, 1975).

15. Ryan, *Womanhood in America*, p. 367, Mary Ryan, "The Projection of a New Womanhood: The Movie Moderns in the 1920's," in Jean Friedman and William Shade, eds., *Our American Sisters* (Boston, 1976), p. 372.

16. Payne study quoted in Sklar, *Movie Made America*, p. 138; Ryan, "Projection of a New Womanhood," pp. 372–73.

17. This discussion of women in film has drawn heavily on two indispensable sources: Molly Haskell, *From Reverence to Rape: The Treatment of Women in the Movies* (New York, 1974), and Marjorie Rosen, *Popcorn Venus: Women, Movies, and the American Dream* (New York, 1973).

18. Haskell, *From Reverence to Rape*, p. 91.

19. Ibid., pp. 99–102; Andrew Bergman, *We're in the Money: Depression America and its Films* (New York, 1971), p. 59.

20. Haskell, *From Reverence to Rape*, pp. 110–11; Rosen, *Popcorn Venus*, p. 171.

21. Haskell, *From Reverence to Rape*, p. 132; Rosen, *Popcorn Venus*, pp. 170–72.

22. For Mae West, see Sklar, *Movie Made America*, pp. 184–87; Rosen, *Popcorn Venus*, pp. 159–64; Haskell, *From Reverence to Rape*, pp. 115–17.

23. Allen, *Since Yesterday*, p. 173.

24. Elizabeth Dalton, "Women at Work: Warners in the 1930's," in Karyn Kay and Gerald Peary, *Women and the Cinema: A Critical Anthology* (New York, 1977), pp. 267–82, covers the Gold Diggers motif well. See also Haskell, *From Reverence to Rape*, p. 145.

25. For *Stage Door*, see Haskell, *From Reverence to Rape*, pp. 147–48.

26. Ibid., pp. 130, 139.

27. Ibid., pp. 133–35.

28. In addition to much material in Haskell and Rosen, see Homer Dickens, *The Films of Katharine Hepburn* (Secaucus, N.J.: Citadel, 1971).

29. Haskell, *From Reverence to Rape*, pp. 215–21; Rosen, *Popcorn Venus*, pp. 177–79.

30. *Life Goes to the Movies*, p. 234.

31. Rosen, *Popcorn Venus*, pp. 193–95; Haskell, *From Reverence to Rape*, p. 123.

32. Haskell, *From Reverence to Rape*, p. 146; Ryan, *Womanhood in America*, p. 181, contains the image from *Footlight Parade*.

33. Rosen, *Popcorn Venus*, p. 191.

34. Sklar, *Movie Made America*, pp. 75, 237; Rosen, *Popcorn Venus*, p. 397.

35. Haskell, *From Revrence to Rape*, p. 151. The epilogue to Rosen, *Popcorn Venus*, "Feminist Footholds in Filmmaking," pp. 389–404, provides an overview of women's roles behind the camera.

36. Anita Loos, *Kiss Hollywood Goodbye* (New York, 1974) is an enjoyable introduction to Loos's career.

37. Frances Marion, *Off With Their Heads! A Serio-Comic Tale of Hollywood* (New York, 1972).

38. Richard Koszarski, "The Years Have Not Been Kind to Lois Weber," in Kay and Peary, *Women and the Cinema*, p. 146–52.

39. Karen Kay and Gerald Peary, "Interview with Dorothy Arzner," in Kay and Peary, *Women and the Cinema*, pp. 153–68; the quotation about Hepburn is from page 163. See also Kay and Peary's "Dorothy Arzner's *Dance, Girl, Dance*," in the same anthology, pp. 9–25.

40. Kay and Peary, "Interview with Dorothy Arzner," pp. 165–66.

41. Marion, *Off With Their Heads*, p. 228; Rosen, *Popcorn Venus*, pp. 153, 181.

42. Sklar, *Movie Made America*, pp. 234–36; Rosen, *Popcorn Venus*, pp. 247–49.

Conclusion

At the beginning of the 1930s, the attention of American citizens was riveted on the Depression. All around was evidence of the greatest economic catastrophe the country had ever faced: 25 percent of the work force unemployed, breadlines and shanty towns in all the major cities, industrial output practically at a standstill. With the economic system of the United States, indeed the world, so out of kilter, many feared the populace would turn to radical alternatives, either revolutionary communism on the left or emerging fascism on the right. But on the whole, people blamed themselves, not the system, for the unemployment, reduced circumstances, and family dislocation they experienced in the 1930s. They would just wait until things got better.

By the end of the 1930s, the Depression had not gone away, but it no longer dominated the national mood. Unemployment was still unacceptably high, and industrial production had yet to reach the 1929 levels. But in many people's minds, the sense of crisis from earlier in the decade had passed. While the Depression stubbornly persisted, the bold, innovative directions of the New Deal gave the impression that conditions were improving.

The growing preoccupation with events in Europe was also pushing the Depression further from the public consciousness by the late 1930s. With the rise of fascism, Hitler's takeover in Germany, Mussolini's in Italy, and the increasing aggressiveness of the Japanese in the Far East, Americans began to feel uneasy. As Hitler seemed intent on conquering the world, people began to revise their previously hard and fast isolationism. Perhaps some wars were worth fighting after all.

The bombing of Pearl Harbor on December 7, 1941, ended these hypothetical debates. The United States probably would have entered the war eventually, but the attack on Pearl Harbor galvanized Americans to make the sacrifices necessary for a total modern war. Ironically, war mobilization finally pulled the country out of the Depression. Many were afraid the depression would return when the American economy demobilized in 1945, but these fears were not realized. Consumer demand, suppressed for so many years by the Depression and wartime shortages and rationing, stimulated the American economy in a dramatic postwar upswing. With European and Far Eastern economies in shambles after the war, the United States was the strongest nation in the world. During the depths of the Depression, few Americans would have predicted so dramatic a turnaround in less than a decade.

The attack on Pearl Harbor and American entry into World War II provide a convenient terminus for the decade of the 1930s. Bounded by two clear and decisive events, the onset of the Depression and the entry into a global war, the decade of the 1930s takes on a unity of its own. Even when prosperity returned after the war, memories of the 1930s continued to influence those who had lived through them. In Caroline Bird's apt phrase, Depression-era Americans would carry an invisible scar for the rest of their lives.

The Depression had a major impact on American culture and society, but women's lives were probably less disrupted by it than were men's. When unemployment hit a family, the husband's world changed radically, but the wife's stayed about the same. At the same time, women as a group made significant (and for the most part unrecognized) contributions to pulling the country through the Great Depression. By substituting their own labor for goods and services previously bought in the marketplace, women often provided the difference between making do and doing without for their families. This substitution represented a break from the general trend toward more labor-saving devices in the home and the removal of family functions to other economic and social institutions. During the Depression, women recaptured some of their vital economic roles within the family.

In general, American society made few attempts to challenge the existing definitions of male and female roles during the 1930s. If anything, the Depression reinforced traditional ideas by giving women larger roles to play in holding their families together in the midst of the economic crisis. In fact, the roots of the Feminine Mystique of the 1940s and 1950s are clearly visible in the preceding decade.

While the majority of American women in the 1930s performed unpaid domestic labor within their homes, a growing minority worked at paid employment outside the home. While popularly held views assumed that women as "marginal" workers regressed during the economic crisis, in fact the opposite was true. Women continued to enter the work force, and the decade posted small but significant gains for women in both blue-collar and professional employment. The percentage of women who worked increased from 24.3 to 25.4 percent, and women's proportion of the total work force rose from 22 to 25 percent. Here the Depression undoubtedly played a role: women like men were forced to seek jobs to support themselves and their families. The increase in the number of married women working, which occurred in spite of strong public opposition, was part of the long-range shift in the female work force from young, single women to older, married women workers. While World War II is usually cited as the beginning of this changeover, the trend was well underway by the Depression.

The other key feature of women's participation in the work force during the Depression is that women as a group often fared better than men. The reasons for this relative success lie in the segmentation of the work force into men's and women's jobs: during the Depression, jobs in heavy industry, where men were concentrated and women rare, were especially hard hit. In contrast, areas where women predominated, such as clerical and sales work, were less affected. This job security, however, came at the expense of heightened sexual stereotyping of men's and women's work: women continued to be shunted into low-paying, low-status jobs in the economy, while skilled and professional jobs were reserved for men. Life was not easy for the woman worker in the Depression in any case: women faced layoffs and periodic unemployment and often worked under unsafe conditions for wages significantly lower than men's. But it is now clear that women were not expelled from the labor force in the 1930s. They held their own, and even made small gains.

Feminism did not die in the decade either, but it was in a period of transition. The old guard of feminists, women like Jane Addams and Charlotte Perkins Gilman who had dominated the women's movement during the suffrage campaign and in the Progressive period, were gone by the 1930s. The next generation of women, those who had come of age in the Progressive era, continued in public life undaunted in the 1920s and 1930s. Many served in the New Deal agencies in Washington, where they continued to work on social welfare issues of concern to women. They kept alive the women's organizations which had been so important to the women's movement in the early twentieth century. Although in the 1930s such groups were mere vestiges of what they had been in the Progressive era, they were important nonetheless. Unfortunately, these same women continued to debate among themselves over the meaning of equality as symbolized by the Equal Rights Amendment.

The next generation of women, those who came of age in the 1920s and 1930s, seem not to have shared the same vision of feminism that had guided their elders. College became a way station before marriage and children, instead of a training ground in feminist ideals. Women graduates planned to work for a few years, but were less willing to make the sacrifices necessary for a professional career. Perhaps historians have been too harsh on these younger women, who seem so pale in comparison to the suffrage pioneers. Even if feminism held less interest for this younger generation of women, it is unfair to blame the decade of the 1930s for the demise of the women's movement. Older women, and some younger ones (notably on the political left), kept the feminist standard flying, providing continuity and laying the groundwork for the revival of feminism thirty years later.

In general, women survived the 1930s in far better shape than has previously been suggested. To be sure, no mass-based women's movement agitated for feminist concerns; women at work faced layoffs and unemployment during the Depression, as well as public hostility engendered by the thought of women holding jobs at all. But women made small gains in almost every arena during the 1930s and large gains in some, notably in the New Deal administration. Instead of a bleak and desolate time for women, the 1930s emerge as a rich, if sometimes contradictory, period of twentieth-century women's history.

Bibliographic Essay

I. GENERAL

Extensive sources are available for reconstructing the history of women's lives during the decade of the 1930s. William H. Chafe, *The American Woman, 1920–1970* (New York: Oxford, 1972) and Lois W. Banner, *Women in Modern America: A Brief History* (New York: Harcourt Brace Jovanovich, 1974) provide comprehensive surveys of the broader patterns of twentieth-century women's history, with special emphasis on their public roles; both books serve as good introductions to developments for women in the 1930s. Also useful is Mary Ryan, *Womanhood in America* (New York: Franklin Watts, 1979), especially for popular culture and society's attitudes about women. Sophonisba P. Breckinridge, *Women in the Twentieth Century* (New York: McGraw-Hill, 1933) discusses women's political, economic, and social roles through 1933. J. Stanley Lemons, *The Woman Citizen: Social Feminism in the 1920s* (Urbana: University of Illinois Press, 1973) is a good source for background on the 1920s. An indispensable source for reconstructing individual women's lives is the biographical dictionary *Notable American Women: The Modern Period* (Cambridge, Mass.: Harvard University Press, 1980), edited by Barbara Sicherman and Carol Hurd Green. Updating the earlier *Notable American Women, 1607–1950* (Cambridge, Mass.: Harvard University Press, 1971), the supplement covers women who died between 1951 and 1975, many of whom were active in the 1930s; it supplies complete biographical material and lists important primary and secondary sources for each woman. Looking through *NAW: The Modern Period* is an enjoyable way to meet many of the major female protagonists of the 1930s.

The 1930s in general, and the New Deal in particular, have been subjected to detailed scrutiny by historians and observers of American politics and culture. The most useful introduction to the New Deal remains William E. Leuchtenberg, *Franklin D. Roosevelt and the New Deal, 1932–1940* (New York: Harper and Row, 1963); more critical of Roosevelt and the limits of New Deal reform is Paul Conkin's *The New Deal* (Arlington Heights, Ill.: AHM Publishing Corporation, 2nd Edition, 1975). Frederick Lewis Allen's *Since Yesterday: The 1930's in America* (New York: Harper and Row, 1939) does not have the brilliance of his earlier study of the 1920s *(Only Yesterday)*, but nonetheless provides an entertaining contemporary account of the decade's concerns, both political and popular. Two books convey the Depression's meaning to ordinary Americans especially poignantly. Caroline Bird's *The Invisible Scar* (New York: David McKay, 1966) captures the mood of the country with special sensitivity to the needs and concerns of women. Equally moving is Studs Terkel's *Hard Times: An Oral History of the Great Depression* (New York: Random House, 1970). In both these books, the voices of the Thirties come alive again.

2. WOMEN FACE THE DEPRESSION

Eleanor Roosevelt, *It's Up to the Women* (New York: Frederick A. Stokes, 1933) and Mary Beard, *America Through Women's Eyes* (New York: Macmillan, 1933) offer contemporary views of the impact of the Depression on women's lives. Also invaluable is Robert and Helen Lynd, *Middletown in Transition: A Study in Cultural Conflicts* (New York: Harcourt, Brace, 1937), which traces the impact of the Depression on Muncie, Indiana, since the publication of *Middletown: A Study in Modern American Culture* (New York: Harcourt, Brace, 1929); both books are superb sources for the values and attitudes of white middle-class America.

How women coped in the 1930s has also attracted the attention of historians and sociologists. An enjoyable source is Jeane Westin's *Making Do: How Women Survived the '30s* (Chicago: Follett, 1976), which brings a wide range of women's experiences to light through oral history; it is especially good on women's day-to-day lives. *Making Do* can be supplemented by Ruth Schwartz Cowan, "Two Washes in the Morning and a Bridge Party at Night: The American Housewife Between the Wars," *Women's Studies* 3 (1976), and Ruth Milkman, "Women's Work and Economic Crisis: Some Lessons of the Great Depression," *Review of Radical Political Economics* 8 (Spring 1976), which describe in more historical terms the contours of women's lives. Winifred Wandersee Bolin surveys similar themes in her article "The Economics of Middle-Income Family Life," *Journal of American History* 65 (June 1978), which forms the basis for her recently published study, *Women's Work and Family Values, 1920–1940* (Cambridge, Mass.: Harvard University Press, 1981). In addition, Caroline Bird's *The Invisible Scar* contains abundant material on women's lives.

Many studies look at the impact of the Depression on American families. The most useful for illuminating women's roles are Mirra Komarovsky, *The Unemployed Man and His Family* (New York: Institute of Social Research, 1940) and E. Wright Bakke, *Citizens Without Work* (New Haven: Yale University Press, 1940). Also of interest are Roger Angell, *The Family*

Encounters the Depression (New York: Scribner's, 1936) and Ruth Shonle Cavan and Katherine Howland Ranck, *The Family and the Depression* (Freeport, N.Y.: Books for Libraries Press, 1938). Although not strictly a sociological study, Louis Adamic, *My America, 1928–1938* (New York: Harper and Brothers, 1938) contains a wealth of information on the Depression's impact on family life. An interesting discussion of the impact of the Depression on the expectations of daughters and granddaughters of women in the 1930s is Sheila Bennett and Glen Elder, "Women's Work in the Family Economy: A Study of Depression Hardship in Women's Lives," *Journal of Family History*, Summer 1979.

To supplement sources which concentrate mainly on the lives of white middle-class urban women, see Margaret Jarman Hagood's wonderful *Mothers of the South: Portraiture of the White Tenant Farm Woman* (Chapel Hill: University of North Carolina Press, 1939) and Nora Miller, *The Girl in the Rural Family* (Chapel Hill: University of North Carolina Press, 1935). Mary W. M. Hargreaves, "Darkness Before the Dawn: the Status of Women in the Depression Years," in Mabel Deutrich and Virginia Purdy, *Clio Was a Woman* (Washington, D.C.: Howard University Press, 1980), also has a good discussion of rural women's lives. For black women, see Charles S. Johnson, *Shadow of the Plantation* (Chicago: University of Chicago Press, 1934); Maya Angelou, *I Know Why the Caged Bird Sings* (New York: Random House, 1969); and Gerda Lerner, *Black Women in White America: A Documentary History* (New York: Random House, 1972).

3. WOMEN AND WORK

The best place to begin an investigation of women's work in the 1930s is with the comprehensive and detailed studies of the Women's Bureau, found in major research libraries and government document repositories, which give extensive data on women's wages, hours, working conditions, and patterns of employment and unemployment. Especially useful for introductory material on the 1930s are "Women in the Economy of the United States: A Summary Report," *Women's Bureau Bulletin #155* (1937); "The Woman Wage Earner: Her Situation Today," *Women's Bureau Bulletin #172* (1939); and "Women's Occupations Through Seven Decades," *Women's Bureau Bulletin #218* (1951). Valerie Kincaide Oppenheimer, *The Female Labor Force in the United States* (Westport, Conn.: Greenwood Press, 1976) and Banner, *Women in Modern America* conveniently summarize women's wage force participation. Ruth Shallcross, *Should Married Women Work?* (Washington, D.C.: National Association of Business and Professional Women, 1940) suggests the decade's hostility to women working during the Depression; for further examples, see Chafe, *The American Woman*, and Lois Scharf, *To Work and To Wed: Female Employment, Feminism, and the Great Depression* (Westport, Conn.: Greenwood Press, 1980).

Much attention has focused on the impact of the Depression on women's work. Grace Hutchins, *Women Who Work* (New York: International Publishers, 1934) provides a contemporary view enriched by examples and statistics available nowhere else. Various Women's Bureau publications, specifically *Women's Bureau Bulletin #103, 108, 113, 139,* and *159,* look directly at women's unemployment. *Women's Bureau Bulletin #165* (1938) gives a comprehensive picture of the black woman worker in the 1930s; Julia Kirk Blackwelder's "Women in the Work Force: Atlanta, New Orleans, San Antonio, 1930–1940," *Journal of Urban History* 4 (May 1978) compares the Depression's impact on black, white, and chicana women. Winifred Wandersee Bolin's "The Economics of Middle Income Family Life" looks at the relation between values and economic need in women's work. An especially important source, one which has significantly influenced my interpretation of the Depression's impact on women's work, is Ruth Milkman, "Women's Work and the Economic Crisis." For a compelling description of what it meant to be unemployed, see Meridel LeSueur, "Women on the Breadlines," *New Masses,* January 1932.

Susan Ware, *Beyond Suffrage: Women in the New Deal* (Cambridge, Mass.: Harvard University Press, 1981) offers an introduction to the New Deal relief programs for women. For a more negative interpretation of their scope, see Genevieve Parkhurst, "Is Feminism Dead?" *Harper's Magazine* 170 (May 1935) and Scharf, *To Work and To Wed.* Mary Elizabeth Pidgeon's Women's Bureau study, "Employed Women under NRA Codes," *Women's Bureau Bulletin #130* (1935), describes the relief program's positive impact on women's work. For another view of the NRA, see Maud Younger, "The NRA and Protective Laws for Women," *Literary Digest* 117 (June 2, 1934).

One of the most significant developments of the 1930s was the growth of organized labor, of which Irving Bernstein's *The Turbulent Years* (Boston: Houghton Mifflin, 1970) tells the stirring narrative. Mary Heaton Vorse offers the view of a participant-journalist in *Labor's New Millions* (New York: Modern Age Books, 1938). For material on women in the labor movement, see Chafe, *The American Woman*; Philip Foner, *Women and the American Labor Movement, From World War I to the Present* (New York: Free Press, 1980); and James J. Kenneally, *Women and American Trade Unions* (St. Albans, Vt.: Eden Press, 1978). Staughton and Alice Lynd's *Rank and File* (Boston: Beacon Press, 1973) contains three interviews with women activists from the 1930s; for individual labor women, see Rose Pesotta's autobiography, *Bread Upon the Waters* (New York: Dodd, Mead, 1944), and entries for Angela Bambace, Dorothy Bellanca, Fannia Cohn, and Rose Pesotta in *NAW* and *NAW: The Modern Period.* Lucy Mason, *To Win These Rights* (New York: Harper and Brothers, 1952) offers another perspective on the rise of the CIO. Westin's *Making Do* contains several informative recollections of the decade's labor struggles. Finally, two documentary films, *Union Maids* (1973), based on the *Rank and File* interviews, and *With Banners and Babies* (1977), covering women's participation in the CIO sitdown strikes, offer unique glimpses of women's vital roles in the labor movement of the 1930s.

4.YOUTH, EDUCATION, AND CAREERS

Maxine Davis, *The Lost Generation: A Portrait of American Youth Today* (New

York: Macmillan, 1936) is the best introduction to youth in the 1930s; see also Lynd and Lynd, *Middletown in Transition*. During the decade, many young people took to the road. Thomas Minehan, *Boy and Girl Tramps of America* (New York: Farrar and Rinehart, 1934) treats women hoboes at some length. A fascinating firsthand account is Bertha Thompson, *Sister of the Road: The Autobiography of Box Car Bertha* (New York: Macauley, 1937).

There is no general study of women in college in the depression, but Mabel Newcomer, *A Century of Higher Education for American Women* (New York: Harper and Brothers, 1959) offers an overview and relevant material about women's collegiate experiences in the decade. Background on college life in the 1920s is well provided by Paula S. Fass, *The Damned and the Beautiful* (New York: Oxford, 1977). *Fortune* magazine's article "Youth in College," June 1936, offers a judicious contemporary view of college life. John Willig's article "Class of '34 (Female) Fifteen Years Later," *New York Times Magazine*, June 12, 1949, traces a group of Seven Sisters graduates from the Depression through the onset of the Feminine Mystique; Mary McCarthy's novel *The Group* (New York: Harcourt, Brace, 1963) fictionalizes the experiences of Vassar's Class of 1933. Both Westin, *Making Do*, and Bird, *The Invisible Scar*, contain material on women in college, with Bird's recollections of her years at Vassar in the 1930s especially pertinent. Mary Beard's *A Changing Political Economy as It Affects Women* (Washington, D.C.: American Association of University Women, 1934) proposes a fascinating yet never realized college course on women's history.

The studies of changing sexual mores that appeared in the 1920s and 1930s make interesting reading. See especially Katherine B. Davis, *Factors in the Sex Life of Twenty-Two Hundred Women* (New York: Harper and Brothers, 1929); Phyllis Blanchard and Carolyn Manasses, *New Girls for Old* (New York: Macauley, 1930); Dorothy Dunbar Bromley and Florence Haxton Britten, *Youth and Sex: A Study of 1300 College Students* (New York: Harper and Brothers, 1938). James R. McGovern, "The American Woman's Pre-World War I Freedom in Manners and Morals," *Journal of American History* 55 (September 1968) dates the "sexual revolution" before 1920. Mary Ryan, *Womanhood in America*, and Linda Gordon, *Woman's Body, Woman's Right* (New York: Penguin, 1976) offer cogent discussions of the growing emphasis on heterosexual behavior. Vern Bullough and Bonnie Bullough, "Lesbianism in the 1920s and 1930s: A Newfound Study," *Signs* 2 (Summer 1977), introduces a group of women in the Salt Lake City area who consciously identified themselves as lesbians in the period.

A good introduction to women's professional work over the twentieth century is Janet Hooks, "Women's Occupations Through Seven Decades," *Women's Bureau Bulletin #218* (1951). For women and the professions, see Cynthia Fuchs Epstein, *Woman's Place: Options and Limits in Professional Careers* (Berkeley: University of California Press, 1970) and Barbara J. Harris, *Beyond the Sphere: Women and the Professions in American History* (Westport, Conn.: Greenwood Press, 1978), although neither devotes extended attention to the 1930s. Chafe, *The American Woman*, contains material on women and careers, as does Barbara Miller Solomon, "Historical Determinants in Individual Life Experiences of Successful Professional Women," *Annals of the New York Academy of Sciences*, March 15, 1973. An article which has greatly influenced my interpretation of developments after 1920 is Frank Stricker, "Cookbooks and Law Books: The Hidden History of Career Women in Twentieth Century America," *Journal of Social History* (Fall 1976). Stricker's article is an excellent place to begin an investigation of women and careers in the postsuffrage period.

Two studies surveyed the impact of the Depression on professional women. *The Trained Woman and the Economic Crisis* (New York: American Woman's Association, 1931) was followed up three years later by Lorrine Pruette, *Women Workers Through the Depression: A Study of White Collar Employment Made by the American Woman's Association* (New York: Macmillan, 1934); both are important sources on white-collar work. *Fortune's* three-part survey of women in business (July, August, September 1935) offers a good introduction to women's growing concentration in office work, as well as information on the leading women in business at the time.

Extended material on specific professions in the 1930s is sparse. The tables in Epstein, *Woman's Place* offer the best material on which to judge women's progress in various fields. See also, for medicine, Mary Roth Walsh, *Doctors Wanted: No Women Need Apply* (New Haven: Yale University Press, 1977); for social work, Frank Bruno, *Trends in Social Work, 1874–1956* (New York: Columbia University Press, 1957), Judith Ann Trolander, *Settlement Houses and the Great Depression* (Detroit: Wayne State University Press, 1975), Clarke A. Chambers, *Seedtime of Reform: American Social Service and Social Action, 1918–1933* (Minneapolis: University of Minnesota Press, 1963) and Chafe, *The American Woman*; for teaching and nursing, Robert W. Smuts, *Women and Work in America* (New York: Columbia University Press, 1959). For women in journalism, Ishbel Ross, *Ladies of the Press: The Story of Women in Journalism by an Insider* (New York: Harper and Brothers, 1936) is a gossipy introduction; a more recent study is Marion Marzolf, *Up From the Footnote: A History of Women Journalists* (New York: Hastings House, 1977). Bess Furman's *Washington By-Line: The Personal History of a Newspaperwoman* (New York: Knopf, 1949) covers her career and mentions many other Washington newspaperwomen; similar information is contained in Doris Faber, *The Life of Lorena Hickok: E.R.'s Friend* (New York: William Morrow, 1980). *NAW: The Modern Period* contains sketches of many newspaperwomen, including Anne O'Hare McCormick, Lorena Hickok, Bess Furman, Dorothy Thompson, May Craig, and Elinore Morehouse Herrick. The best discussions of women in academics are found in Newcomer, *A Century of Higher Education*; Jessie Bernard, *Academic Women* (New York: Pennsylvania University Press, 1964); and Patricia Albjerg Graham, "Expansion and Exclusion: A History of Women in American Higher Education," *Signs* 3 (Summer 1978).

5.FEMINISM AND SOCIAL REFORM

Several studies have surveyed the state of feminism in the 1930s. Genevieve Parkhurst, "Is Feminism Dead?" comes to rather pessimistic conclusions; so do Chafe, *The American Woman* and Scharf, *To Work and To Wed*. A more optimistic assessment of the survival of feminism is found in Susan Ware, *Beyond Suffrage: Women in the New Deal*. For women in politics during the decade, see Breckinridge, *Women in the Twentieth Century*; Eleanor Roosevelt and Lorena Hickok, *Ladies of Courage* (New York: G.P. Putnam's Sons, 1954); Martin Gruberg, *Women in American Politics: An Assessment and Sourcebook* (Oshkosh: Academia, 1968). See also Eleanor Roosevelt's articles in *Good Housekeeping*, 110 (January, March, April 1940); and Marguerite J. Fisher and Betty Whitehead, "Women and National Party Organization," *American Political Science Review* 38 (October 1944).

For women in the New Deal, see Ware, *Beyond Suffrage*. Individual women in the New Deal are treated in Joseph P. Lash, *Eleanor and Franklin* (New York: W.W. Norton, 1971); George Martin, *Madam Secretary: Frances Perkins* (Boston: Houghton, Mifflin, 1976); Elaine M. Smith, "Mary McLeod Bethune and the National Youth Administration," in Deutrich and Purdy, *Clio Was a Woman*. Some of these New Deal activists left autobiographies tracing their careers: Mary Anderson, *Woman at Work* (Minneapolis: University of Minnesota Press, 1951); Rose Schneiderman, *All for One* (New York: Paul S. Eriksson, 1967); Frances Perkins, *The Roosevelt I Knew* (New York: Viking Press, 1946); Eleanor Roosevelt, *This Is My Story* (New York: Harper and Brothers, 1937) and *This I Remember* (New York: Harper and Brothers, 1949); Florence Jaffray Harriman, *Mission to the North* (Philadelphia: J.P. Lippincott, 1941). *NAW* and *NAW: The Modern Period* contain entries for most of these women as well.

General information on women's organizations in the 1930s is contained in Breckinridge, *Women in the Twentieth Century* and Chafe, *The American Woman*. Women and pacifism are treated in Gertrude Bussey and Margaret Tims, *The Women's International League for Peace and Freedom, 1915–1965* (London: Allen and Unwin, 1965) and Dorothy Detzer, *Appointment on the Hill* (New York: H. Holt, 1948). For the birth control movement in the 1930s, see Linda Gordon, *Woman's Body, Woman's Right*; and James Reed, *From Private Vice to Public Virtue* (New York: Basic Books, 1978). Mary Anderson, *Woman at Work* covers the Woman's Charter. A good summary of the battle over the Equal Rights Amendment is chapter 5 of Chafe, *The American Woman*; the *Women's Bureau Bulletin #157* (1938) surveys the legal status of women, state by state. On black women's organizations in the 1930s, see Lerner, *Black Women in White America* and Jacquelyn Dowd Hall, *Revolt against Chivalry: Jessie Daniel Ames and the Women's Campaign Against Lynching* (New York: Columbia University Press, 1979).

6.WOMEN ON THE LEFT

Two articles are indispensable for reconstructing the experiences of women on the political left in the 1930s: Jayne Loader's comprehensive eighty-page annotated bibliography, "Women on the Left, 1906–1941: Bibliography of Primary Sources," *University of Michigan Papers in Women's Studies* 2 (February 1974) and Robert Shaffer's excellent article, "Women and the Communist Party USA, 1930–1940," *Socialist Review* 46 (May–June 1979). The comparison between the Old and New Left was suggested by Loader, and Ellen Kay Trimberger, "Women in the Old and New Left: The Evolution of a Politics of Personal Life," *Feminist Studies* 5 (Fall 1979). Mary Inman's *In Woman's Defense* (Los Angeles: The Committee to Organize the Advancement of Women, 1940) presents a broad theoretical basis for expanding women's initiatives by the Communist Party; Margaret Cowl offers clues as to why Inman's ideas remained ignored in her retrospective "Women's Struggles for Equality," *Political Affairs*, May 1974. Vivian Gornick's *The Romance of American Communism* (New York: Basic Books, 1977) supplies a general introduction to the Communist Party and its members. Dorothy McConnell, *Women, War, and Fascism* (New York: American League Against War and Fascism, 1936) demonstrates women's antifascist concerns during the popular front period. Mary McCarthy remembers the 1930s in "My Confession: One Writer's Encounter with Communism," *Reporter*, December 22, 1953, and January 5, 1934; see also her fictional *The Company She Keeps* (New York: Harcourt, Brace, 1942).

For the lives of individual women active on the left in the 1930s, see Ella Reeve Bloor, *We Are Many* (New York: International Publishers, 1940); Al Richmond, *Native Daughter: The Story of Anita Whitney* (San Francisco: Anita Whitney 75th Anniversary Committee, 1942); Vera Weisbrod, *A Radical Life* (Bloomington: Indiana University Press, 1977); Bloor and Elizabeth Gurley Flynn in *NAW: The Modern Period*. Highly recommended is Peggy Dennis, *The Autobiography of an American Communist: A Personal View of a Political Life, 1925–1975* (Westport, Conn.: Lawrence Hill, 1977). Jessica Mitford's *A Fine Old Conflict* (New York: Knopf, 1977) does not cover the 1930s. The interviews with Christine Ellis and Stella Nowicki in Alice and Staughton Lynd, *Rank and File* throw further light on the activities of the Communist Party. *The Long Loneliness: The Autobiography of Dorothy Day* (New York: Harper and Brothers, 1952) is a compelling introduction to her life; see also William D. Miller, *A Harsh and Dreadful Love: Dorothy Day and the Catholic Worker Movement* (New York: Liveright, 1973).

7.LITERATURE AND FINE ARTS

For general background on the impact of the Depression on cultural expression, William Stott, *Documentary Expression and Thirties America* (New York: Oxford, 1973) provides an excellent introduction; see also Richard Pells, *Radical Visions and American Dreams: Culture and Social Thought in the Depression Years* (New York: Harper and Row, 1973). William F. McDonald, *Federal Relief Administration and the Arts* (Columbus: Ohio State University Press, 1969) gives a detailed, almost encyclopedic, description of the federal arts programs. Useful monographs on the arts program include Richard D. McKinzie, *The New Deal for Artists* (Prince-

ton: Princeton University Press, 1973); Marlene Park and Gerald E.
Markowitz, *New Deal for Art* (Hamilton, N.Y.: The Gallery Association of
New York State, 1977); Jane DeHart Mathews, *The Federal Theater,
1935–1939* (Princeton: Princeton University Press, 1967); Jerre Mangione, *The Dream and the Deal: The Federal Writers Project, 1935–1943*
(Boston: Little, Brown, 1972); Monty Noam Penkower, *The Federal Writ-
ers Project: A Study in Government Patronage of the Arts* (Urbana: University
of Illinois Press, 1977). Daniel Aaron, *Writers on the Left* (New York:
Harcourt, Brace, 1961) describes the general intellectual milieu; Anzia
Yezierska, *Red Ribbon on a White Horse* (New York: Charles Scribner's,
1950) provides an autobiographical account of her time on the New York
Writers Project.

The sources for women and literature in the 1930s are rich, starting with
the novels and short stories cited in the text. A stimulating introduction is
the extensive *Women and Literature: An Annotated Bibliography of Women
Writers* (Cambridge, Mass.: Women and Literature Collective, 1976, 3rd
edition). This bibliography contains summaries of women's major works,
as well as biographical information about many of the little-known au-
thors. As the members of the collective found, however, many of these
rediscovered books are long out of print. Loader's "Women on the Left"
also provides suggestions of artists and titles to pursue. Rather than list
thirty or forty women's novels from the 1930s, let me suggest two which
reflect the concerns of many women writers at the time: Tillie Olsen,
Yonnondio: From the Thirties (New York: Dell, 1974) and Meridel LeSueur's
Salute to Spring (New York: International Publishers, 1940). For black
women writers, see Margaret Perry, *Silence to the Drums: A Survey of the
Literature of the Harlem Renaissance* (Westport, Conn.: Greenwood Press,
1976) and Robert E. Hemenway, *Zora Neale Hurston: A Literary Biography*
(Urbana: University of Illinois Press, 1977).

The story of women in the arts in the 1930s is an exciting one, and the
best place to begin is with Karal Ann Marling and Helen Harrison,
7 American Women: The Depression Decade (Poughkeepsie, N.Y.: Vassar College Art Gallery, 1976), which provides an overview of the decade and
biographies of seven representative women artists. Another important
source, for the 1930s and women artists in general, is Ann Sutherland
Harris and Linda Nochlin, *Women Artists, 1550–1950* (New York: Knopf,
1977). See also Eleanor Munro, *Originals: American Women Artists* (New
York: Simon and Schuster, 1979); Elsa Honig Fine, *Women and Art*
(Montclair: Allanheldt and Schram, 1978); Donna G. Bachmann and
Sherry Piland, *Women Artists: An Historical, Contemporary, and Feminist
Bibliography* (Metuchen, N.J.: Scarecrow Press, 1978). A good introduc-
tion to documentary photography in the 1930s is Karin Becker Ohrn's
Dorothea Lange and the Documentary Tradition (Baton Rouge: Louisiana State
University Press, 1980). See also *NAW: The Modern Period* for information
on Lange and Margaret Bourke-White.

Lillian Hellman's two memoirs, *An Unfinished Woman* (Boston: Little,
Brown, 1969) and *Pentimento* (Boston: Little, Brown, 1973) offer glimpses

of the New York theater world. Hallie Flanagan's *Arena* (New York: Duell, Sloan and Pearce, 1940) describes the innovations of the Federal Theater Project; for biographical material on Flanagan, see *NAW: The Modern Period*. For women in music, the best general introduction is Christine Ammen, *Unsung: A History of Women in American Music* (Westport, Conn.: Greenwood Press, 1980). Also useful are Jo Ann Skowronski, *Women in American Music: A Bibliography* (Metuchen, N.J.: Scarecrow Press, 1978) and Adrienne Fried Block and Carol Neuls-Bates, *Women in American Music: A Bibliography of Music and Literature* (Westport, Conn.: Greenwood Press, 1978). *NAW: The Modern Period* discusses the careers of Ruth Crawford Seeger, Marion Bauer, Ethel Leginska, and Florence Price; see also Barbara Jepson, "Ruth Crawford Seeger: A Study in Mixed Accents," *Feminist Art Journal*, Spring 1977. The moving documentary by Judy Collins and Jill Godmilow, *Antonia: Portrait of a Woman* (1977), introduces Antonia Brico to the wider audience she deserves.

8. POPULAR CULTURE AND POPULAR HEROINES

The best introduction to the popular culture of the 1930s is to browse through back issues of *Life*, the *Saturday Evening Post*, *Ladies Home Journal*, and *Good Housekeeping*. Maureen Honey, "Images of Women in the *Saturday Evening Post*, 1931–1936," *Journal of Popular Culture*, Fall 1976, focuses on short stories and fiction. Frederick Lewis Allen's *Since Yesterday* provides a broad and readable introduction to popular culture in the decade. For women's fashions and styles, see Banner, *Women in Modern America*; Alice Lessing, *Sixty Years of Fashion, 1900–1960* (New York: Fairchild Publications, 1963).

For women in sports, two recent books are very helpful: Ellen Gerber, *The American Woman in Sport* (Reading, Mass.: Addison-Wesley, 1974) and Stephanie Twin, *Out of the Bleachers: Writings on Women and Sport* (Old Westbury, N.Y.: The Feminist Press, 1979). See *NAW: The Modern Period* for more on Babe Didrickson Zaharias and Sonja Henie. A recent book on aviation, Wendy Boase, *The Sky's The Limit: Women Pioneers in Aviation* (New York: Macmillan, 1979), pays substantial attention to the 1930s. For Amelia Earhart, see *NAW;* George Palmer Putnam, *Soaring Wings: A Biography of Amelia Earhart* (New York: Harcourt, Brace, 1939); Amelia Earhart, *Last Flight* (New York: Harcourt, Brace, 1937).

Material on movies in the 1930s is quite extensive and rich, as are the movies themselves. A very good overview of movie culture and its impact on American life is Robert Sklar, *Movie Made America* (New York: Random House, 1975). See also *Life Goes to the Movies* (New York: Time-Life Books, 1975) and Andrew Bergman, *We're in the Money: Depression America and its Films* (New York: New York University Press, 1971). Two surveys of women's treatment in films provide excellent material on the exciting period of the 1930s: Molly Haskell, *From Reverence to Rape: The Treatment of Women in the Movies* (New York: Penguin, 1974) and Marjorie Rosen, *Popcorn Venus: Women, Movies, and the American Dream* (New York: Coward, McCann and Geoghegan, 1973). Karyn Kay and Gerald Peary,

Women and the Cinema: A Critical Anthology (New York: E.P. Dutton, 1977) has several relevant articles, as does the journal *The Velvet Light Trap*. Mary Ryan, in *Womanhood in America* and in an earlier article, "The Projection of a New Womanhood: The Movie Moderns in the 1920s," in Jean Friedman and William Shade, eds., *Our American Sisters* (Boston: Allyn and Bacon, 1976), analyzes how movies affected women's aspirations and dreams. Important in tracing the careers of women backstage are two autobiographies: Anita Loos, *Kiss Hollywood Goodbye* (New York: Viking, 1974), and Frances Marion, *Off With Their Heads! A Serio-Comic Tale of Hollywood* (New York: Macmillan, 1972). For Dorothy Arzner, see Clair Johnston, *The Work of Dorothy Arzner* (London: British Film Institute, 1975) and Richard Koszarski, *Hollywood Directors, 1914–1940* (New York: Oxford, 1976). The epilogue of Rosen, *Popcorn Venus* also contains material on women's behind-the-camera roles. In the end, there is no substitute for seeing the films themselves, a truly enjoyable introduction to the decade of the 1930s.

Index

Abbott, Berenice, 143
Abbott, Edith, 79, 104
Abbott, Grace, 79, 89, 104, 111
Abortion, 7, 34, 63, 124
Academics, women in, 79–81
Actresses, film, 179–88, 189, 190, 191, 192
Addams, Jane, 65, 99, 104, 111, 200
Agriculture, xii, xiv; women in, 10–11, 12, 24, 31, 41
Akins, Zoe, 162, 189, 190, 191
Alice Adams (1935), 186
Allen, Florence, 73, 90
Amalgamated Clothing Workers of America, 44, 45, 49, 156
American Association of University Women, 69, 71, 98, 106
American Federation of Labor, 42, 43–44, 48, 49, 104
American League Against War and Fascism, 106, 119, 131
American Writers' Congress, 131–32, 157
American Women's Association, 71, 72
Ames, Jessie Daniel, 103
Anderson, Marion, 172
Anderson, Mary, 49, 89, 106, 107, 110

Angelou, Maya, 11, 13
Anna Christie (1930), 190
Anna Karenina (1935), 190
Anti-lynching, 102–103
Arden, Elizabeth, 75
Arthur, Jean, 183
Arts, government patronage of, 141–52
Arzner, Dorothy, 190–91
Association of Southern Women for the Prevention of Lynching, 103
Athletes, women, 173–75. *See also* Sports, women in
Aviation, women in, 176–78
Awful Truth, The (1937), 185

Balch, Emily Green, 65, 98
Ball, Lucille, 184
Bambace, Angela, 42
Banister, Marion Glass, 90
Barnes, Djuna, 162
Barton, Ann, 127
Bauer, Marion, 163
Baum, Vicki, 189
Beach, Amy (Mrs. H. H. A.), 163
Beard, Mary, 79
Bellanca, Dorothy, 45, 49
Benedict, Ruth, 79
Bengelsdorf, Rosalind, 145